The ESSENCE OF SPIRI

Other books by Haridas Chaudhuri

THE INTEGRAL PHILOSOPHY OF SRI AUROBINDO: A SYMPOSIUM
MAHATMA GANDHI: HIS MESSAGE FOR MANKIND: A SYMPOSIUM
THE PHILOSOPHY OF MEDITATION
INTEGRAL YOGA: THE CONCEPT OF HARMONIOUS AND CREATIVE LIVING
BEING, EVOLUTION AND IMMORTALITY
MODERN MAN'S RELIGION
MASTERING THE PROBLEMS OF LIVING
SRI AUROBINDO: THE PROPHET OF LIFE DIVINE
THE RHYTHM OF TRUTH
PRAYERS OF AFFIRMATION
THE EVOLUTION OF INTEGRAL CONSCIOUSNESS
PHILOSOPHY OF LOVE

The ESSENCE OF SPIRITUAL PHILOSOPHY

HARIDAS CHAUDHURI

Edited by DIONNE SOMERS

with the assistance of JO IMLAY

First published 1990
in association with the
California Institute of Integral Studies
and the Cultural Integration Fellowship

© **Bina Chaudhuri 1990**

All rights reserved. No part of this book
may be reproduced or utilized in any
form or by any means, electronic or
mechanical, including photocopying,
recording, or by any information storage
and retrieval system, without permission
in writing from the Publisher.

British Library Cataloguing in
Publication Data

Chaudhuri, Haridas, *1913–1975*
The essence of spiritual philosophy.
1. Man. Mind, body & soul
I. Title
128

ISBN 1-85274-074-4

Crucible is an imprint of The Aquarian
Press, part of the Thorsons Publishing
Group, Wellingborough,
Northamptonshire, NN8 2RQ, England

Printed in Great Britain by Mackays of
Chatham, Kent
Typeset by MJL Limited, Hitchin,
Hertfordshire

1 3 5 7 9 10 8 6 4 2

CONTENTS

About the Author   *Page 9*

Acknowledgements   *Page 11*

Editor's Introduction   *Page 13*

1
Today's Need for a Spiritual Renaissance   *Page 19*

2
Search for Ultimate Reality   *Page 29*

3
Preservation of Values   *Page 38*

4
Existentialism and Kierkegaard   *Page 39*

5
Albert Camus and Buddhism   *Page 49*

6
Karma   *Page 56*

7
Limitations of the Rational Mind   *Page 64*

8
Mysticism of the Logos   *Page 65*

9
Kali *Page 72*

10
Faith as Existential Choice *Page 74*

11
Free Will and Determinism *Page 81*

12
Doing Our Own Thing *Page 89*

13
Self-Consciousness *Page 96*

14
The Problem of Guilt Feelings *Page 98*

15
Maya: The Eternal Feminine *Page 107*

16
How to Transform the Ego *Page 113*

17
Integrating the Extremes of Life *Page 122*

18
Secrets of Self-Control *Page 125*

19
The Conquest of Death *Page 131*

20
Meditation as the Art of All Arts *Page 137*

21
Aspects of Spiritual Unfolding *Page 145*

22
Meditation and Self-Discipline *Page 151*

23
Samattva — Evenness of Mind *Page 156*

24
Dialectics of Spiritual Growth   Page 157

25
Metaphysics of Dreams   Page 166

26
Existence, Consciousness, and Joy   Page 172

27
The Power of Silence   Page 173

28
Intuition   Page 182

29
Integral Theory of Immortality   Page 186

30
Mysticism and Depth Psychology   Page 195

31
Psychology of Energy Centers   Page 201

32
Meta-Therapy   Page 209

33
Reflections of *The Tibetan Book of the Dead*   Page 216

34
Aspiration and Divine Grace   Page 254

ABOUT THE AUTHOR

Haridas Chaudhuri was born in May of 1913, in Shyamagram, East Bengal. Although orphaned at an early age, he was self-directed towards meaningful achievements. In 1929, he won the Ramtanu Gold Medal in Bengali literature when he graduated from high school. He went on to receive his B.A. and M.A. with honors in Philosophy and Religion from the University of Calcutta in 1936. There he received the Gold Medal for highest scholastic achievement, as well as the Silver Medal from his department. In 1948, he received his Ph.D. for the dissertation "Integral Idealism" from the same university. Dr Chaudhuri then became a member of the educational service of the Government of West Bengal and chairman of the Department of Philosophy at Krishnager College.

In 1951, Dr Chaudhuri came to the United States at the nomination of the great Indian sage, Sri Aurobindo, and at the invitation of Dr Frederic Spiegelberg of Stanford University to teach at the American Academy of Asian Studies. From this experience, he went on to become the founder of the Cultural Integration Fellowship, dedicated to the promotion of intercultural understanding East and West and a center of universal religion. Further, he founded and served as President (as well as Professor of Philosophy) at the California Institute of Asian Studies, the name of which now is the California Institute of Integral Studies.

Dr Chaudhuri wrote and published a dozen books, some fifty articles, and lectured widely around the world. He was a member of the American Philosophical Association and the American Oriental Society.

He passed on in June of 1975, leaving the world with treasures to be discovered and used within the philosophical wisdom he embodied and conveyed.

ACKNOWLEDGEMENTS

This work was developed from graduate classes and public lectures given by Haridas Chaudhuri. I especially want to acknowledge the excellent editorial assistance given by Jo Imlay, and am also grateful to Joanne Keaney and Elliott Isenberg for their editorial contributions. In seeing this publishing project through to the end, I have appreciated the encouragement of Bina Chaudhuri, the support of John Broomfield, and the permission of the Board of Directors, Cultural Integration Fellowship, to include talks given under its auspices.

DIONNE SOMERS

EDITOR'S INTRODUCTION

This book speaks to the quest for higher values in our age. Through the vehicles of comparative philosophy and psycho-spiritual inquiry, Haridas Chaudhuri's message comes through clearly: wholeness, balance, harmony and integration are master keys for us in moving into the twenty-first century.

As a philosopher whose approach integrates Eastern and Western thought, Dr Chaudhuri's focus is on the search for authentic spiritual values relevant to us now and in the future. He brings out precious truths found within different religious, philosophical and psychological views as representations of a still larger reality, which is boundless. He shows the remarkable similarity of concepts found in Eastern and Western philosophical systems and describes the context in which varied philosophical points of view formed.

In developing the East-West synthesis, Dr Chaudhuri worked with a few basic assumptions regarding the nature of reality and the human being which form a *leitmotiv* throughout his thought. Let us explore some of these, for they will rhythmically ebb and flow throughout this work.

First, Dr Chaudhuri perceived that Truth is more than conceptual. Ultimate reality is more than any one way in which it can be conceived of or described. Any system of thought falls short of authentically expressing the basic essence of reality. This is so because ultimate reality is transconceptual. However, only through the development of perceptions and the translation of perceptions into words can our experiences and ideas be communicated. Statements such as, 'The map is not the territory,' and 'Truth is nonverbal,' have been attempts to capture this view. However expressed, the implication is that reality is more than our rational mind can comprehend — it is 'a thought-plus, a word-plus, a system-plus.'

Through Dr Chaudhuri's eyes, the basic structure of reality is Unity-in-Diversity. Ultimate reality is an interrelated unity of all that is. Under whatever name we give it, this unity is both self-existent and dynamically creative; it is unchanging and forever changing in all that can be known and experienced. As a spiritual unity, reality is a multidimensional whole; it is nondual.

In its dynamic form, this unity manifests into diversity — or the realm of matter and duality — through creating bipolarities or polar opposites, which are experience on every level of existence. This expression is an essential part of movement and change. A single pole, apart from its opposite, is a half-truth. Paired, they are the Yin-Yang, or the Shiva-Shakti of the universe.

If reality is a nondual unity which also polarizes within its structure and process, it is both an integrated whole and dynamic synthesis of opposites. Reality is both one and many, nondual and dual, absolute and relative, infinite and finite, spirit and matter. Moreover, all aspects and levels of reality are actively interrelated.

Dr Chaudhuri also saw the basic nature of reality as comprised of multidimensional continuums of energy which are perceived from a multiplicity of perspectives. Unbroken continuums extend throughout the fabric of reality, such as the nature-human-spirit continuum, the physical-emotional-mental-spiritual continuum, the unconscious-conscious-supraconscious continuum, the individual-group-society-nation-world continuum, and the continuum of human values.

Although ultimate reality transcends all viewpoints and conceptual models, in its relative nature it can be approached from many perspectives, each having some validity and truth. These multiple perspectives range from a common sense orientation to that of mystical experience, from conservative to liberal attitudes, and include all of humankind's philosophies, methods, systems, and ideologies.

Dr Chaudhuri made great use of the dialectical process. While conceptions of the dialectic have changed over time, they appear to reflect existing and emerging paradigms. Through his own unique philosophical perspective, Dr Chaudhuri contributes to an understanding of this concept as it is beginning to be perceived more widely at the present time. He saw the dialectic as an eternal process which occurs on all levels of subjective and objective reality and as a spiral movement of energy creating progressively more rich and open-ended syntheses. His view brings together 'Marx's dialectical materialism, Hegel's dialectical idealism, and integrates their rationalistic approach with the nondualistic ontology of the East.' While other writers have addressed the dialectic primarily in its relation to nature, logic, human history, and social thought, Dr Chaudhuri saw great value in consciously using dialectical synthesis as a fundamental universal principle which can be brought into practical experiences of day-to-day life.

In Dr Chaudhuri's view, an evolution of consciousness is taking place on both the individual and collective level. For him, as with his teacher Sri Aurobindo, evolution *presupposes* involution. It is actually the descent or involutionary movement of spirit within matter which prompts the evolutionary process. Specifically, he saw the progressive movement of evolution extending from matter toward life energy, and then toward a sentient mind, to a rational self-consciousness, and finally to an integral consciousness. As humans we presently exist predominately on a rational level of awareness and this, as such, does not represent the summit of our evolutionary potential. Rather, the growing edges of the human evolutionary process are seen to be in the unfolding of a state of consciousness which truly integrates spirit within matter on all levels of personal and social existence.

Since we are, in essence, spiritual entities, our main task on earth is to become what we essentially are. We are to discover and live by our true identity, which is an undivided whole. As human beings we have physical, emotional, mental and spiritual dimensions which are expressed through an unconscious-conscious-supraconscious continuum of experience. Born with a range of potentialities, our responsibility is to actualize them, because each aspect of our nature has a legitimate contribution to make in our growth. None of these aspects should be suppressed, but rather transformed to a higher level of functioning.

Whether we know it or not, our whole life is a process of growth. Through all our experiences, we are potentially enriching our life. However, when the process of inner evolution is brought into our awareness, and growth becomes the purpose of our life, our consciousness is intensified and expanded. We voluntarily choose the path of self-cultivation of our energy and begin to work with the tools of wisdom, love, nonattachment, inner silence and spiritual intuition. Living in such a conscious way means to become truly free and the master of our fate. Through having the ability to act with a creative purpose in life, we have the potential to achieve immortality here and now in *this* world.

This evolution of consciousness is also expressing itself with a movement into an age of synthesis on all levels of our collective structure. Presently, our social being is going through a quickening — a highly volatile and transitional process of old patterns dying in order for the new evolutionary promptings to emerge more fully. Yet universally and with increasing pervasiveness, ecological, educational, political, social and psycho-spiritual movements are aspiring for a sense of wholeness, integration, and unity. The challenge of the emerging age is to be aware of and to actualize this collective potential.

In moving to this higher level of awareness, Dr Chaudhuri would have us remember that it involves more than formulating the most excellent plans and invoking the highest human aspirations; for we as humans are reaching the unfulfilled limits of the upward striving of our rational minds, when this process is relied upon by itself. To attain this new level of consciousness implies an opening and surrendering to higher forces of the universe. It means allowing spirit to become truly involved and integrated within the material forms and processes of life on a fully conscious basis. As this union comes about, planetary evolution will be able to fulfill itself, with a major practical manifestation being the achievement of authentic human unity — a kingdom of heaven on earth. The realization of this experience will come as individuals throughout the world learn to be in dynamic union with that which is the ground and summit of all existence, and to share this union through consciously participating in the evolutionary flow of life.

DIONNE SOMERS
MILL VALLEY, CA.

1

TODAY'S NEED FOR A SPIRITUAL RENAISSANCE

There is a great need today for the reconstruction of religious ideas in accordance with modern developments of thought within the different branches of the sciences, in psychology and in philosophy. Even though truth is eternal, from time to time we need to reaffirm eternal truth in a language which is intelligible to a particular age.

Why do we need religion? We hear a good deal about the death of our religious ideals. When we analyze it, we find this movement goes back to the German philosopher Nietzsche who presented the matter dramatically in *Thus Spake Zarathustra*. In this book one morning an old man got up from bed. Even though it was a sunny day, he took a lamp in his hands and stepped out of his home. He seemed to be excitedly in search of something. He was shouting, 'Where is God?' As he proceeded through the streets to the marketplace, people gathered around him — they thought he must be a madman. Then he shouted, 'God is dead! They have killed God! I can still hear the sound of the gravediggers!' Nietzsche believed this was the biggest event of the century, but the news would take centuries to reach the masses of people — just as when a remote star explodes in outer space, even though the star is gone, the light takes hundreds of years to reach our planet. Confronted with this line of thinking, naturally we ask ourselves, 'What is the meaning of it all? Is there any need for religion?'

When I say spiritual renaissance, what I have in mind is this: In every age old ideas about God to some extent die out, but new ideas have to be found. Old gods die in a sense. But at the beginning of every age, a new god has to be born. That is to say, new ideas, new formulations of the supreme truth have to be made. But we can never do without God, the reality of God. Human ideas of God die, and they are reborn. But the reality behind such ideas is beyond life and death. It is never born and therefore never dies. It is eternal.

Let me affirm this again: We can never do without the reality of God. Nietzsche's life itself is an illustration of what happens if the spiritual value goes out of life. He was a genius, as we all know. With his penetrating insight, he vividly depicted the spirit of the age and the shape of things to come. But despite his brilliancy, Nietzsche eventually was brought to the verge of insanity. He followed a path of terrible loneliness, leading him to insanity, and he perished under the weight of that loneliness.

This is an illustration of what happens if we lose our spiritual insight, our vision of the reality of God. In some directions we may gain something, just as Nietzsche did. He had a wonderful concept of self-existence and freedom, but having lost his spiritual insight, he began to feel the crushing weight of loneliness. When spiritual value goes out of our life, it becomes empty and shallow. Life can never be fulfilling and enriching. Extreme rationalism digs the grave of God and sounds the death knell of spiritual values. Extreme rationalism is based on the belief that with the help of reason, we can fathom the mystery of existence and know everything that is knowable or worth knowing. This belief is fatal to our spiritual understanding. Why is it so?

There are many things to be said in answer to this question, but let me tell you the main reason. When we proceed to understand life and reality on a rationalistic, intellectualistic basis, what is the assumption? It is that truth and reality can be understood by intellectual analysis. When we finish our job of intellectual analysis, the truth stands in front of us in all its nakedness as an object of observation and intellectual understanding. The basic assumption of rationalism is a subject-object orientation, a belief that truth is an object which can be grasped by a subject, the human knower.

When we proceed in this manner, it is only natural that God will always elude our grasp, because God is not an object. God is anything but an object. Whatever is an object is a creature, not the Supreme Creator. Therefore, if we hope to have any understanding of spiritual reality, we have to transcend this dualistic thinking of the intellect with its subject-object orientation. We have to realize there is another approach in our knowledge, another mode of procedure of another power within us by which we can become aware on a level beyond the dualism of the knower and the known. This is what religions throughout the centuries have tried to discover. Some have called it faith. Some have called it mystic experience or intuition. Throughout the ages the endeavour of the great spiritual leaders has been to open a door for the human spirit by which we can transcend this dualism and contact the Supreme Being on a higher level of consciousness.

Here I would like to introduce a little of Sri Aurobindo's line of thinking. He said that in order to achieve this spiritual renaissance of reawakening, three things are essential. First of all, religion must develop a universal outlook. In the twentieth century, we cannot afford to be sectarian, dogmatic or fanatical. If we are to vindicate the truth of spiritual values, we must discover them in a universal form, rising above sectarianism and dogmatism. Secondly, we need an evolutionary perspective. I mentioned the need for the reconstruction of spirituality in keeping with modern developments. Science and scientific philosophy have given us this evolutionary perspective, which gives us an understanding of the value and importance of time. Thirdly, we need what I may call existential depth.

I should like to explain briefly these three fundamentals of spiritual reawakening. Let us consider universality of outlook. The best way I can explain what I mean is to tell you a story which Mahatma Gandhi shared. In 1947 in New Delhi, representatives of the different world religions were participating in a conference. During a recess some of the delegates were drinking water at a fountain. They were all thirsty, and they all drank the same water. But speaking different languages as they did, they expressed themselves in different ways. They referred to the same substance by using different words. Gandhi said that therein lies the essence of a universal outlook. When people become religious-minded or spiritually-oriented, they feel the thirst of the soul. They are on the lookout for a fountain to satisfy their thirst.

These spiritually thirsty people in different countries and in different ages were perhaps mysteriously guided by God to discover that fountain. But speaking different languages as they did, born in varied historical circumstances, growing up in different cultural systems, they expressed themselves in different ways. In consequence, we have different theological systems in different countries. Underlying these different notions of God there is only one reality.

Similarly, we find that in different religions, ultimate reality is expressed differently. Taoism in China speaks of the way of nature. In Buddhism, it is called *Tathata*, pure existence. In Hinduism, ultimate reality is called *Brahman*, the great, the eternal. In Christianity, this reality is called the Heavenly Father and the Trinity; in Judaism, Jehovah; in Islam, Allah; in Zorastrianism, Ahura Mazda. These different concepts emphasize this or that aspect of the Supreme Being. But underlying all these divergent theological notions there is one ultimate reality which alone is capable of satisfying our spiritual thirst.

This point has been emphasized by the great leaders of what we call the spiritual renaissance in India. Vivekananda, Tagore, Gandhi and Aurobindo all emphasized that we live in a time when it is important to acknowledge the one supreme truth behind all apparently conflicting theological doctrines.

As for evolutionary perspective, the existentialist philosophers of our day agree on one point, and that is the unconditional reality of our existence in this world here and now. This implies concern for conditions of living in this world and fulfillment of our destiny in the world.

When we study the Middle Ages, we find an interesting phenomenon in the West and the East. We find a great preoccupation with the supernatural in some form or another, either as the supernatural kingdom of heaven somewhere beyond the material world or as the transcendental, beyond space and time. In the Hindu-Buddhist tradition, there was preoccupation with the transcendental. In the Judeo-Christian tradition, there was preoccupation with the supernatural.

In the Hindu-Buddhist tradition, due to this preoccupation with the transcendental, there was an emphasis on the unreality of this world. People of that period were concerned with spiritual truth, but they negated the world. They believed God alone is real and this world is unreal. In Europe, we find that the supernatural is the only reality and the natural order is evil. There was this concept of the perpetual struggle between the flesh and the spirit. Only by killing the flesh, eliminating the impulsive side of nature, can we realize the spirit within us. In the East, the natural order was regarded as unreal, and the transcendental alone as the single reality.

In this century, the great existentialist leaders such as Karl Jaspers and Martin Heidegger fulfilled an important task. Drawing inspiration from the beginning of the Western culture, they reaffirmed the reality of this world and the significance of our life in this world. Heidegger said Western culture is great because it began great. The great beginning of Western culture is to be found as far back as original thinkers such as Heraclitus and Parmenides, who had an insight into Being. At that time the foundation was laid for Western culture. After that, many philosophers lost sight of that original ontological insight of Being. They intellectually tried to reconstruct an image of ultimate reality in different ways. The existentialists said it is time for us to restore that original ontological understanding, which gives us the joy of living.

In the Middle Ages people lost the joy of living. They believed we can know God only through mortification of the flesh, absolute renunciation and rigid austerities. They forgot the joy of living. They forgot the fullness of the supreme spirit. There was a separation between nature and spirit in the Middle Ages. But this was not always so. In the beginning we find a wonderful vision of the unity of nature and spirit.

Sri Aurobindo said a similar thing about India. When you go to the beginning of Indian culture, you find an integral vision of ultimate reality. God was experienced as operative in nature, in the world. Let me tell you one passage from a famous Upanishad. 'It is out of the fullness of joy in the heart of reality that the world springs into existence. In joy, everything abides. Into joy, everything is fulfilled.' That is an optimistic view of life and reality emphasizing the joy of living and participation in this wonderful cosmic drama that God has sent for us. In keeping with this, Tagore, the great poet-philosopher, said that to be born in this world is to be invited by God to participate in the festival of light and joy that this universe is.

This is the second point which I am trying to make — affirmation of the reality of this world. In the Middle Ages, that idea of reality and the divine significance of the world somehow was lost due to preoccupation with the transcendental and the supernatural. It is time today to reaffirm this original insight and to understand the divine significance of this world. If we understand this and if we take care of our life here and now in the present, the future will take care of itself. This is a very important principle.

In continuation of this, a further point is the evolutionary perspective. In other words, not only is the world real, it is ever-changing. A wonderful process of evolution, of progressive development is taking place. In order to understand this, we have to understand the scientific theory of evolution on a spiritual basis. Here, evolution is not to be understood as a mechanical process controlled by blind physical forces. The divine significance of evolution is that this universe is a medium of progressive manifestation of the eternal. The process of evolution is increasing manifestation of the glory of the spirit in the realm of matter.

As we look back through history, we find how higher and higher powers of consciousness were brought forth into manifestation. This is a marvelous understanding in which science, religion and philosophy can join hands. When we scan the process of cosmic evolution, we find different stages of unfoldment of matter, life, mind, reason, and spirit. We may go back to the condition of the earth in its simplest expression, when there were only the material elements. In the course of evolution, as the different elements of matter entered into more complex configurations, at a certain stage life appeared on the scene. Life, with its subconscious vital energy, gave rise to a new order of creation — the plant kingdom. This subconscious vital energy had characteristic functions entirely different from the qualities of brute matter. Then when conditions were suitable, a higher degree of complexity of structure and function appeared on the cosmic scene, laying the foundation for the animal kingdom. The animal was born with a higher power of consciousness. Gradually higher and higher species of animals came into being.

At a still higher stage humans and their still higher power of reason and self-consciousness appeared on the scene. Animals are conscious; they know. But humans know that they know. This is self-consciousness. This unique power of self-consciousness is at the root of the efflorescence of human cultural development and creativity in science, art, religion, morality, and other spheres.

By understanding evolution we find how higher powers of consciousness become manifest, laying the foundation for higher orders of creation. This is what Aurobindo meant when he said the cosmic process of evolution is the medium of the increasing manifestation of the inexhaustible glory of the spirit in the realm of matter. This is the stupendous mystery of creation and evolution.

In his view, humans are not the last word in the wisdom of God. Humans are a transition, a link, a preparation for a still higher order. The most wonderful thing is that the next big step in evolution is possible for us to take. It is within our power to transform ourselves into divine humans. Why? Because we are self-conscious. The next step has to be taken through our own free co-operation. Creative freedom is a characteristic of self-consciousness.

According to Sri Aurobindo, human self-consciousness is a lower mode of operation of a higher consciousness, what we may call divine consciousness, cosmic consciousness or supermind. Humans evolved out of animal when self-consciousness was manifested. Humans will be transformed into divine humans, laying the foundation for a unique world order when the cosmic consciousness or supermind becomes fully operative in our life and society.

The most important thing to contemplate is that it is possible for us to co-operate intelligently with the divine power working in nature and evolution. Through what we call religious effort, spiritual discipline and commitment to higher values, we can co-operate with the force of evolution to bring about the manifestation of the supermind in our life and society. This is the evolutionary perspective. The most creative energy in us is revealed when we can look forward meaningfully to our future. When we know something glorious is ahead of us, we release creative energy. Many people have a philosophy of despair. They believe life is meaningless. As they look to the future, they don't see anything to inspire them. Therefore, an important factor in spiritual reawakening is to be able to cultivate a meaningful vision of the future on the basis of our understanding of the divine significance of cosmic evolution.

Finally, I shall say a word about what I call existential depth. There is a common saying: 'The proof of the pudding is in the eating.' The philosophical implication is that the ultimate criterion of truth is experience. We hear a lot of things and they may sound good. But until and unless we experience something, we refuse to be convinced completely. We may give brilliant discourses on God, on the Absolute, on the higher self. They may be intellectually stimulating, but our mind may be filled with scepticism and assailed with doubts. In the absence of any personal experience or realization, this is just high-sounding talk.

The greatest spiritual leaders of the world have emphasized this need for personal realization or for personal communion. This is the goal of our spiritual search. Ultimately, every individual has to work out his or her salvation and come to the point of participating personally in the divine life. In the absence of that personal participation of inward experience, God is hearsay. God is a theory. When something is a theory, we may take it or leave it. Therefore, the most important thing in our religious life is to transform the status of God from rumor or hearsay to personal experience. Then God becomes a reality, a dynamic force in our life.

In our religious life, it is necessary and natural to start with faith. But we must not end just with faith. Swami Vivekananda put it this way: It is all right for people to be born in a mosque or a temple or a church, but for heaven's sake let them not die there! In other words, we may be brought up in a certain faith, but let us not end our life there. The fundamental spiritual task in our life is to transform that faith into living, flaming personal realization. Then God becomes a tremendous reality in our life. This is what I call existential depth.

This is when we need spiritual discipline to reorganize the affairs of life in accordance with our spiritual ideals. By following a certain discipline, we can have some inward experience of God. We can encounter the Supreme Being. All the great spiritual leaders and religious founders were mystics in the true sense of the world. Mystic implies a personal encounter with the supreme.

Every human being has a profound spiritual potential. By actualizing that potential we can enter into direct communion with God. This is our highest spiritual destiny. By doing so we can live and function with the totality of our being.

What happens when we have direct contact with the Supreme Being? How should we regulate our spiritual discipline so we fulfil our destiny in the right way? When we enter into direct communion with ultimate reality, our egocentric individuality is dissolved. Out of the ruins of the ego is reborn our higher self, our spiritual individuality. We can understand this from the analogy of resurrection following the crucifixion. Out of the crucifixion of the egocentric individuality is born the true spiritual individuality. Whether we say Christ is born in us or Buddha is born to us, the fact is, the divine child is born. We discover the higher self within. This is the goal of our spiritual effort. At this stage we learn how to participate in the divine *lila* and join forces with God, who is engaged in this process of cosmic evolution.

Let me close with another story. One time a sincere and serious spiritual seeker was engaged in an all-out spiritual quest. He went to the Himalayan mountains and engaged in deep meditation in a cave. After a long process of self-searching, he had a great illumination and was very excited. He went to the summit of the mountain and saw there a beautiful small temple. The man knocked at the door of the temple, and a voice from within inquired, 'Who are you?' He replied, 'It is I.' The presiding deity of the temple replied, 'Go away! The temple is very small. There is no room for a second person here.'

The man was greatly disappointed. He re-entered his mountain cave and plunged himself into deeper meditation. After another long period of search and contemplation, he had a wonderful realization. Again he went to the temple and knocked at the door. The same voice inquired, 'Who are you?' This time he said, 'Thou.' The door of the temple immediately opened. He entered into the temple and became one with the presiding deity. He came out of the temple reborn as a new personality. He went to the plains and sought the company of people. He began to work with the people, out of a desire to help transform human society into an image of the divine.

This illustrates the different stages of spiritual enlightenment. First, the realization comes when we catch a glimpse of the Supreme Being. But still there is a sense of separateness between 'I' and 'Thou.' We have a vision of God, but we think of God over and above us, outside of us. The next stage comes when the sense of separation is gone. Then we realize God as the Self of our self, the Being of our being, the Consciousness of our consciousness — that we all live and move and have our being in the cosmic medium of this one Supreme.

In the Middle Ages becoming one with the supreme was considered the final goal. But a still higher idea is to come out of the temple. First we must rise up to the highest plane of consciousness, encounter the Divine in the fullest measure, and realize our oneness of being with the One. But then it is imperative that the ascending movement of consciousness is followed by a descending movement of consciousness. That is to say, out of this union we are reborn and are able to bring some of the power and glory of God into the sphere of human relations. After this realization we begin to work in the world as an instrument of the divine, as a channel of expression of the higher values of life. This is our way of participating in the creative process of cosmic evolution, by joining with God toward the fulfillment of human destiny.

2

SEARCH FOR ULTIMATE REALITY

When you know the Ultimate, it becomes your master key to the whole universe and all that is worth knowing. You can call it the Ultimate; you can call it ultimate reality; you can call it Being; you can call it the Absolute. Whatever you call it, the search for the Ultimate is the central motivation of philosophical thinking.

We find this in all cultures. In India, sages searched for the Ultimate from the objective standpoint. For example, ancient Vedic sages searched for the Ultimate by observing the beauty and sublimity of the world around them. They looked with wonder at the things in nature. As they appreciated the beauty and sublimity of cosmic nature, they were inspired to carry on their search for truth, for the Ultimate. This is the objective approach — observing, appreciating and analyzing the things of the natural world.

The subjective, psychological approach came afterward in the period of the Upanishads. Having explored the outside universe, humans looked within to find the ultimate unifying principle of their existence. By following the objective approach, they discovered a principle of unity behind the endless pluralities of the universe, which they called Brahman. Then, following the meditative, subjective approach of exploring the different realms of inner consciousness, they eventually discovered the principle of unity behind the plurality of psychic life, of the mind-body. This was called the Atman, the Self.

It is interesting to note how the human mind has functioned

historically. As we explore the deeper and higher realms of consciousness, ultimately we discover the Atman, the Self, the principle of unity behind the plurality. Finally comes the synthetic approach, the integral approach, the holistic approach. By following the holistic approach, we think of the relationship between the subjective and the objective. One day we make a surprising discovery, that the Self, Atman, and Being, Brahman, are one and the same, not different. The great discovery that they are nondual is a grand synthesis.

Nondual is different from the word 'identical.' For example, there are identical twins in a family. Identity still presupposes two. There are two persons. We say they are identical because they have close similarity, but there is an existential difference. Identity presupposes existential difference. But when we say nondual, it does not presuppose existential difference. Nondual means the same reality. This is why Indian philosophers say nondual or *advaita*. It means the same reality, not two different realities.

It is also important to note that they do not even say 'one.' The highest philosophical expression of Indian thought is not called monistic or monotheistic. It is called nondualistic. Why? Because one presupposes many. 'One' and 'many' belong in the realm of relativity. 'One' is one of the numbers. It presupposes other numbers, so it is relative. One is relative to many. When we say 'nondual', we refer to a reality to which number does not apply.

Number is a category of the human mind which is applicable only to the finite beings of the world. It does not apply to ultimate reality. God has no number. Human beings have numbers, which signify limitation. God, being unlimited, has no number. So from a philosophical standpoint, it is meaningless to say God is one or two or many. God is beyond all this. Number does not apply. Quantity does not apply. Quality does not apply. All these are categories of the human mind, which do not apply to ultimate reality. The ultimate ground of the psychological or subjective world on the one hand, and the physical or objective world on the other, are manifestations of the same reality, which is called Atman-Brahman.

Let me tell you a story from the Upanishads which beautifully describes the human search for ultimate reality. It is such a significant story that its content perfectly fits into the history of philosophy, both Eastern and Western.

There was a young man whose name was Bhrigu. His father was Varuna, a God-realized person. When Bhrigu was going through school, suddenly one day a deep philosophical quest appeared in his mind. He had a strong desire to know Brahman, ultimate reality. He had been reading and gathering information about life and things of the world for so long. Suddenly one day he thought, 'I have knowledge of the different things of the world, but what is beyond all this? What is the nature of the ultimate ground of life?'

It was well known that guidance is necessary to pursue this philosophical quest, the inquiry into Being. So he tried to think of a suitable guru. Suddenly it came to his mind, 'I do not have to go far. Right in my home there is a great teacher — my own father.' With due respect and reverence, he told his father he wanted to know Brahman. But in those days, gurus did not believe in spoon-feeding. They believed that people who easily find the truth, also easily forget it. Spiritual truth has to grow from within. The teacher is simply there to help in this growth process.

Gurus also did not talk too much. So his father said, '*Tapas*, Brahman.' This means those who want to know Brahman have to practice *tapas*, self-discipline. They must organize their whole life in accordance with this one over-mastering impulse of God-realization. If they discipline their lives and pursue the right kind of study and meditation, they will know Brahman.

Bhrigu plunged into a long, hard search for the supreme truth. After a period of self-discipline and meditation, one day he made his first important discovery. It was a landmark in his search. 'Everything in this world, all the multitudinous phenomena of life and existence, sprang into being out of universal matter. In matter they abide. Into matter they go back again.' This means Brahman is universal matter.

He was very excited with this discovery. He found that every living thing lives by matter, by eating food and breathing air and drinking water. That is our nourishment. Then eventually we go back into the elements of nature. He reported his discovery to his father, and Varuna simply smiled a little. Bhrigu was disappointed because he thought is father would be excited, too. He thought he would get a pat on the back and did not understand why his father did not join him in celebration.

After a period of contemplation, doubt entered his mind. In our mature spiritual growth, doubt and critical thinking are important. This is what distinguishes a true spiritual search from an emotional, religious approach. In the religious approach, we often are asked to accept something on faith. But it is not our own. If we accept a tenet on blind faith, it does not become a part of our being. That is why a gulf exists between the inner being and the outer life in many people's lives. Truth does not become one's own. In a true spiritual search, we do our own thinking and complete an evaluation of things. Naturally, we encounter doubt.

In a vague way, Bhrigu felt many things could not be explained in terms of matter. He told his father, 'I know I have not yet found the truth. Would you kindly instruct me?' His father again told him, '*Tapas*, Brahman! Search more. Concentrate your energy more on your quest.' So Bhrigu again plunged into deeper meditation and thought.

After a period of time, he made another discovery. He said, 'Everything comes into being out of life energy. Everything is sustained by the vital energy. And everything is dissolved again into the universal flux.' His father again only gave a faint smile. And again Bhrigu felt the inadequacy of his findings.

His next discovery was this: 'Ultimate reality is cosmic mind, universal mind. Out of that everything comes. In that everything abides. Into that everything is fulfilled.'

It is interesting how the story proceeds. First of all, he makes a discovery, and for some time he is happy. Then doubt enters his mind, and he becomes aware of the inadequacy of his findings. Then again he is inspired by his father to plunge deeper into the spiritual search.

This is the history of the whole human race's search for the truth: These are the milestones and landmarks in our philosophical quest. First is materialism, because to one school of philosophy, matter is ultimate reality. In every country, in every culture this distinct school of philosophy represents a particular stage in our search for the truth. Then humans discover life energy, which is another school and gives rise to what is called vitalistic philosophy. For example, in the West, Henri Bergson was a great, contemporary, vitalistic philosopher. In his book, *Creative Evolution*, he pointed out that ultimate reality is not matter; rather it is the *élan vital*, the universal life force, which is a creative, vital impetus. This is analogous to Bhrigu's second discovery. Then the third discovery is cosmic mind. In every culture, there also is a school of idealistic philosophy,

But after another period of searching and meditating, Bhrigu found that even mind is not ultimate. He discovered a higher principle beyond mind: 'Ultimate reality is universal reason.' Some refer to this as objective idealism, whereas the view which focuses on mind is known as subjective idealism. In the West, subjective idealism was propounded by Bishop George Berkeley, among others, and the outstanding example of the school of objective idealism is Hegelian philosophy.

After further searching, Bhrigu went beyond reason. He said, 'Ultimate reality is *ananda.*' *Ananda* means infinite joy, love, and beauty. When we rise to this level of consciousness, ultimate reality appears as absolute beauty, absolute bliss, and absolute love. Most mystics in various countries have this *ananda*-level experience.

This experience is symbolized in Hindu philosophy by Krishna, the god of love, joy and beauty. The idea is that Krishna is not stern. Krishna is the divine playmate of humans. He is friend, philosopher and guide. He is neither aloof nor commanding. He is the voice of love. To use the expression of Alfred North Whitehead, 'God is persuasive agency,' not stern command. This idea is embodied in the Western tradition in Jesus who went beyond the previous concept of God as justice and law to the discovery that God is love.

Bhrigu's story ends by saying that he eventually went beyond even the *ananda* level, but what that is cannot be said. Something beyond it cannot be put into words. It is indescribable. As we catch a glimpse of it, we are struck dumb and cannot speak. We have no words to express our inner experience. All we can say is that the reality behind it is 'the great silence.' It is an unfathomable mystery.

The *ananda*-level experience gives rise to spiritual philosophy and is the source of inspiration to the great mystics the world over. It is their aspiration to experience reality on this level. Then they are led spontaneously beyond this level to catch a glimpse of that which is beyond it. The element of mystery becomes important. Some refer to it as the Godhead beyond God, and others call it 'the deep, dazzling darkness.' Those who reach this level believe that what they are experiencing is not all. Beyond that there is a great unknown, an unfathomable mystery. This makes them humble. And this is the difference between a true knower of the truth of ultimate reality and a pseudo-knower, or a pseudo-mystic. A person who has real, authentic knowledge always becomes humble.

Bhrigu's story from the Taittiriya Upanishad is significant and interesting because it shows the different stages in our search for the Ultimate. There is level beyond level — the physical, the vital, the mental, the purely rational, and beyond that, the intuitive or mystical. This is a wonderful story since all of the different schools of philosophy and spiritual thought can be classified under these five general areas.

From the standpoint of integral philosophy, there is no incompatibility or mutual exclusion among the materialistic, vitalistic, the idealistic, and the mystical schools of thought. When we analyze closely with a broad, open mind, we find there are precious elements of truth embodied in all these different thought systems which can be brought together in a comprehensive, harmonious whole of cosmic vision and experience. All these are different, interrelated dimensions of the same universe.

A major thesis of integral philosophy is that the universe in which we live is not one-dimensional, but rather, it is multi-dimensional. It has many different aspects. Just as in religion it is said there are many rooms in the house of God, so there are many dimensions of this universe, which is the house of the cosmic spirit. They are interrelated and intersupporting.

You can easily understand this interrelatedness by looking within yourself. Within your own life and existence you will find different aspects — your body, your life, your mind, your reason, your spirit — which are interrelated. All these are different aspects of your total reality. Corresponding to these different aspects of your being are different aspects of the universe. You are a microcosm representing the macrocosm.

We can follow a dialectical method to establish this. This is not dialectical materialism, but spiritual dialectics. An essential feature of the dialectical method is completing a circle. We come back to the point from which we started, but in a larger and richer form. The circle is an accurate geometrical representation of the perfection and completeness of reality.

The first important stage of spiritual dialectics, or what I like to call integral dialectics, is to follow the method of *via negativa* — *'neti, neti'* — not this, not this. Mystics the world over have followed this in their search for the truth. This is the method illustrated in the story. Bhrigu first finds matter in his search for ultimate reality. Then he says, 'No, it is not this. This is not enough.' This is the method of negation. In the search for the Ultimate, we constantly negate that which is not ultimate in order to go beyond it. This is the path of organic self-transcendence. In our search for the Ultimate, we keep going beyond and beyond and beyond.

First we follow the path of negation to arrive at 'the great silence.' Some stopped at the level of *ananda* and referred to ultimate reality as *Satchitananda*, existence-consciousness-bliss. Others, especially in Buddhism, did not stop at bliss. They went beyond it. They talk about emptiness — the great silence. They emphasize *nirguna* — the formless — that no word is enough.

We are climbing the rungs of the cosmic ladder. This is called the ascending process, and we have peak experiences as we reach higher and higher summits. Having reached the highest peak, people often say, 'Ah, this is wonderful! This is what I have been looking for all of my life.' They feel perfectly happy because they have reached the summit, and that fills their whole being with ecstatic joy and indescribable bliss. What else can they want? They are on top of the world.

But in the dialectical approach, the ascending process is followed by a descending process in order to complete the circle. In other words, we are not just concerned with the highest but with the whole. The total mountain includes the summit and the base and the body. So *'neti, neti'* is followed by *'iti, iti'* —

enlightened affirmation of the whole. In other words, after having reached the highest, we must glance back and pay attention to all other levels we have rejected or passed by. Nothing should be rejected completely from our life. Everything has its own place.

For example, let us say we rejected material life. Where we first said, *'neti, neti,'* now we say, *'iti, iti'* — 'This too, this too.' In other words, we say, 'I first rejected matter in my search for the Ultimate. However, I now recognize it as having an important reality. It is a form of manifestation of the Ultimate, of Being. Nothing is outside of Brahman, or Being.' Then we turn to life energy, *élan vital*, and we say, 'This also is a form of manifestation of Being. It has its own value. It had its own proper place and function in the total scheme of existence.' We no longer reject it. We affirm everything, recognizing how everything is closely interrelated. The circle is completed.

Another important structural feature of the dialectical method is what is called triadic rhythm: a movement through the triadic process of thesis, antithesis, synthesis; position, opposition, reconciliation; affirmation, negation, reaffirmation. This is the triadic rhythm of the dialectical process of growth. It is the natural course of things.

As we begin our life, we live in the material world, and we identify with our body, which is matter. We appreciate and enjoy the material values of life. This is the thesis, our original position. Everybody starts life this way. The first things we notice and understand to be real are our body and this material world with its different physical things. We not only enjoy it, but we also are attached to this world. We have an instinctual identification with the material body and with the material world. For a period of time, things go fine. We are eating, drinking, and being merry. We want to enjoy more.

As we develop intellectually and spiritually, a disenchantment takes place within us as physical pleasures cannot give us the happiness for which we are looking. Deep down in our hearts, this realization dawns. As our soul becomes hungry, we look beyond purely material values. Some say, 'I don't care for money or possessions. Let me go to a quiet retreat. Let me search for truth there for some time, at least.' That is antithesis,

SEARCH FOR ULTIMATE REALITY 37

negation. This is an expression of *'neti'* in their lifestyle, which is called renunciation.

The third stage is synthesis, coming back to the thesis in a larger form. Having gained supra-physical experience, whether vital, mental, or spiritual, then we take another look at matter. We look at it in a different light. It does not look like the same material world which we left. It is clothed in a new significance because we see how it is a meaningful field of manifestation of the supreme spirit.

From the integral or holistic standpoint, the whole of life and the whole of the universe has great significance. Everything has its proper place and function in the total scheme of existence. It is like a cosmic stage on which a divine drama is being enacted and in which we join and participate in a divine play.

3

PRESERVATION OF VALUES

Everything that is born dies. There is no escape from that. This is the inevitable characteristic of all that is finite and limited. In the process of evolution of nature and life, we find old and worn-out forms dissolve so that out of their ruins new forms, values, and patterns of existence emerge into being.

Yet, in spite of all this dissolution and change, there is a divine assurance of preservation. Supreme values are preserved in the midst of all changes and mutations. Just as in science we have a law of conservation of energy, in spiritual philosophy we have a fundamental law of the conservation and preservation of values. Everything good that you do, every noble thought that passes through your mind represents values which are preserved in the tablets of eternity.

4

EXISTENTIALISM AND KIERKEGAARD

The approach of the great Danish philosopher Soren Kierkegaard has stimulated the thinking of many intellectuals and spiritual seekers today. Without an understanding of his thoughts and ideas, it is not possible to understand many contemporary movements in philosophic and religious thinking.

Existentialism is an important contemporary philosophy, in which, broadly speaking, there are two schools. One is the religious or theistic school, and the other is the non-religious or atheistic school of existentialism. Kierkegaard is regarded as the father of the modern theistic or religious form. If you study his writings, you will find he was a great poet, philosopher, prophet, and above all a supremely religious man. He emanated some fruitful and powerful thought vibrations into the cosmic atmosphere. At the same time, I also shall call attention to some of his limitations. Understanding those limitations allows us to see some great lessons from his life and from his philosophy, because we are able to learn from both the positive contributions and the defects of a great thinker.

Kierkegaard was born in Denmark in 1813 and died in 1855. If I have to choose one line by way of summing up his philosophy and his religious viewpoint, that line would be, 'Exist as an individual self.' What does it mean to 'exist as an individual'? First of all, Kierkegaard said that in order to exist as an individual self, we must renounce insincerity and false pretense. By way of elucidating this point, he made a severe, prophetic attack upon the official Christianity of his time. He called it bourgeois Christianity and said that when we try to understand the sayings and the writings of many so-called Christians, we find a lot of falsification and insincerity. In the strict sense of the term, few people can be called true Christians because most just pay lip homage to the basic principles of Christianity without putting them into practice. So he did not really attack Christianity. He attacked the false practices of Christianity and those who passed themselves off as Christians, whom he called hypocrites. Instead of being Christian, they were great enemies of Christianity.

Kierkegaard said that the essence of Christianity lies in existential living. If we have knowledge of the truth, if we know something to be true, the most important thing from the standpoint of religion is to live on the basis of that conviction. To put those beliefs into practice is what he called existential living. Without this existential living, those beliefs are mere ideas in our minds which do not affect our pattern of living or the substance of out inner existence and consciousness. Therefore, those beliefs mean nothing.

Let me tell you a story in this connection. A pastor once asked a little girl, 'Do you know what is in your Bible?' The girl replied, 'Sure I do. I know everything that is in the Bible.' The pastor was amused and asked her to tell him a little of what she knew. She said, 'My mother puts receipts in the Bible, but my father will not put anything in the Bible. My sister's snapshots of her friend are in the Bible. And a lock of my hair which was cut off when I was a baby is in the Bible.'

Kierkegaard would say that many people who memorize Bible sayings without putting the basic principles and truths into practice have the same attitude to the Bible. Divorced from our actual day-to-day living, our inner ideas and beliefs mean nothing. They don't represent truth. As Kierkegaard said, 'Real truth is subjective and is not just an objective idea.' The real truth is subjectivity. If we do not acquire ever-deepening awareness of our own subjective nature, if we do not know how to transform our personality in the light of the truth that we experience, then it is no truth at all.

Further, Kierkegaard said that the fundamental religious issue is not what you believe, not what you know and not what you have. The fundamental religious issue is to be or not to be what you are. If we do not pay attention to this fundamental question — how to be one's self and how to become harmonized with the essence of one's being — then we do not understand the meaning of religion at all. He pointed out that Christians often talk about Christianity and then live a superficial life of enjoyment without the sincerity and the courage to fight for the truth which they believe. They live with a false sense of respectability. They think that because people accept them and fear them, that is the essence of their religious life. Misled by this false sense of responsibility, they lack the courage to fight, lest their respectability or their popularity be disturbed.

Secondly, he said that in order to exist as an individual self, one has to renounce mere intellectualism, because this is a great hindrance to existential living and to establishing an existential relationship to God or ultimate reality. In this respect, he severely attacked the philosophy of the great German thinker Hegel. Hegel is regarded as the leading spokesman of idealistic philosophers. He built up a wonderful philosophical structure, the philosophy of objective dialectical idealism. The fundamental maxim or tenet of Hegel was, 'Reality is identical with thought,' with reason, idea. According to Hegel, 'All that is real is rational; all that is rational is real.' This is the essence of rationality, of the rationalistic approach to life and reality. By applying his dialectical method, Hegel built up a magnificent philosophical system in which he believed the deepest secret of reality, the nature of God, was expressed completely.

Kierkegaard pointed out that this is extremely misleading to the true spiritual seeker. It is not enough to know everything about a philosophical system, if it does not help you to transform your own existence and your own subjectivity, your inner nature and consciousness. On the contrary, it is just misleading. This was the essence of his criticism of Hegelian idealism and intellectualism. However clever and profound your philosophical ideas may be, however powerful your language and expression, the nature of reality or the nature of God can never be expressed adequately through human intellect and reason, Kierkegaard said. By its very nature, that is impossible. Why impossible? Because at the heart of reality a supreme paradox defies human understanding and outsoars logical conceptions of the human mind. It is an impossible task to express the nature, the depths and the mystery of reality in a philosophical system.

Moreover, Kierkegaard said such an attempt distracts attention from the fundamental religious task of inner growth, self-development and self-realization. He claimed our philosophical thinking is a transition from reality to possibility. By conceptual thinking and philosophizing, we enter into a realm of imagination, and we deal with infinite possibilities. This is a transition from reality to possibility, whereas true existential living is a passage from possibility to actuality, in actualizing the possibilities of life. In order to actualize the dynamic possibilities of our own existence, we need something other than mere contemplation. We need choice. We need intelligent selection. We need to go through pain and suffering, doubt and despair.

Thirdly, Kierkegaard said, in order to live and exist as an individual self, one had to renounce outward social bondage and emotional attachments. In this respect, he is in line with the Neo-Platonic view. The Neo-Platonic view is that in order to realize God, we must fly alone to the Alone. In the course of the pilgrimage of the soul, we have to strip ourselves of all external wrappings, ties, bonds, and fetters and prepare ourselves to meet the supreme reality alone. This is another essential condition of inward spiritual realization. Until and unless we have the courage to do so, we cannot realize God in the full sense of the word. If we cannot realize God in the full sense of the word, we cannot realize our inward selves either. Self-realization, the attainment of authentic existence, is impossible without realizing God — and we need to realize God alone.

Let me tell you some facts about Kierkegaard's life to illustrate this point. At the age of 27, he fell in love with a woman. For some time he was thrilled with the idea of married life and of establishing an organic relationship with society and with the world. But after a year, he suddenly broke off the engagement. A great conflict was going on within him. On the one hand, he felt the religious impulse to make an all-out effort to realize God, to know God — what we may call a passion for the Absolute. On the other hand, he had a wordly desire, as he called it, to get married, to have a family and to establish a relationship with the social environment.

Finally he made a decision. He said that his goal was God-realization, and in order to achieve that ideal, he decided not to marry. But because he really loved the woman and did not want to make her unhappy, he did something else. Not only did he sacrifice her, he sacrificed his own image in her mind. He sacrificed her goodwill by painting himself in such black hues that she broke off the engagement. He thought his action would save her from disappointment and unhappiness so she could marry somebody else. So he set both of them free through this double sacrifice.

He wrote about a parallel to this situation, the sacrifice of Abraham. As you know, Abraham dearly loved his son, Isaac. One night Abraham had a dream or a vision in which God commanded him to sacrifice his beloved son to prove his utmost loyalty to God. Abraham was torn by his great love for his son and his utmost loyalty to God, but his loyalty to God came first. The next morning he took Isaac to the top of a mountain. He built a fire and an altar. When everything was ready, Isaac said, 'Father, here is the fire and the wood, but where is the lamb to be offered?' Abraham said, 'God will provide the lamb.' You can imagine the breaking of his heart as he tied his son's hands and placed him on the altar. He raised his knife, and just at that moment a voice called out to him. 'Abraham! Don't do anything to your child. You have been tested, and God has been much pleased to see your loyalty.' Then Abraham heard a noise, and he found a ram caught by its horns in a nearby thicket. The ram was brought out and became the offering.

Kirkegaard saw the similarity to his own life between his loyalty to God and his love for a woman. But after making his decision, he felt great despair, unhappiness and suffering. He thought that just as Abraham got his son back, so, too, might his fiancée return. But that did not happen.

Let us try to analyze the working of his mind. As you can see, he thought his fiancée was a rival for God and that to serve God, he had to sacrifice her. He thought he was confronted with an exclusive alternative, but was that true? Is there, in fact, polar opposition, an exclusive destruction between such alternatives? Can a human being really be a rival of God? Is it not rather the truth that loved ones have been created by God so that through our acceptance and love of them we can reach God more easily? That is the question to think about, because here lies the fundamental defect of Kierkegaards's philosophical attitude, for which he suffered a good deal. He construed the whole situation as a disjunction, a mutual opposition, as if anyone can rival God.

Another limitation of his outlook was that he thought of God as the radical opposite of nature. His fiancée symbolized the spirit of nature, our organic relationship with society and the universe. Kierkegaard's assumption was that we have to sacrifice the one for the other. Is that true? Does not God live in nature? Is there not profound wisdom in the heart of nature? Nature is our great teacher. The Tantric philosophy of India tells us that in order to enter into the kingdom of heaven, we must place ourselves in the schooling of nature and obtain our own graduation.

Kierkegaard also pointed out that while Hegel and other philosophers talk about the categories of philosophical thinking, there is another set of categories which is of greater importance. These are the categories of existential living, personal realization, inner growth and our approach to the infinite. We all go through anxiety, despair, guilt, inner suffering, and torment, a dark night of the soul, being limited and human as we are, in our journey toward the kingdom of heaven. We have to understand properly the significance of these stages in our inner growth as we strive for self-realization and God-realization. These are some of the essential conditions of increasing self-awareness and approach to God. The moment we become aware of our freedom and decide to tread the path of freedom, great anxiety develops in our minds. This is the anxiety of freedom. We know we may wrongly use our freedom, that we may sin by exercising our freedom. This anxiety is inseparable from freedom.

Despair also grows. As we become aware of our own inner nature, our attention is drawn to our limitations, our defects, our shortcomings, and we face a growing sense of despair within us. As long as we do not think about these, we are fine. But eventually we must begin to come to terms with our inmost self, our actual nature.

Then there is discontent. As we catch a glimpse of the infinite and become aware of our spiritual potential, the possibility of approaching God, the more discontent we feel. When we are no longer satisfied with ourselves as we are, we begin to strive for something higher, greater and nobler. We experience 'divine madness,' to use Plato's term. This carries with it a sense of guilt in the philosophical sense of the word. According to Kierkegaard, as we stand in the presence of God, the infinite, as finite beings, we experience 'fear and trembling.' Just as Abraham had 'fear and trembling' when he was in the presence of God and was about to sacrifice his son, we react with 'fear and trembling' as we are confronted with standing alone facing God. We experience the nothingness of our own existence in the august presence of the Supreme.

That is our first existential experience. Afterward, we may have the wisdom to accept ourselves just as we are, with all our limitations and shortcomings. This acceptance soothes us. We accept ourselves as we are and offer ourselves to the divine. We surrender to God. When we have this attitude of self-acceptance and self-offering to the divine, something miraculous happens. We begin to experience the grace of God. We know that in spite of all our nothingness and unworthiness, we are acceptable to the divine. This is the third stage. As we experience divine grace, we witness a transformation of our being and the birth of a new self. We come to understand the meaning of self-realization. A new self is born in us, a transformed personality which is the synthesis of the finite and the infinite, of the actual and the ideal. This new self is the result of our contact with and our offering to the divine.

But Kierkegaard said this self-realization is not a static thing. It is a dynamic process, a continuous struggle toward the fulfillment of the divine in our lives. Kierkegaard used two expressions to describe his transformation — 'reduplication' and 'repetition.' 'Reduplication' means putting into practice the basic spiritual principles, trying to live in an existential way. The highest fulfillment of this reduplication is what he called 'repetition' — that is, repeating the divine pattern in our own life. The repetition also may be called transfiguration of personality or the birth of a new self within. But we must understand that in his concept of self-realization, the self does not mean a mental concept or the soul. The self here means a dynamic relationship between body and soul or between us as finite beings and God as an infinite reality. It is relationship. And it is through our contact with the divine that this relationship is established and this new self is born within us.

Now I shall make some brief points of criticism of Kierkegaard's philosophy. First of all, we shall find that his religious experience was limited, although certainly he had a profound religious experience in his life. It was a particular type, a particular phase of religious experience that was conditioned by circumstances of his own life. Kierkegaard, being the youngest of seven children, was emotionally attached to his father. Instead of having much companionship with the other children, he considered his father to be his main companion. After his father died, he was terribly shaken and moved to the depths of his being. In the course of time, his religious thinking mainly took the form of longing for his father. Consequently, the fulfillment of that religious experience mainly came as the reunion with God, the Father. That is how he refers to God — as God, the Father. In this way, his spiritual experience was limited and conditioned or determined by these material facts of his own life.

Also, much of his religious thinking is dominated by the concepts of guilt and sin, gloominess, melancholy, and despair. This is certainly an unhealthy thing. But that also is to be understood with reference to his own life. From his childhood, he lived under the shadow of sin and guilt. He had a terrible guilt consciousness which is one reason why he thought he should not live a normal life and chose to abandon his fiancée. His father once told him a great secret which had a devastating effect upon the boy. The father confided that after his first wife died, he raped a servant woman and later married her; by her, he had the seven children. The boy thought that as a result of his father's great sin, the curse of God was upon the whole family.

So he grew up with a great sense of melancholy, sin and guilt which produced a terrific conflict within him.

Whatever psychological factors were involved, there is no doubt Kierkegaard was a God-intoxicated man. All his passion and all the libido energy of his soul were turned to God. As some would say, he was crazy for God. But he did not know how to handle this spiritual seeking, because he did not have the training to come to terms with this great passion within him.

Those of you who have read Tantric philosophy will remember that when this passion for the infinite is awakened, it is called *kundalini*. Or you may call it the awakened and spiritually oriented libido energy. But Hindu philosophers point out that even this passion for God has to be handled carefully and kept under control. Otherwise, it will consume you. It will destroy you. It may sound paradoxical, but that is the truth. That is what happened to Kierkegaard. He had no way of controlling and properly balancing this infinite passion within him, and consequently, he was consumed and devoured by that passion. It had a shattering effect upon his health, and he died a premature death at age 42 in a devitalized condition. That is where the need for a teacher arises. Sometimes an individual does not know what to do, but with the proper guidance of a good teacher, this awakened passion for the infinite can be channelled properly and kept under control so that harmony and balance can be established in life.

Finally, I shall mention that Kierkegaard, in criticizing the philosophy of Hegel, committed another mistake in his concept of irrationalism. For Kierkegaard, the supreme task of religious life was to accept such things as revelation or divine incarnation as absurd, irrational phenomena. He said, how can the infinite be manifested in the form of the finite? How can the eternal be manifested in time? By reason, we cannot understand it, but still it is true. It must be true. By faith we have to accept, for example, Jesus Christ as the manifestation of the infinite in the finite. Kierkegaard said this is just an absurd phenomenon which we have to accept by faith. So this is irrationalism.

I am reminded of a story in this connection. A Chinese visitor to the United States was asked his impression of Americans. He said, 'Americans are funny people. They keep their rooms overheated, and then they eat ice cream to feel cool. They pour lemon juice into water to make it sour, and then they add sugar to make it sweet. They take wine and say "Here's to you," and then drink it themselves!' This too, appears to be irrationalism, but, of course, it is not really so.

I would say that Kierkegaard considered the manifestation of the infinite in the finite irrational only because of the strong dualistic assumption with which he started. Who said that the infinite is the opposite of the finite? Who said there is a radical gulf between God and humans?

I would say this is only one side of the picture. It is true God is infinite, and we are finite. Therefore, as we comprehend the infinite distance that separates the finite and the infinite, we have the sense of nothingness. We feel very small against the great immensity of God. That is true. But the other side of the picture is that there is no unbridgeable gulf between the finite and the infinite. The finite is a form of manifestation of the infinite, and the infinite is seeking to express itself in and through the finite. Consequently, as we reflect upon our relationship to God, the infinite, we have a sense of closeness and affinity because we are children of the infinite, children of immortality. We don't exist separate from God. We exist and live and have our being within the all-comprehending consciousness of God. As a result of this feeling of being rooted in divine consciousness, we feel great joy and infinite security.

5

ALBERT CAMUS AND BUDDHISM

It is fascinating to observe how some of the brilliant minds of today have rediscovered truths which reaffirm the ancient wisdom of great sages. This meeting point of modern thought and ancient wisdom is an intriguing study. As you know, Albert Camus was a brilliant thinker and writer of modern times. He died young, but in a short time he made a valuable contribution to civilization, in recognition of which he won the Nobel Prize. I will discuss some of these truths he articulated and then note the striking similarity that exists between his thinking and Buddhism.

First, I would like to tell you about his doctrine of innocence. Camus drank deeply at the fountain of nature, and he saw truth in its beauty and sublimity. As a lover of nature, he protested against theological preoccupation with sin and the doctrine of the sinfulness of humans.

Much of theological thinking, and this is true of Christian theology, is sin-ridden. There is too much emphasis upon the basic sinfulness of humans. The psychological truth is that when you hammer too much upon sinfulness and crime, you may become sinful. As Buddha once said, humans are what they think. If we think we are good for nothing, worthless and sinful, we become those things. But if we have a positive approach, contemplating the higher values of life and valuing the assets of our personalities, these are the things which come to the fore of our consciousness and become dynamic forces in our lives.

Consistent with this discovery of modern psychoanalysis, Camus believed much of the criminality of human nature is due to a sickness of the mind. Therefore, we should feel sympathy and compassion and not be angry and mete out harsh punishment. We certainly do make mistakes and sometimes commit horrible crimes, but basically human nature, which is part of cosmic nature, is innocent.

In nature, there is no sin — there is innocence. In this dynamic interplay of different vital forces, there is no such thing as sinfulness. What we call good, what we call evil, what we call virtuous or sinful, are products of the interaction of the individual human nature with the social environment. We grow up in a certain community, and from our childhood we unconsciously imbibe the cultural patterns and ethical norms of the society to which we belong. As a result of this interaction between the individual and society, we generate emotional and ideological conflicts, which humans are not always able to solve. Anti-social activities and criminal tendencies are the result of these unresolved conflicts in the depth of our unconscious mind.

In order to cure this, we have to look deep into human nature and understand the dynamics of the human unconscious so we can eliminate and resolve these conflicts. We have to turn inward and know ourselves, and by the power of truth we shall be saved. This was the great achievement of the Buddha, which is an interesting point of comparative study. Buddha said all the sinful, anti-social activities and tendencies of humans can be traced back ultimately to their primal ignorance.

This is called *avidya* in Sanskrit. Many people miss the central point of the theory of ignorance as the source of evil, so I would like to explain this. We know from experience that when we are confronted with different alternatives and courses of action, we often realize that one is good and one is not good. Even so, we may choose the wrong path. Often that happens because of certain strong impulses within us. This is a common experience.

In view of this fact, how can we say that ignorance is the cause of wrong doings? Why do we knowingly choose the path of evil? In order to understand the theory of Camus and Buddhist and Hindu philosophers, we have to do some deep thinking.

Let us say someone thinks about robbing a bank or stealing from her neighbor. She knows this is evil, but still she chooses that path. If we analyze this person, we will find conflicts within her. Somehow she feels justified in stealing. Somehow she feels the existing social order, the status quo, is not good. She has been cheated by society. In her mind, she may feel that many people are making a lot of money, but they have made their money by exploiting the poor. Inside she somehow feels she could make better use of the money for herself as well as for others who are in similar circumstances. She feels somehow a higher law makes her action right.

Thus the whole concept of good and evil is in question. We have to rethink this value distinction. From the ultimate standpoint, what is good and what is evil? What is right? What is wrong? This is the doctrine of *avidya*. The idea is that when we talk of ignorance, we do not mean empirical ignorance. We mean the crime of fundamental ignorance about the ultimate value of life and the true nature of the society in which we live. *Avidya* is ignorance about our place, function, and goal in the total scheme of the universe. Ignorance about these things makes us evil or makes us choose the wrong path.

According to the teaching of Buddha, when people become aware of the ultimate meaning of life and the purpose of existence, they cannot commit any evil. The light of truth saves them. As soon as they have a vision of the truth, their whole being is filled with the spirit of love, because love is the other face of truth. As soon as you know the truth, you cannot but be motivated by the spirit of love. Your whole being is filled with the spirit of compassion, and good deeds spontaneously flow from your vision of truth and the spirit of love.

That was also the teaching of Socrates. He said, 'Knowledge is virtue,' but this statement also has been much misunderstood. Again, we know what is right and what is wrong, but still we often choose wrong. So how can Socrates say knowledge is virtue? By knowledge, Socrates did not mean superficial intellectual knowledge, secondhand knowledge or book-learning knowledge. By knowledge, he meant the inward vision of the truth, which is an absolute, which is a power of the total self, of a person's whole character. According to Socrates, when people have this inward vision of truth, they are necessarily virtuous.

Let me also point out that Buddha did not merely affirm that all criminal tendencies are ultimately traceable to primal ignorance. Buddha was a practical teacher. He chalked out in definite terms the eight-fold path which can lead to the liquidation of ignorance and the attainment of enlightenment. This enlightenment fills our whole being with pure compassion and love, which is the essence of goodness and virtue. There can be no goodness or virtue apart from the spirit of love in the human heart. And there can be no genuine self-love without knowledge of the truth. These are all interconnected.

Secondly, I should like to tell you about the existentialist strain in Camus's thinking. He said the human situation is absurd because it is paradoxical. For example, we are involved in many vicious circles. One vicious circle is war and peace. At the end of every great war, we think we are through with this nasty business of war. New hope springs in our minds after a bloodbath, but the march of time shows it is a vain hope. After another period of time, another war breaks out. Thus it goes, the vicious circle of war and peace, peace and war.

As we look back to the beginnings of civilization, we find this has been a recurring cycle. Is it possible there may be the dawn of an entirely new world order where war will be eliminated? We do not know. All we know is that we move through constant fluctuations of joy and sorrow, pain, and pleasure — another vicious circle. This is the absurdity of life.

With the help of Greek myths, Camus dealt elaborately with the nature of the human condition. He told us the story of Sisyphus, a powerful king who had great scorn for the gods, for which he was severely punished. It was the punishment of a thankless task. He had to push a heavy boulder to the top of a hill, only to have it fall back to the bottom. Then he had to start from the beginning again. In his book, *The Myth of Sisyphus*, Camus pointed out that this story describes the human condition. When you think about it, the life of the average human is a humdrum existence. We get up in the morning, rush to work and go through a lot of drudgery. Then we go to bed, only to start the same routine the following day. This story is repeated day after day.

Camus also told another myth from ancient Greece, the story of Tantalus. Most of these tragic heroes had great contempt for the gods or supernatural deities, for which they were punished. But Tantalus also committed the crime of cannibalism. His punishment was to be placed in the midst of a pool of clear, pure water. Whenever he was thirsty and bent down to drink, the water would sink beneath the ground and disappear. Overhead were branches of trees laden with delicious fruit of all kinds. However, when he would reach for the fruit, the branches flew away from him.

Visualize his situation. He is slowly dying of hunger and thirst. Water, water everywhere, but not a drop to drink. Camus said that this too is the human situation. Our souls are athirst for higher values, but still we are dying of loneliness. We are dying from the pangs of alienation from our fellow beings and estrangement from the ground of existence. It is the same situation. The age-old aspiration running through the human heart is for love, immortality, peace, harmony, equality, justice and fraternity. These are the fruits hanging in front of us, tempting us. But as soon as we reach out for the fruits, they fly away.

The Greeks believed this condition was due to strange, supernatural forces. Camus, however, said we do not know whether or not there are supernatural forces. All we can say is that this life belongs to us. We have to live this life and to accept life in all its facets. Camus said that when Sisyphus clearly realized this was his life, he gained peace of mind. By becoming aware of his situation, he conquered the situation.

Camus did not give us a solution, but offered an idea upon which to reflect. The idea is that the human situation is paradoxical. We are involved in what Buddhism calls *samsara*, the cycle of being born, dying and being reborn, the cycle of pain and pleasure, joy and sorrow, love and hatred, war and peace. Camus tried to tell us not to blame the situation upon anything remote. It is not the gods or supernatural fates. We do not know whether those things exist. What we know is that this is part of human life. Understand it as it is. Try to live it heroically.

Buddhism also does not believe in a supernatural fate and

has an optimistic message for us. The message is that ultimately all the happenings of life are traceable to karma, and even karma is ultimately due to ignorance. Therefore, the most inspiring message of Buddhism is that it is possible for us to lift that veil of ignorance to attain an unclouded vision of the truth as it is. By doing so, we can conquer our karma and discover a new source of higher values, light, joy, love, and peace. That is the great spiritual potential which is within our power to actualize.

Camus also explicitly raised and discussed the question of how to remedy the human situation. What is the exit out of it? One ancient and traditional solution is supernaturalism. Ordinary religious, theological teaching says life is full of sorrow, suffering and dark forces operating in the natural order of existence. The best solution is to believe that beyond the frontiers of the natural order is a supernatural kingdom. If we reorganize our lives, eventually we can pass on to this kingdom.

Camus, however, did not accept that solution. He said life is one. The world is one. There is no dualism between the natural and the supernatural. There is just one continuous, unbroken world order. In line with most other contemporary philosophers, he said that the supernatural order is the product of humans' wishful thinking.

Another solution which has been suggested is utopianism. Some philosophers do not believe in the supernatural kingdom, but instead believe in a glorious utopian future of mankind. In the course of time — we may not know exactly when — a wonderful new age is going to dawn. We have to look forward to that new age, and the utopian kingdom will be ushered into existence. We also may take some steps toward that, they say.

According to Camus, communist ideology is one such utopian ideology. Communism, he said, is based upon certain scientific doctrines such as survival of the fittest and determinism. Camus said that the trouble with utopians is that in extending their vision to a hypothetical future, they often feel justified in indulging in war and violence in the present. Utopians take their stand upon the ethical doctrine that the end justifies the means. If a classless society is the goal, we can rob Paul in order to help Peter.

Like Gandhi, Camus said that if the end is to be good, the means also must be good. He did not believe that the end justifies the means. In the name of a remote future, we certainly are not justified in committing acts of violence, in supporting or encouraging the slaughter of people. He believed in the doctrine of noble means for a noble end. This line of thinking is in conformity with ancient wisdom. By adopting the wrong means, we ruin our end. This is a profound truth. From that, Camus concluded that the most important ethical theory or rule of life is to live in the present. If we know how to live our life correctly and do things which are noble in the present, the future will take care of itself.

Let me tell you a story from an ancient book about the importance of the present as against the past and the future. A village woman was carrying a jar full of oil on her head to the marketplace. As she walked, she daydreamed about the future and about how much money she would make by selling the oil. She figured that in one month she could make at least 100 rupees. Soon her dreams expanded to how much she could make in a year or two. Then she figured that in ten years she would be able to buy a home. As she visualized that, she started dancing in joy and the jar of oil fell to the ground. Her dreams lay in ruin at her feet.

That often happens in our lives as we try to escape from the present. We cast our glance backward at the past and become preoccupied with the good old days. Or, we project ourselves far into the future and forget what we need to do in the present. Either preoccupation ends in catastrophe. We have to learn our lessons from the past, and we also must keep alive in our prayers a healthy hope and aspiration for the future. But essentially we must concentrate on the present, doing the things that have to be done now.

If we train ourselves to take full care of the living present, the future takes care of itself. We creatively advance into the future, because that is the nature of time. As we do things right in the present, we creatively allow the future to build itself for us. That is a great message from Camus upon which we can reflect.

6

KARMA

Karma is a Sanskrit word meaning 'action.' However, even people who have studied Hindu philosophy often have misconceptions about the true meaning and significance of the law of karma, which is a fundamental spiritual principle.

The law of karma implies that the universe is an eternal moral order. The law of karma contrasts with the mechanistic conception of material science. Science tells us the world is controlled by natural forces, specifically particles of matter combining and recombining with one another in accordance with blind physical forces. Chance presides over this casting and recasting of the cosmic weather. In other words, the world is just a big machine.

Karma tells us that even behind these apparently blind, mechanical forces, there is a principle of cosmic intelligence, a power, which controls the operations of nature and guides the destiny of humankind. The power accords with what Plato called the 'idea of good,' the principle of goodness. Plato gave a masterful analogy to the structural principles of our life when he pointed out that the root and principle of the whole universe is the idea of good.

Even though in other great religions the word karma may not be used, the idea is there because this is a fundamental spiritual law, a basic premise of all religious or spiritual outlooks. The fundamental truth of natural science is faith in the conservation of energy, which means that the sum total of energy in this universe remains constant. Not an iota of energy is ever lost. All the changes we see are in the nature of transformation of energy, energy passing from one form to another. This is the basic assumption or postulate of science. Likewise, a fundamental principle of religion is faith in the conservation of the higher values of life. These values such as truth, beauty, goodness, freedom and honesty are powerful, dynamic forces not only in society, but in the universe as a whole. The world in which we live is not just a mechanical structure. It is not a field of accidental forces blindly jostling at one another, but is ultimately determined by a supreme spiritual being. When we understand this, other expressions of the law of karma become clear.

You are familiar with the expression, 'As you sow, so shall you reap.' This is the second implication of the law of karma. The law of karma tells us we live in an eternal moral order. From that it follows that whenever we do something which disturbs the moral balance of the universe, the moral balance vindicates itself by reacting upon the evil-doer. Let me give an illustration of a person who decides to rob a bank. He makes his plans down to the minutest detail. He is shrewd and intelligent. He is familiar with the ways of the world, and he also knows where the police are and how to operate the safe. With all these things at his disposal, he successfully robs the bank. As a result, he has a lot of money in his pocket, and he probably can buy many material goods. To all appearances, he has been totally successful. This is as far as our observation goes at first.

But the law of karma tells us that he has disturbed the moral balance of the universe. According to this law, the moral balance will vindicate itself by reacting violently upon his personality. Consequently, he will suffer in various ways. He will reap as he has sown. First of all, he will suffer in a spiritual way. This action produced a considerable drop in his level of consciousness. Such things as happiness and joy depend upon our level of consciousness, the plane on which we think and live. This lowering of the level of consciousness will bring in its trail other disastrous consequences.

When we study criminology, we find that criminals often betray themselves. Eventually they may think that anything, even the ultimate punishment, capital punishment, would be far better than suffering the terrible anguish of the soul which is brought about by their criminal actions.

To understand fully the law of karma, we must distinguish it from the law of causality in science, the idea of fate in ancient Greek philosophy and another similar idea in Islamic theology called kismet. If we distinguish karma from these, we will be in a position to understand some concrete, practical principles.

Causality is the law of cause and effect. According to the law of cause and effect, everything has a cause. Nothing happens out of the blue. Whatever happens, whatever exists, must have a definite cause to account for its existence and to account for its specific nature. This is the first implication of the law.

Secondly, the same cause must produce the same effect. Let us again consider the example of the bank robber. From the standpoint of the law of causality, what counts is intelligent planning and sureness, the ability to escape the attention of the police, the command of the details of action. Karma says that is not enough. The moral quality of the action, the intentions and the motives are important factors in the procession of events, in the causation of things in life and in nature. Moral qualities are not ineffective things. They are not simply our mental ideas. They are objective forces in life and nature. That is the distinction between karma and causality.

In connection with this, we are all familiar with the advice of Christ to turn the other cheek when someone slaps us. That is an application of the law of karma. If someone hits me, I feel like hitting back. Somebody hits me; somebody is an enemy. I have a tendency to return enmity with enmity. What happens? Both of us get involved in a vicious circle. As I hit back, the other person begins to hit me all the more. As I see my enemy's blows growing in intensity, my hits also become all the more intensified.

What is the spiritual principle? If somebody hits you, it is not only good but also wise, taking a long-range view of life, to return that hit with love. This is not just a moral platitude. This principle of wisdom is based upon great insight into the law of the universe. When you return a hit with love, that alone can help you to break the vicious circle by appealing to the inner goodness of the other person and disarming his or her enmity and hatred. You will be on your way to converting that enmity into friendship, because love is a dynamic force. This is how we find love can conquer hatred, and truth can conquer falsehood.

If some people have cheated me or have been dishonest, a natural tendency is to react with anger and antagonism. But when we react in an antagonistic way, we do not help those individuals to overcome their shadow side, their negative side. If we want to achieve our point and to have them as friends, the best way is to appeal to their inner goodness. We should not emphasize whatever negative feelings they might have inside but instead appeal to the bright side of their nature.

Mahatma Gandhi applied this principle not only to individual, interpersonal relations but also to international relations and politics. He conducted the freedom movement of India armed with the principle of karma. Even in fighting political enemies, his firm conviction was that the irresistible, all-conquering power rested in truth and nonviolence. The more we succeed in eliminating hatred from our minds and in giving out the positive force of love and truth, the more we prepare in an invisible way the conquest of our enemy.

Now let me distinguish karma from fate. In ancient Greek philosophy fate was conceived as an irresistible supernatural power which controlled the destiny of humans. There were good people. There were bad people. There were great heroes. The Greek tragedies tell us that in spite of their inner strength, heroism, and supreme moral qualities, humans were dashed tragically against the stone walls of fate. Fate was visualized as an all-conquering power over which humans had no control. The notion of fate as a supernatural force was at the basis of their idea of tragedy.

In both karma and fate, individuals have their lives determined by an invisible force over which they do not seem to have much control. But according to the law of karma, the invisible force which seems to control our lives from day to day is not a supernatural, external power with which we have no organic connection. Instead, the invisible force is the outcome of various actions we performed in the past, because humans are the architects of their own virtue. In the past, we contributed to the formation of that invisible force which holds sway over us today. In other words, fate does not leave room for the creative freedom in humans, whereas the law of karma is perfectly compatible with it.

The same distinction can be made about karma and kismet. In Islamic theology, Muslims believe the lives of all individuals are rigidly and rigorously predetermined from the cradle to the grave. This invisible force is not a blind natural force, nor is it a supernatural power which is independent of humans or God. It is a supernatural force which is rooted in the will of the all-powerful God. Consequently, what we may perceive to be our freedom is an appearance only. Actually humans have no freedom. We are subjected to that order of predetermination.

Karma says no, humans have freedom. What appears in our life today to be an invisible force is the result of our past actions. What we are today is the result of a continuation of our long past. By virtue of what we do today, we creatively advance into and determine our future. The law of karma also implies that in the course of our spiritual growth, there comes a time when we rise above karma. So long as we are in a state of bondage and suffering, we are subjected to the law of karma, over which we have not much control and of which we have little knowledge. But as we advance along the road of spiritual development, we gain insight into its mode of operation. Once we rise above the law of karma, we attain liberation or salvation in the full sense of the word. Then the only spiritual force or power which is dominant in our life is the will of God.

Until we reach that point, we often get caught in the meshes of karma, and we have difficulty getting out of the net. In this connection I would like to share a story of Abukashan, a famous and wealthy merchant of Baghdad. Abukashan had a fortune, but he was stingy. He had a notorious pair of slippers he used to wear wherever he went. These slippers were completely worn out, but still he thought it was not yet time to give them up. Abukashan's slippers were the talk of the town. People said, 'Even a beggar would not like to be found lying dead in slippers like those.'

But Abukashan was extremely lucky. One day a big perfume store went into liquidation, and Abukashan had the good fortune to buy a huge consignment of crystal jars and perfume. He bought these things for a song, and he was very happy. Any other merchant on an occasion like that would invite close friends for a banquet, but not Abukashan. He thought, 'I have great fortune now, and I'm going to celebrate by visiting the public bath.' As he went, a friend drew his attention to the miserable condition of his slippers. The friend said, 'It is long overdue that you give up those slippers. You are a wealthy man. What will people think of you?'

Once at the bath, Abukashan left his slippers outside and went into the shower. A few minutes later the judge of the town entered the bath, leaving his brand new shiny slippers. When Abukashan came out of the bath, he did not see his slippers. Instead he found a new pair of slippers. Abukashan thought, 'This must be due to the kindness of my friend who gave me a bit of advice. He must have left these for me as a gift.' Without much ado, he put on the new slippers and went away.

A little later the judge found his slippers had gone. His attendant said, 'I can't find your slippers, but here are Abukashan's slippers. Most probably there has been a mistake.' When Abukashan was found wearing the shiny slippers, he was brought to court for trial. The judge was furious and imposed a heavy fine in light of Abukashan's vast wealth. Abukashan was sorry and tried to explain. The more he tried to explain, the more ridiculous his story sounded. No one was in a mood to believe him. So he paid his fine and went home wearing his old slippers, which were returned to him.

Feeling angry about this matter, Abukashan threw the slippers from his window into a river. The slippers got caught in a fisherman's net. At first the fisherman thought he had caught a big fish, but instead he found the slippers, which had damaged the net. Naturally the fisherman was angry, and with great force he threw the slippers back into Abukashan's house. Abukashan had spread the valuable crystal jars on a table. The slippers dashed against the bottles and broke them, spilling all the perfume. In a twinkle of an eye, his whole fortune was ruined.

Abukashan was mortified beyond expression. Now his problem was how to get rid of the slippers. He went to a nearby village and threw the slippers into a pond. But as luck would have it, the slippers lodged themselves in a pipe which supplied drinking water to the villagers. The villagers inspected the pipes and found the slippers which they knew belonged to Abukashan. They lodged a complaint in the court, and again a heavy fine was imposed on him.

What was Abukashan to do? He said, 'I am going to burn these nasty slippers.' In order to burn them, he put the slippers on the roof to dry. Then a peculiar set of circumstances took place. The neighbor's cat saw the funny-looking things and began to play with them. Just then a woman was walking along the road carrying a heavy load on her head. As the cat was playing, the slippers fell and landed with some force upon the head of the woman. Unfortunately, she happened to be pregnant, and she suffered a miscarriage. Again Abukashan went to court. A still heavier fine was imposed upon him, and he got his slippers back again.

Late in the evening, he decided to bury the slippers in his garden. The neighbors in a village are always curious about what goes on, so Abukashan's neighbors saw him digging. They thought perhaps he was burying a wonderful treasure. According to the law of the country, citizens must notify the government and pay a tax on any treasure. The neighbors informed the government, and Abukashan was again brought to court. He tried to explain, but no one would believe he was trying to bury an old pair of shoes. Considering Abukashan's wealth and the treasure which he must be hiding, the judge once more levied an enormous fine on him.

That was the last straw. Abukashan was nearly brought to his knees. With tears in his eyes, he appealed to the judge. 'Let this be the last penalty. I don't know what to do with my shoes. Please be so kind that if anything else happens to me on account of these slippers, I shall not be held responsible. Will you please take custody of me along with my slippers?'

The point here is that our actions get us involved in a circle, and if it is too late, it is difficult for us to get out of the circle. The lesson is that we always should be on the alert to give up our old shoes at the right time. Hindu philosophy tells us that if we understand the law of karma, we shall realize that an important spiritual principle in life is the principle of non-attachment. As we go through life, we acquire different things, different positions, and we must remember to be thankful God has showered these things upon us. But at the same time, we must not be attached to them. We must make allowance for the fact that just as good things come to us, they also go. When they come, welcome them and enjoy them. Make good use of them. When they go, do not hold on to them. Non-attachment is accepting things as they are and as they come without being attached to them. If we can practice non-attachment, we can go through the changing circumstances of life without suffering the adverse consequences of them. This is the principle which is expounded elaborately and brilliantly in the Bhagavad Gita.

According to the law of karma, even though we have a kind of destiny, we also have freedom. When we understand the law of karma, we find that destiny, properly understood, is not incompatible with the creative freedom of humans. Rather, it is the outcome of freedom. By our free actions in the past, we create our destiny. By our free actions in the present, we create our future. As we evolve and grow along spiritual lines, eventually we can rise above subjection to the law of karma.

All Eastern systems of spiritual philosophy say that when we realize the supreme spiritual truth and become integrated with absolute spirit, the bonds of karma are shattered. When the fire of illumination kindles in our hearts, the bonds of karma turn to ashes. We gain full spiritual freedom and are not subjected any more to external destiny. We become the masters of our own destiny. Without being affected by adverse circumstances or by external forces, our lives become like lotus leaves. The lotus leaf floats on the water, but not a drop of water clings to its surface. It floats freely. Similarly, when we attain God-realization, we rise above the law of karma and are united with supreme reality.

7

LIMITATIONS OF THE RATIONAL MIND

In spite of our best efforts to be good and to love each other, every now and then we fight with each other, we experience brush fires, and wars break out in different parts of the globe. In spite of our best intentions to live together in harmony and peace, reason has not the power to unify our forces. Rational mind, by its very nature, is dualistic. It operates in dichotomies. Consequently, through reason we cannot unify the dichotomies of our inner nature. Rational mind, with all its glory, is an inferior mode of operation of a higher power of consciousness which has not yet been manifested fully. In the course of further evolution, it is quite possible within the range of human potential that integral consciousness will be brought forth into manifestation in our lives. Evolution is necessary for that. A change of heart is necessary. Inner change of consciousness is necessary. We must advance to this higher level in order to unify the entire human race.

8

MYSTICISM OF THE LOGOS

There is a vast amount of literature on the mysticism of the logos, which is also known as the creative word. For example, we find it in the Vedas, in the writings of Philo of Alexandria and in the Book of John. The opening of the Gospel according to St John says: 'In the beginning was the Word. The Word was with God and the Word was God.' First of all, logos implies the creative sound or the creative word; secondly, it implies absolute reason, divine wisdom, absolute idea and thought; thirdly, it implies the unity of different powers, spiritual laws and forces operating in the universe which guide and sustain the world process.

Fundamentally, logos means the creative sound. In the Vedas, this has been called *Shabda Brahma*. *Shabda* means sound or word. It has been stated that the first primordial manifestation of the supreme spirit was the creative sound. Sanskrit literature says that the closest human approximation to creative sound is '*Om*.' The first manifestation of the spirit, by whatever name you call it, is cosmic sound vibration. The theory is that at the beginning and at the very root and basis of the universe is the supreme spirit or creative energy.

Regarding the concept of Brahman in the ancient scriptures of India, a great modern scientist has written that what was probably meant by it was the total field of energy. Of course, according to the sages of the past and the spiritual leaders of the world, this energy is neither blind nor mechanical but is profoundly intelligent. There is great wisdom in this energy because it is essentially spiritual.

The first manifestation of this supreme creative energy is cosmic sound vibration with creative potency. Therefore, we can visualize sound as an ocean of energetic vibrations. All objects and creatures that live are different manifestations of this absolute energy. In every object and living being, there is a unique configuration of vibrations. This special constellation of energy produces a unique rhythm in each individual. Every being has an essential sound of its own. From this, every human life has its own song. His or her life evolution is an unfoldment of the seed word, the seed sound within.

Studying the writings of the mystic poets, we find confirmation of this view. For example, Walt Whitman was fascinated by nature. He said he used to hear the sound of everything. Every tree had its own sound, its own music. The mountain had its sound. Even the tiny blades of grass had their own sound. *Leaves of Grass* portrayed his enchantment with the music of nature in which every blade joined its voice in the music of the spheres that Plato talked about. The more we grow spiritually, the more our inner hearing becomes attuned to this music. We begin to hear the unique rhythm and music of every individual thing.

Some people who have had occult experiences also give testimony to this. They speak of what is called akashic records; that is to say, the eternal sound of the void. The idea is that none of the happenings of nature or of this world completely dies out. These happenings are recorded in the eternal tables of nature, in the void. Those who develop spiritual hearing find they hear the voice of heaven. Most of the founders of the great religions had this capacity; they heard the voice that comes from the akashic records which is also connected to the doctrine of cosmic sound.

In Hindu symbolism, we find that the great god Shiva has in one hand a drum and in the other hand a flame. The drum is the creative sound symbolizing one expression of the divine. It represents the creative sound which attracts, fascinates and binds together different things, bringing together conflicting forces. In space and time, this attraction assumes the form of gravitational pull. Different heavenly bodies attract each other.

In Shiva's other hand is the flame which represents the opposite process of dissipation and dispersion. Scientists speak of the expanding universe. Within a particular solar system, different heavenly bodies attract each other. But between different solar systems we find there is a repulsion, a dispersion. In consequence, the whole universe both is expanding like a balloon and at the same time tearing apart. These are opposite forces, but in the divine both of these forces are reconciled. God is the balanced unity of opposites.

When we study the Old Testament, we find the concept of different messengers of God, different angels. If we take it literally, it would not make much sense to most modern people. But if we probe more deeply, we find a great truth. God is the supreme transcendental power which can act in finite beings, through the medium of certain finite limited forces. In Biblical times, the Supreme Being emanated spiritual powers. People thought of these powers as angels which were really symbols for the laws that controlled the operations of nature and the destiny of history. Philo has pointed out that all these different spiritual forces which emanate from God are not separate things but are unified in the wisdom of God that sustains the world. Logos is the unified wisdom and the ultimate spiritual unity of the different powers that function in nature. It is through the power of logos that divine power becomes operative in nature and the world. Logos therefore mediates between the infinite and the finite. Through logos we can reach out toward union with the infinite.

The second way that logos can be viewed is as reason and will. It is absolute reason united with divine will. What is divine will? Many of you know this statement: 'At the beginning God said, "Let there be light." And there was light.' As soon as the divine word is uttered, immediately it is fulfilled and there is light. In our case, on the relative level, there is a time gap. We say, 'Let me do this' — whatever it is — and after the wish is formulated, time passes. We have to do appropriate things and make some effort. We have to take suitable steps in order to fulfill our wish. It will not just fall into our lap.

But the divine will is an absolute will. The will of the supreme is effortless, because it is beyond time. Consequently, there is no time gap between the divine will and its fulfillment. As soon as the will is expressed, it is fulfilled. This is logos, the effortless expression of the will of God. Not only is it effortless, it is desireless also. This is an important concept to assimilate. Will, truly speaking, is different from desire. Desire is an expression of the ego; it is selfish. It is a manifestation of the vital nature. But the will of God is not the expression of any ego. It is unmotivated, pure will. Another way of expressing this would be to call it the will of love, an unmotivated love expression.

In the mind of the Absolute, when there was the will to create a diversified universe, there was an emanation of light — that is to say, wisdom — from its transparent spiritual essence. This emanation of light was intended to create and maintain, to regulate and govern the universe. This is the logos, the divine wisdom as it emanated from the essence of the Supreme toward the creation, preservation and regulation of the universe. This is what Hegel would call the 'absolute idea'; the Supreme as the absolute idea is logos, the wisdom which sustains this universe and controls the destiny of all living creatures and individual beings.

Let me call your attention to a related idea. When we ordinarily use the expression 'divine word,' we have a tendency, because of the weakness and narrowness of our human nature, to interpret it in a sectarian way. The followers of different religious sects interpret the divine word according to their own liking. For example, the Muslims interpret the divine word as the Qur'an. In the same way, Christians have a tendency to think that the Bible represents absolute truth, and Hindus may think the whole of divine wisdom is embodied only in the Vedas. Because of our intrinsic narrowness, we have a tendency to interpret the logos in a parochial manner, equating it with a particular scripture. This is the fallacy of false equation and false identification operating in our unconscious mind. The divine logos is immeasurable and boundless. The great scriptures of the world are manifestations in different countries and at different times of this one logos. All these scriptures are revelations in history, through different prophets, of the wisdom of one Supreme Being. A true understanding of the divine logos will enable us to understand that very precious truths are to be found in all the great scriptures of the world and that these represent fragments of the infinite light of the Supreme. This is the metaphysical significance of the doctrine of the logos.

Lastly, what does logos mean from the standpoint of our growing spiritual unfoldment? Let us consider three of the important centers of consciousness in the human system and how the logos can be experienced and understood within them. The first is the heart. Some very profound experiences of humankind center around the opening of the heart center. Another is the eyebrow center. This is why you find many gods and illumined beings represented with a third eye, the eye of wisdom. Another, the highest center, is within the top of the skull.

Those who have had personal spiritual realization testify that when the heart center opens, we feel the true spiritual flame of divine love. A person experiences the genuine love of God, purged of all selfish motivations and egotistical desires. As a result of the opening of the heart, a person enters into an intimate communion with the divine. He or she establishes a unique relationship of love and devotion with the infinite. A person hears what is called the music of the infinite. It is because of this that in Hindu mythology, Krishna, the god of absolute love and beauty, is always represented with a flute in his hand. The flute portrays the music of the infinite. In Sanskrit this music is called *anahatha*, which means sound that is not created, the uncreated word. In contrast, the sound we normally hear is created, creature sound. When I talk, there is friction between my tongue and palate and lips. Vibrations are produced on account of this friction, so you hear a sound. In contrast to creature sound, creative sound is heard through the development of spiritual potency. When the heart center opens, we have for the first time a transcendent experience of the creative word or sound. Before this, life revolves around the ego. Our thoughts are motivated by ego desires. But as soon as this experience happens, there is a transition from the egocentric to the cosmocentric. There is a shifting of the center of gravity from the ego to the divine. A true transvaluation of life takes place at this stage.

According to the mystics, in the course of further development the eyebrow center opens, and another aspect of the logos is unveiled. We make a fresh contact with the divine from another standpoint by hearing the divine command. This is why this center is called *ajna*, which means divine command. In other words, the divine word, logos, comes to us in the form of a command. This means the disclosure and revelation in our inner consciousness of our specific destiny in life. As we grow, we come to a point when we become fully aware of the specific purpose and mission of our life. Life assumes a tremendously profound meaning. It becomes divinely significant. Consequently, we experience a free flow of creative energy. We have a strong, clear sense of direction sanctified by the experience of this command.

Finally, in the opening of the *sahasrara*, the highest center of consciousness at the top of the skull, there is the crowning fulfillment of the mystic realization of which humans are potentially capable. We enter into an intimate communion filled with the rapture and bliss of the supreme godhead. This is the goal toward which the power of logos leads us, bringing into our life the ultimate fulfillment of our spiritual longings. So from a spiritual standpoint, we see that at different stages our experience of the logos is different.

In our spiritual practice, the power of the mantra, the holy word, is very important and effective as a point of concentration in order to experience the creative sound. One which can be adopted is 'Om sri hari om.' The meaning of *om* is the most sacred and the most powerful syllable in Sanskrit literature as it is the sound symbol of the absolute. In this mantra, the first *om* expresses that we have a genuine, sincere aspiration for union with the divine, so we start with it. *Sri* means divine power, the power of love and wisdom. It is not a blind power, not controlling or physical. *Hari* means God as wisdom and God as love. The last *om* means dynamic union with the divine, the ultimate fulfillment of spiritual longing. The more we repeat this mantra and others like it, the more our whole being is filled with harmonious and peaceful sound vibrations.

A mantra is like a golden thread or rope, with the help of which we rise up to higher levels of consciousness. As we soar more and more with the help of the power of the sound, our different centers of consciousness are opened, resulting in our penetration into the mystery of existence and increasing union with ultimate reality.

9

KALI

In Indian mythology, Kali is an aspect of the divine mother, who represents death and destruction. But her hidden meaning often is not understood. Because of this, it may seem confusing that many great mystics drew abundant inspiration from concentration on her.

Creation requires destruction. In order to create something good and noble, the forces of dark and evil have to be subdued and conquered. When we understand the significance of Kali, we also understand the significance of Easter, of crucifixion followed by resurrection, or death followed by new life.

Kali comes from the word *kala*, which means time. Kali means that power of the divine spirit which devours time and helps the spiritual seeker to enter into the plane of the timeless. Preoccupation with the perishing things of time is devoured. This results in the discovery of the realm of the eternal.

When we enter into that higher plane of consciousness, we have a strange and mysterious experience. We both die and we live, for death and life are combined together. What does this mean? The human being has a dual nature. On the one hand, we are a creature of time. On the other hand, we are a child of eternity. We are phenomenal beings and we are also transcendental entities. We are bound by changing circumstances and we belong to immortal reality.

So long as our timeless aspect is a closed book to us, we do not do anything about it. As long as we just live on the plane of time, we are in a state of bondage and we suffer. We are affected by the changing happenings of life. When there is a set of circumstances which are agreeable, we feel happy. When we enter a new set of circumstances which are not agreeable, we become unhappy. That is how we go, vitally affected by the continually changing experiences of life and by the vicissitudes of our fortune.

In the course of our spiritual growth, there comes a moment when we die as a phenomenal being, when we cease to become preoccupied with the changing and perishing values of life. However, on the heels of the death of our temporal existence, a completely new set of values is unfolded. We contact the realm of eternity and realize ourselves as spiritual beings. This is the new life and the resurrection. There cannot be a new life without this kind of death. There cannot be resurrection without crucifixion.

This is the mystical significance of Kali. Through contemplation of her, we keep in view the great spiritual ideal of life. This is what we are trying to do — to rise above the plane of time and discover the kingdom of heaven which is within our own being.

10

FAITH AS EXISTENTIAL CHOICE

Faith is the beginning and the end of spiritual living — the alpha and omega of the growth of personality when we properly understand what it is. In simple terms, faith may be defined as that by which we live. It is the sustaining principle of life and of our inner spiritual evolution. We are familiar with the saying that we do not live by bread alone. The most distinctive characteristic and central trait of human reality is that we are able to cultivate a sense of higher values, an inner vision of something greater and nobler than ourselves. This sense of higher values sustains us in our effort, in our striving and in marching forward toward our true destiny in life.

Authentic faith implies a sense of higher values. Every human being has some idea in his or her mind of the ultimate goal of existence. It may be highly developed or undeveloped and inchoate. It may be comprehensive or partial and fragmented. I am reminded of Aldous Huxley who once said, 'It is not a question of philosophy or no philosophy. It is a question of good philosophy or bad philosophy.' As Martin Heidegger put it, 'Man is essentially a metaphysical being.' In other words, we never come across any human being who is absolutely void of all philosophy. All human beings have some idea in the back of their minds about what the meaning of life is. They have some idea of the nature of the universe in which they live and what they are going to do here. They may be misguided or they may be right, but they have some idea. In the same way we may state that it is not a question of faith or no faith; it is a question of good faith or bad faith. Well thought-out, all-embracing faith or poorly conceived faith — that is the vital issue in our spiritual life. A sense of values is at the very center of human existence. These values regulate our action in our life and our thinking all the time.

Faith also implies determination, a resolute will to follow what we consider to be our highest value, the chief good of life. This is our commitment, our existential choice. As we make this choice, we pull all the energy of our existence into it. It is existential, because it is a matter of life. We stake our being on what we consider to be of supreme value. This existential choice is the essence of faith. It is not enough that we consider something to be good or valuable. Of course that counts, but it is not enough. After we have considered and understood something to be a great truth of life, we may make a resolute wish. We say, 'I freely choose to accept this value as the ideal and goal of my life,' and we put all the energy of our existence into it. So from this standpoint, faith is the centered movement of our total existence toward a freely chosen set of values. But as I say, this may be good faith or it may be bad faith; it may be a well thought-out value or it may be a poorly conceived value.

Faith is not a static thing. It is not a question of accepting some beliefs, ideas and creeds. It is a living, dynamic experience. As we evolve inwardly, our faith also evolves. It undergoes a gradual transformation, a refinement and expansion. It acquires more and more depth. So this history of human self-development is the history of the gradual flowering of faith within us.

Let us look at different kinds of faith. We sometimes think that only a person who is pious and religious or who accepts a particular scripture or who belongs to a particular temple or church has faith. But from the definition of faith that I have given, you will understand that every person has some faith, whether we consider it right or wrong.

First of all, of course, there is the orthodox, popular meaning of faith. A particular individual is born in a particular religion and has the faith of that religion. He or she subscribes to certain creeds and theological doctrines. To a certain extent, all individuals imbibe unconsciously from their childhood varied articles of faith and certain creeds. The more they grow, the more their ideas may become clear and refined. Eventually they may go beyond these ideas and have some personal realization of the truth which is beyond all dogmas.

Those who have rejected the popular credal faith do so on account of a different faith of their own. For example, today among intellectuals, scientists, and artists, we come across people who are atheists in their outward faith. Yet even atheists, who have rejected a theological conception of God, also have some kind of faith. For many of them, the faith which is operative in their consciousness is what is called humanism. They believe in the welfare of humanity, the full development of the human potential and the efflorescence of human culture. They would say the essence of spirituality is bending all our energies to the fullest development of humankind to establish peace and order.

Even confirmed skeptics have hidden in them somewhere some kind of faith. There may be skeptics who deny everything. Their whole mind is permeated with doubt. They may refuse to believe in anything. They may feel humans are too powerless to have any real knowledge whatsoever. Yet they have some kind of faith which comes out on occasion, especially in moments of distress. One writer captured the flavor of this attitude in an anecdote about a confirmed skeptic who did not believe in anything — not in God, not in a higher self, nor in immortality. But even this skeptic prayed when in distress. And do you know what the prayer was? 'Oh God, if there be a God, take my soul, if there be a soul, and lead me to heaven, if there be a heaven.'

Within our younger generation today there are many rebels who have an intense consciousness of their own. They are often rebelling against the time-honored institutions of social existence. Outwardly they seem to have a complete loss of faith, but even behind this loss of faith there is some kind of faith which is prompting them. They are disenchanted and may feel that those who are in control of affairs are hypocritical. They feel that by rebelling, by bringing to collapse the present order, a new world order can be created which would be free of hypocrisy and sham respectability. Not all of them know what they are looking for or what will achieve this goal. But one thing they know is that the existing order is wrong. Another thing they know is their faith in unrestrained freedom and free self-expression. For some this freedom has no positive content because it is not sustained or nourished by any clear sense of higher values. But still they are guided by a great faith in limitless freedom.

In whatever people are doing, they have some kind of faith. The great spiritual task of life is to guide this faith because it is a living and growing process. It has to be nourished toward its proper fulfillment of expression in our day-to-day existence.

What are the different stages involved in the process of evolution of faith within us? From the authentic spiritual standpoint, the most important thing is not what we outwardly believe, what our creed or dogma is. The most important thing is an inner growth of consciousness. As we grow and evolve, our consciousness expands. It rises to higher and higher levels. As we go through this evolution of consciousness, we find we have left behind some things which we believed yesterday. Certain ideas which appeared so important are now on the periphery of our life. We do not have an inclination to cling to them any more. So we experience a sudden transformation of our inner existence as a result of this growth of consciousness. As our consciousness begins to be elevated to higher levels, new energies surge up from within in a miraculous way. A new joy of life, a new vision of truth well up from the depths of our being. The dynamics of this experience may be completely beyond our comprehension. This is also the truth behind what is called a religious conversion, which is a mysterious process of spiritual growth.

Because faith is a growing and dynamic phenomenon, we have to do something to bring about its evolution and development within us. The first important factor in faith is free choice. Faith is not faith at all if it is not a matter of free existential choice. We must freely choose a particular way of living and not allow faith to be simply a matter of thinking or accepting something.

Ordinarily we do not think of faith in this way. Usually we think that we are born in a particular religion, and therefore we have that faith. A particular person may be born in a Christian family. The basic truth about Christianity is a belief in God conceived in a certain way and accepting the spirit of love as the way of living. Suppose this person as she lives from day to day is guided in her activities by violence and hatred. She may have been told that God is love, but in her own way of doing things she does not believe this. So she is not really a Christian at all. Christianity as a religious faith is not a mere accident of being born into a Christian family. It is a matter of free existential choice.

The second important factor is dynamic self-opening. The inner self opens to the light of truth and love of the ultimate. In order for faith to be a living, growing process of spiritual development, we have to keep an open mind. We cannot accept any creed to be the last word of wisdom because this amounts to stagnation, mental calcification and spiritual death. The most important thing in spiritual life is growth and evolution. We must have an attitude of appropriating and assimilating the light of truth from wherever we find it.

Truth is universal. Treasures of truth have been found embedded in unexpected quarters, in different parts of the world and in different cultural scriptures. We must have the mobility, dynamism, and openness to assimilate these precious elements of truth from all different sources without any bias or prejudice. This is dynamic self-opening, and it is an important factor in the gradual unfoldment of our inner being. This is what we need to do on the physical plane; this is how we grow and nourish our body. And we need to do the same thing on the spiritual plane.

What do we do on our physical plane? A modern person is a citizen of the whole world. The world has become small today. The different nations and peoples have come together so that even the remotest part of the globe is now our next-door neighbor. In order to have a balanced diet, we gather the elements of nourishment from all available sources throughout the world. This is also what we can do on the spiritual plane by keeping our eyes and ears open to gather in truth relevant to our existence.

The third factor in the cultivation of faith is constructive self-development. All human beings have some positive aspects of their personality and some potential of their own, just as they have some shortcomings and drawbacks. An important step in spiritual growth is increasing awareness of the potentialities of one's own nature and concentrating on the development of these. Sometimes people think they want to do good for others, but forget that we cannot really help others very much unless we develop our own selves. We can help society best by offering only the best within us. For example, people who suffer from inner conflict and despair, even with the best of intentions, cannot really help other people. Unconsciously they infect other people with their own misery. All individuals carry an atmosphere of joy and inner peace or an atmosphere of inner conflict, distrust and despair. Without development of the positive virtues of our nature, we cannot offer our best to society. Our activities become self-defeating.

A fourth factor is what has been called selfless action. This logically comes after self-development. We may develop ourselves and rest content with that. We may say, 'I have developed good qualities and abilities, and now I just want to enjoy them.' That defeats the spiritual purpose of life. Self-development needs to be followed by selfless action. In other words, we develop the potentialities of our nature, and the next step is to share our blessings of life with fellow beings. We must contribute in a humble measure in our own little way to the welfare of society.

Finally, for the full flowering of faith, some form of daily spiritual practice is also important. It is important for our full growth that we set up some time every day or whenever we can for quiet contemplation of the divine, for sincere inquiry into the inmost center of our own being, toward a deeper awareness of the presence of God within us. Through such silent self-communion, more and more our faith is transformed into a living experience of the fundamental spiritual truth of existence. Faith is brought to full fruition through prayer, meditation and contemplation, because it is with the aid of such practices that what we talk about is transformed into the reality of actual experience. God becomes a living reality in our life.

The most important thing about spiritual practice is that we do not simply talk about God; we do not simply think about the higher self; we do not simply conceptualize or verbalize a higher spiritual reality. We go beyond conceptualized thinking. We encounter the ultimate spiritual truth. We find ourselves in the immediate presence of God. We exist alone in the presence of the Alone. This is the existential fulfillment of our faith.

When faith is transformed into this living experience, we discover the supreme values of life. We also succeed in applying our best, our latent energy toward the fulfillment and realization of the inner vision of the higher values of existence. Spiritual life begins with faith, and spiritual life ends with faith. True spiritual life begins with faith in the sense of existential choice, and it ends with faith in the sense of existential encounter with the supreme reality which we call the divine.

11

FREE WILL AND DETERMINISM

The issue of free will and determinism is a fundamental and perennial challenge in ethics and religion. Both seem to be genuine facts of life and experience. On the one hand, there is the scientific law of cause and effect. There is some kind of universal determinism which philosophy would say is the expression of the fundamental rationality of life, of reality, of the universe — because law is the expression of reason. On the other hand, we also know and experience the freedom of the life force, the free expression of the spirit, the *élan vital*, the vital urge, which is at the root of this universe. Often there seems to be a contradiction between conformity to law — determinism — and the freedom of self-expression on the part of every living being and also on the part of the spirit.

First of all, let us try to understand what we mean by freedom. The eagle is regarded as a symbol of freedom, free movement or a free-flying bird. When we imagine a bird flying in the sky, this brings into our mind the vision of freedom. Therefore, in the mythology of all countries, the bird is a symbol of freedom. There are two factors here when we consider it. First, this is the movement of a living being without any resistance, without any restraint, without any obstacles or impediments. The sky is free from all obstacles. But there is a deeper factor. Henri Bergson, the French philosopher and biologist, discussed at great length the fundamental freedom which we notice in the movement of all living beings. This is the freedom of the vital urge, the *élan vital*.

When we study this free movement of the birds from one standpoint, it is subject to causality. The law of causality is a universal law which holds sway in all physical phenomena in the entire realm of matter, including control of the movement of the bird. All its movements at different positions in space can be explained in terms of cause and effect. Science explains how the law of gravitation offered by the air and atmosphere works upon it and how the muscles of the bird generate motor energy. So here is a picture of determinism as well as freedom.

Bergson said if we go deeply into the matter, we shall come to the source of this freedom. In this bird there is a vital energy, a life force working and spontaneously expressing itself. As it is expressed in the shape of movement in the physical world, certainly this expression obeys the laws of nature. But the power which expresses itself, the life force, is free. The two are not incompatible. The freedom which we see and admire is the free expression of the life impulse working in the bird. The bird is flying with the universal life force by virtue of its possession of this life impulse, which is free creative energy. This is a profound mystery of life, how life expresses itself freely and how the expressions in the physical world become subjected to the law of causality.

Now let us take a simple illustration. When I move my arm, you can look at this phenomenon from two standpoints, the outward and the inward. From the outward standpoint, this movement of my arm is a physical phenomenon. It is subjected to the law of cause and effect. My muscles contract and the movement generates motor energy. I also am countering the law of gravitational pull. Anything subjected to the law of causality is a physical expression taking place in the realm of matter.

Viewed from the inward standpoint, we find a deeper factor operating, and that is my free will to move my arm. My free will to move is radically different from physical phenomena. Something is essentially different. Bergson tried to convey this using the words '*élan vital*', which is a free, unfettered, creative force. This freedom of the life force is what he called 'absolute freedom,' and this is a concept which has greatly influenced existential philosophy. The freedom of the life force, the freedom of the spirit, is a pure freedom. What does he mean by pure freedom? He said the freedom of the life force is free from both mechanical and teleological determinism, the two kinds of determinism. When I give a push to the table or to a ball, it moves. This is mechanical determinism. The mechanism or force imparted to the object sets it in motion. The ball begins to move as a result of a mechanical force which works upon it. It is being driven from behind.

Another kind of determinism is teleological determinism. You form a desire in your mind, for example, 'I want to go to a movie tonight.' Your activities of the day become determined by an idea working in your mind, a plan regarding the future. In effect, the future is determining your actions in the present. This is the opposite of mechanical determinism. In mechanical determinism the past determines the future. That is to say, anticipated forces working in the present determine what happens later on. Here, the future determines the present. Your vision of the future determines your whole course of activity. So this is teleological determinism. 'Teleos' means 'end' — an end with regard to the future.

But the freedom of the life energy which works throughout nature is a different kind of freedom. It is not determined by anything, neither by the past nor by the future. Nature does not plan. The sun shines without any plan because its nature is to shine. The flower blooms in your garden because its nature is to bloom. It is free, unfettered, unconscious self-expression — without any consequence, without any plan, without any deliberate effort in a particular direction. This is what Bergson called pure freedom.

We humans also experience such free self-expression on certain occasions. You are all familiar with the saying that the highest virtue is that which is performed unconsciously, without any direct effort at virtue. When you make a plan to get something, the plan often detracts from the value of your virtue. You are most virtuous when your left hand does not know what your right hand is doing. Pure freedom is not a matter of deliberate effort and conscious planning, but a free self-expression of your inmost nature.

Many other instances illustrate this concept of freedom. For example, you may feel happy and joyful. Spontaneously you begin to sing or play the piano. You are singing or playing out of the fullness of joy in your heart. There was no previous planning here. It is a spontaneous act of self-expression. You had no idea to achieve this or that, to affect anybody in any particular way. This act is a free self-expression of your inner nature, the same pure freedom expressed by the blooming of a flower, the shining of the sun or the singing of a bird.

Similarly, true artists paint or write poetry out of the depths of their inner nature, not because they are going to achieve something or earn money. They are simply expressing their deep aesthetic urge to create. God-realized persons also are freely expressing people who live and act spontaneously, without any inhibition and without any plan. But their whole nature acts in accord with the cosmic welfare.

I have given certain instances of freedom within nature. Now let me take some other instances of the freedom of the spirit. Let us take the case of a mentally disturbed person who is walking around on the street. He moves freely, first laughing, then crying or frowning. He is unpredictable. In a sense he acts free, without giving the least thought to what you might think about him. He acts without hesitation, without any inhibition, without any taboo. In a way, this is free will.

But how are you to compare this behavior with the idea of spiritual freedom? Or the freedom of the will, which is an ethical issue? The great Hindu philosophers would say that this person seems to have freedom. But this is not true freedom because there has been a violation of the inner nature in this individual. This is an important concept, namely, that freedom is the free expression of the *inner* nature of an individual, of a living thing. Hinduism uses the terms '*swabhava*' and '*swadharma.*' Swabhava means the inner nature, and *swadharma* means inner becoming, the inner law of self-development and growth.

What is the inner nature of humans? This inner nature is our power of self-organizing. We must learn to organize the different impulses, desires and drives of our personality in order to reach the maximum fulfillment of our potentiality, to achieve our highest good. Psychotic persons may appear to act as freely as they like or desire. But their inner nature has been violated because of the lack of integration. Their impulses and desires are not organized toward the fulfillment of the main purpose of existence.

We can apply this criterion to many other instances. Sometimes we think people who act as they please are a picture of freedom. But freedom does not lie there. Freedom does not mean a protest against all law or determinism. The ability to act whimsically or arbitrarily is not the true concept of freedom.

Freedom also is a kind of determinism. It is a great mistake on our part radically to separate the two. Freedom is inner determinism, the ability to determine your life, to organize your life, to live your life in accordance with your highest good. This is self-determinism, what Spinoza called 'inner necessitation.' This is the essence of freedom. The more you succeed in doing so, the more you are able to organize the different impulses, desires, wishes, thoughts and drives of your nature on the basis of a freer understanding of the main purpose, goal and chief good of your existence. Freedom itself becomes determinism of the highest form.

We can extend this idea to the case of so-called free thinkers who place the highest value on uninhibited personal expression. However, often something is lacking. True human nature is not expressed in licentiousness, for example. In many cases you will find that such people are expressing an inner hostility and antagonism to others, of which they are not even aware. Deep feelings of anger and rebellion are being expressed in that apparently free nature. Why? They are not aware of how best to achieve authentic freedom. *Swabhava*, the spiritual essence, allows us to become more and more aware of our inner motivations. We know what we are doing; we know in what direction we are going. More and more we become aware of our chief good. More and more we become aware of the meaning of life as a whole and the meaning of our own life in the context of the cosmic whole. We become more free as we succeed in fashioning our life and determining the course of our living on the basis of understanding the meaning of existence.

Let us take the case of ascetics. They too are trying to express freedom. They renounce society and go to a deep forest or a mountain cave in the hope of attaining spiritual freedom and living free from all social taboos and conventions, free from all worries and anxiety, free from all the pressure of problems and actions that come from society. They go far away from the maddening crowds.

Let us try to understand to what extent they succeed in achieving freedom. There is an aspect of relativity in this matter, as you can well understand. They feel they are gaining freedom because they are relieving themselves from the worries and anxieties which come from living in society. Freed from these, they have time to do whatever they please. They can dance, sing, cry, study, or meditate, whatever it may be. When we approach this from the standpoint of *swabhava* and *swadharma*, we find there is a relative measure of freedom, but there may not be full freedom. People may renounce the whole world, but even in absolute solitude their minds still may be overcrowded with desires, impulses and wishes which are unfulfilled. They carry with them all the problems and anxieties of social existence. If they are not integrated within, if there are many repressed desires and unsolved conflicts, then no matter where they go, they carry society. This is not freedom. The most important thing for all of us is to solve the problems in our heart. Unless we succeed in doing so, we cannot have true freedom. This is the number one reason why an ascetic may not achieve freedom.

Let me mention another point. Consider a person who is a free-acting criminal at large in society, doing things according to his or her personal desire or whim. Then let us take the example of someone like Mahatma Gandhi. When he felt an unjust, false law in society had been imposed by the government, he decided to break the law, knowing that as a result of his violation the government would put him in jail. But he embraced that consequence, and he went ahead and broke the law. The government put him in jail and restricted his freedom of movement. But he freely chose to stay in jail with that restricted movement.

If you compare these two examples, you will understand the true meaning of freedom of will as distinguished from freedom of movement. People may freely move, but they may not be spiritually free. They may be slaves of their passions, conflicting emotions and disorganized compulsive urges. They may be slaves, even though they freely move in society. But in going to jail, Gandhi expressed a free will. He freely embraced the consequences of his actions out of his vision of the good of society as a whole. Freedom of movement was not present, but the freedom of will was expressing itself triumphantly.

People also may choose to embrace death. In embracing death they may express the freedom of their will out of a vision of the cosmic good or out of a vision of the will of God in their life. By embracing death they conquer all outward restrictions. By embracing death they conquer death. We may say Jesus Christ was trying to protest certain existing social beliefs or certain laws. By protesting he chose to be crucified. In doing so, he conquered death and expressed his freedom. When we have the right understanding of this freedom of the spirit, then we conquer all outward oppositions. Finally, we even succeed in conquering death.

I do not mean that we repress or suppress our wishes or desires. I am saying we are rational beings. The more we succeed in intelligently organizing the basic desires, aspirations and drives with a view to the fulfillment of our highest potential, the more we achieve freedom. Further, the more we understand the meaning of life as a whole and the meaning of our life as individuals in the context of the whole, and succeed in living on the basis of this understanding, the more we achieve freedom and express it. This is the spiritual content of freedom. This freedom expresses itself in the intellectual sphere in the shape of freedom of thinking. It expresses itself in the emotional sphere as free expression of organized emotions. It expresses itself in the sphere of action as the ability to make decisions in accordance with our highest good.

As freedom is the expression of our true inner nature, we may realize how meditation can help us tremendously in gaining insight into the dynamics of our personality and the deepest potentialities of our being. It gives us increasing insight into our deepest aspirations, our possibilities and an understanding of the meaning of life. We come to see the purpose of our existence and the main direction of our living. The more we have a clear idea of this, the more we express and realize it.

The more we have self-knowledge and knowledge of reality, the more we realize freedom. On the basis of this understanding and knowledge, we can fashion wonderfully our own life energy for the true welfare and enrichment of ourselves and others.

12

DOING OUR OWN THING

There is a great truth behind many things we talk about and want to apply in our life. But at the same time there is also the possibility of our abusing and misunderstanding it. Truth is not to be found in any set of words, any slogan or phrase. Truth is an attitude of our understanding. We may read a wonderful book, but whether we find the truth within it or not depends on how we understand it. This is important to remember, especially if we are concerned with personal growth, spiritual development, and self-realization.

Let me give you an illustration. A man was very depressed. He suffered from an inferiority complex, from a feeling of inadequacy and sinfulness, so he went to a great master for instruction. The teacher looked within him and wanted to inject in him some positive thinking. The teacher said that in ultimate essence, 'Thou art That. *Tat twam asi.* Thou art Brahman.' The way the guru said it and the atmosphere in which it was conveyed immediately had a great impact upon the man. He felt lifted into a higher level of consciousness. All of his feelings of littleness, helplessness and nothingness vanished in an instant.

In great joy he rushed out into the street and happened to see a big elephant coming. He decided this was a chance to test whether he was, in fact, Brahman. He stood in the middle of the street and shouted to the elephant, 'No farther!' The elephant's trainer yelled from a distance, 'Stand aside! Give way to my elephant!' But the man was not in a mood to do that.

He felt he was Brahman, and therefore the elephant should listen to him. Fortunately for him the elephant was a trained animal. The elephant gently took hold of him with his trunk, put him aside and went his way.

But the fellow felt insulted and bewildered. He went back to the teacher and demanded an explanation. The guru said, 'My son, it is true you are Brahman, but in the same way that you are Brahman, the elephant also is Brahman, and the driver of the elephant is also Brahman. Why did you not pay attention to the driver Brahman, and why did you not show some respect for the elephant Brahman?' Finally the man gained the proper perspective.

'Thou art Brahman' is the truth, but what is the meaning of this truth? What is its application? We have to understand in what sense it is true. This is what we may call the doctrine of the paradox of truth or the doctrine of the ambiguity of true statements.

In the same way, I want to discuss another truth — namely, that of 'doing our own thing.' There is a truth behind this cliché. What is that truth and what is its application? Again, it depends upon our understanding. If we understand it correctly, it can be a wonderful principle of self-development and self-expression. But if we do not understand it correctly, it can hamper our personality growth.

A great American philosopher, Josiah Royce, developed this concept well in his book, *A Concept of God.* He pointed out that every individual has a unique, unrepeatable, unduplicable essence of his or her own. He said this principle of the uniqueness of individuality actually follows from the very nature of God as love. Love is individuating. When you love an individual, you love an individual as an individual. Royce gave a nice analogy. If you give a child a lot of toys, soon the child will choose one in particular as his or her favorite. Even after it has become old and ragged, the child still loves it, prefers it, hugs it more than the others. This is because the child's love individuates. When we lavish our love upon anything or any being, the object of our love gains a unique value which cannot be replaced.

Royce asked us to imagine that the toy has been broken. The

child becomes overwhelmed. The child's parent may say, 'Don't cry. I will give you a better toy.' But the first impulse of the child is, 'I don't want a better one. I want this one!' This is the principle of how love individuates. As Royce put it, the motto of love is 'There shall be no other.' That is the dogma of love — the unrepeatable, irreplaceable value of the object of love.

This follows from the concept of God as absolute love. When there is love within love, there is the principle of diversification. Out of love, God has produced all kinds of individuals. But because God is love, God cares for every individual, regardless of how many individuals there are. This is the attitude of love. As a result of this cosmic love in the heart of reality, every individual has a unique essence.

When I say every individual has a unique essence, it may seem to imply that he or she is a static being. But all of us also have the aspect of becoming. We grow and we develop; we become gradually what we essentially are. Nobody stays put anywhere. Everybody moves, lives, develops, evolves, and is in a process of growth. Every individual has a unique law of becoming his or her own.

The great spiritual truth behind this is that all of us should have an opportunity to find our own true self and to be able to grow freely and independently, following the rhythm of our own being. By following the line of our own self-development, we can reach the height of our potential and function at the optimum level of efficiency.

What is the historical and ideological root of this concern with doing one's own thing? When did we develop this stress upon individuality? Today we are living in an age of mass culture. We find overpowering, gigantic structures and institutions in society. Everything is huge, wherever we go. Pretty soon we discover we seem no longer like individuals but like numbers that have been given to us from the records. We may feel lost and become reduced to faceless, anonymous units of existence. This can happen at a factory, university, corporation or anywhere in mass society. What counts is not a matter of our personality but of how much energy we put forth to keep the machine going.

Confronted with the danger of being lost and reduced to a faceless unity, naturally the minds of every one of us rebound to the search for individuality. We may ask, 'Who am I then?' What shall we benefit by seemingly gaining in the materialistic world but losing our own soul? We come back to this inquiry into the meaning and value of individuality and of doing as one pleases.

Yet we can also overdo this. 'Thou art Brahman' is wonderful. But when we misunderstand and misapply it, it becomes a real impediment to right perspective and proper growth. This is the danger that we have in respect to every great formula, truth, principle or creed.

Let me explore some of the abuses to which we can put this principle of independent and free self-development by following the rhythm of one's own being. For example, some people see this as a matter of just following their passing impulses. Perhaps some may have the impulse to get drunk, so they get drunk. Others may have the impulse to do daring driving on the highway. Some may follow the impulse of sleeping until noon and spending the rest of the day in leisure. Or some may drift endlessly, not knowing where they are going.

One may ask, 'What is wrong with this? I am doing just what I wish.' What is wrong is that there is a misinterpretation of an important spiritual truth. The spiritual truth is to be your own true self. In order to be your own true self, you must have some idea of what your true self is. Is your self a mass of instincts and impulses? What is your true self?

Actually to do one's own thing, one has to inquire into the purpose of his or her existence in the total scheme of the universe. It imposes a great responsibility on us, a challenge to look within ourselves. When we believe we should follow passing impulses, we often have poor conceptions of ourselves. The self then becomes nothing but a bundle of passing impulses, desires and instinctual drives. Instead of being free, we become slaves of our passing impulses. We become victims of the chaos of conflicting desires that arise at different moments.

Great thinkers and spiritual leaders tell us that the true self lies deeper than what we see on the surface. It is not to be understood as a mere mass of impulses and desires, which are part of our being, no doubt. In order to understand our true self, we must organize our lives in such a way that we can gain more and more insight into ourselves. We need to do some serious thinking, reading and meditation to see ourselves and how our behavior affects others.

Here I shall bring out another point. As we inquire into the true self, we find that it is not a self-enclosed atom. Within the essence of an individual is a sense of oneness with others, and awareness of the spiritual unity of all humanity. This essential relatedness to our fellow humans is an important ingredient of our own authentic being. To the extent that we do not understand this, we are violating our true self. There is no true self apart from our relationship with others. There is no true self apart from our awareness of the spiritual unity of all existence. The more we have this awareness, the more we have the spirit of love. And when we have regard for the welfare of others, we can no longer do things in utter disregard of the well-being of others. When we disregard others, we disregard our own true self. It sounds paradoxical, but it is a real spiritual truth.

One way of expressing this truth is to say that our authentic self has three essential and inseparable aspects. One aspect is uniqueness. Every individual has a uniqueness of his or her own. Another aspect is universality. Every individual is related to other individuals. There is an interlinkage of interest, a close interrelatedness of all human beings, so together we form the human total. Still another aspect is what we may call transcendence. Everyone is rooted in ultimate reality — in cosmic consciousness. This rootedness in the supreme is an essential ingredient of our authentic self. To the extent that we are oblivious of this relationship, we have not realized our true self. The more we become aware of our relationship to ultimate reality, the more our real self begins to blossom.

What are some of the positive implications of this principle of doing our own thing? Every individual has a special potential, a unique combination of qualities, attributes and possibilities. Therefore, the first important thing is to become aware of your own true potential. What are the positive qualities of your nature, and what are your drawbacks and shortcomings?

Once you gain insight into your potential, you can focus on its actualization. If, for example, a child is cut out to be a musician, the sooner he or she becomes aware of it, the better. The most important thing is to cultivate your own qualities and not to follow the principle of imitation or be allured into some other avocation — no matter what the pressure of life circumstances may be.

Another implication of this principle of self-development is that every human being has been given the power of independent thinking. Humans are thinking animals. This is our prerogative and a most precious gift God has given us. Under no circumstances, therefore, should we sacrifice our power of independent thinking, for it would amount to selling our souls for a mess of porridge. It is the divine right of every individual to develop the power of free thinking and not to be a slave in his or her thought to any outside authority. So often we have a tendency to sacrifice this power for security. We do it to escape, because free thinking imposes responsibilities. It is also strenuous. Initially in life, we are not yet ready to accept this responsibility, but we cannot develop our full personhood until we do so. Authoritarianism, totalitarianism, dictatorship and fascism come to dominate the lives of people because they are often too inclined to sacrifice their power of independent thought.

Over the centuries, spiritual leaders have tried to emphasize this. For example, once a Buddhist monk was doing everything possible to advance spiritually. He went to a teacher and said, 'Please tell me how I can be a light on to Buddha.' The teacher immediately saw how overwhelmed the monk was by the personality of Buddha. So he said, 'What do you think is the teaching of the Buddha? What did he emphasize most in his talks?' Then the teacher pointed out that Buddha had said to his disciples at his deathbed, *'Atma dipa bhava'* — 'Be a light unto thyself.' This was his great teaching. He showed the path, but each of us has to take the path. Over and over again he emphasized that the light of truth is in the heart of every one of us. Buddha came to show how we can discover that light; but we have to discover the light by ourselves. That is really being a light on to Buddha. Doing our own thing is to discover the light which shines in the depths of our soul, by following the example which has been indicated by the great masters of the world.

Another implication of this is the courage of conviction. When we know for ourselves what the truth is and have given it some serious thought, then we must have the courage to speak up and be counted. This is doing our own thing, and everybody in greater or lesser measure can do this.

Finally, the more we look within ourselves, the more we organize our life in accordance with spiritual ideals, the more we do our own thinking and the more we practice silent communion with the inmost depth of our being, the more we begin to see the direction and guidance of the inner light. This guidance is there in every human being, no matter in what language we express it. In religious language we say that God is there within us and shows us the light. But if we set aside religious language, we may say the human psyche is a self-guiding, self-regulating principle and power. There is a profound wisdom in the unconscious mind of humans. As we commune with the depths of our own inner being, the more this inner light surfaces and shines out, telling us what is really doing our own thing.

13

SELF-CONSCIOUSNESS

Language is ambivalent. The same word can have so many different meanings. Self-consciousness today has acquired a negative meaning. Sometimes we find that individuals are preoccupied with themselves. They are always wondering what others will think of them if they adopt a certain line of action. They lose spontaneity and drive. They are inhibited and cannot go ahead. Self-consciousness in that sense is a limitation. It is born of morbid self-concern and too much preoccupation with what other people will think.

But in the philosophical context self-consciousness does not mean that at all. Here self-consciousness has a positive meaning. It means that at the human level the whole creative process of universal life comes alive. For the first time in the history of terrestrial evolution, nature becomes aware of its own creative impulses, of its own inherent purpose. Therein lies the power of humans.

Previously, nature was working through the instincts of animals and they are bound to do what they are motivated by instinct to do. They are compelled to do certain things. They do not raise any questions about their actions or the purpose and meaning of anything. But there comes a stage, a moment, in human development when suddenly we raise a big question to ourselves: 'What is the purpose of it all?'

As a result of this question, we as humans are able to catch a glimpse of the meaning of this creative force of evolution. The universal life force has become conscious at the human level. It is up to us to cooperate with this creative force and march forward or to withdraw cooperation. This is the deep significance of self-consciousness.

14

THE PROBLEM OF GUILT FEELINGS

Guilt and the consciousness of sin is a fundamental psychological problem of human existence. Here I want to explore different types of guilt feelings and the problems connected with these, in order to see what we can do about them.

A distinction has been made in psychology between guilt feelings and inferiority feelings. Guilt feelings and inferiority feelings often sound alike. A person who is suffering from a sense of guilt says something like this: 'I am no good. I have done something terribly wrong. I am ashamed of my evil nature. I deserve to be punished.' A person who suffers from inferiority feelings says something like this: 'I am weak. Others consider me "chicken." I am ashamed of my weakness and have got to do something about it.' When we compare the language of guilt and the language of inferiority, we see that both express a sense of shame and a desire for self-condemnation. Both are saying, 'I am ashamed of my nature.' One is ashamed of evil, and the other of weakness. Both, therefore, condemn themselves. This is why we so often confuse the two.

However, these two feelings produce distinctly different patterns or modes of behavior. People who feel guilty and want to condemn themselves for their evil nature usually become submissive. They frequently want to punish themselves. They may avoid competition and ambition because of their guilt. Sometimes their desire for punishment may lead eventually to suicidal tendencies. But people who feel inferior might think, 'I am weak. Other people are stronger than me. They insult and berate me. But poor me, I cannot do anything about it. I cannot even raise my little finger as a way of protest.' On the basis of this feeling, their destructive, aggressive tendencies surge up now and then, and they may harbor vengeance. They may become domineering and take every opportunity of dominating, thereby affirming themselves and overcoming their agonizing feelings of inferiority.

Understanding this distinction, we can concentrate on the actual feeling of guilt, the feeling of sin. Again it is important to distinguish between a normal sense of sin or guilt and pathological, morbid feelings of guilt. Most of the emotions that are natural in people have an important function to fulfill in our development and in our struggle for existence. Guilt has a value. As the great Danish philosopher Kierkegaard points out, guilt or sin is a fundamental existential category. He is saying that guilt is an essential factor in realizing our existence and in developing our nature. This is what distinguishes humans from animals. Consciousness of sin is a distinctive feature of humans alone. When it operates within normal bounds, it can spur tremendous growth of personality. It can become a source of inspiration as we strive for the fulfillment of higher goals of life and for the realization of the latent potentialities of our human nature. This can be essential to self-improvement and self-perfection.

Let us say you express a harsh word to a friend and feel guilty later. You may say, 'Why did I do that? He is a sincere, well-meaning, close friend of mine. It was not necessary for me to hurt his feelings.' You feel guilty about it. This is normal. If guilt is kept within normal bounds, you will analyze the situation, think why you were prompted to act in this way and tell yourself that in the future you will not unnecessarily hurt the feelings of another person, especially a friend who is well-meaning. The guilt feeling urges you to tutor yourself, to rectify the shortcomings of your nature and to open the way for further development.

Some of the noblest deeds of humans have been inspired by guilt feelings. Take, for example, Albert Schweitzer, one of the greatest men of our time. At the height of his achievement, a terrible sense of guilt began gnawing into his heart and invading his mind. One day he saw a statue of a black man in a humiliating position, and it reminded him of the injustice Europe had done to underdeveloped countries. The colonial policy of some European nations was represented in his mind with guilt. He felt he also shared that responsibility and told himself, 'This is a picture of man's inhumanity to man.'

This is normal guilt feeling. As a matter of fact, the more people advance morally and spiritually, the more they share a sense of responsibility for the whole of humanity. As a result of this guilt feeling, people say, 'Yes, I am my brother's keeper.' This is what we find when we study the lives of all truly great people.

Albert Schweitzer's guilt was a normal feeling of an ethically sensitive person. This guilt feeling had no paralyzing effect upon him. He did not become depressed. He did not retire into solitude and become inactive. He wanted to do something constructive to atone for it, so he dedicated himself to the service of humanity. He vowed to do something constructive, something noble, some act of self-sacrifice for the good of humanity. The rest of his life became the answer to this feeling. You may call it sublimation, how some feelings are channelled toward the fulfillment of higher aims of life. Whatever way you explain it, we find how guilt feelings can become an agency of constructive and fruitful action.

Let me give you a second illustration of another great man of our times, Mahatma Gandhi. He urged his followers to strive for the freedom of their country entirely on a spiritual basis of love, truth and nonviolence. He said that if we want to be successful, we must have love in our mind and in our speech which is then reflected in our actions. We must not harbor any thought of hatred or revenge toward a perceived enemy. Success will depend upon it. This was his gospel.

We know how human nature is. Every now and then Gandhi would see that in spite of the training and instruction he offered, some of his followers would do something vindictive or would express some hatred against the enemy. Consequently, he would have a sense of guilt himself. He felt he had been inadequate in properly training them. Or he would feel that because all people were part of the same human family that their wrong was also his wrong. He would fast for some time in order to atone for the guilt of his followers. By doing so, he generated a tremendous spiritual force and succeeded in imparting a great momentum to the whole movement.

But guilt feelings can become abnormal and pathological. Abnormal guilt feelings often rob us of our happiness and obstruct our self-development.

Let me offer a few illustrations of this dynamic. A college student had a peculiar habit of biting his hand. This biting was a compulsive urge within him, and he did not know why he did it. He struggled with himself to stop, but every now and then he had a terrible urge to bite his hand. An ugly scar appeared as a result of his constant biting. He wanted to hide himself. He felt he could not go to his classes and when he did go, he wore a glove, even when the weather was hot. Finally he went to a doctor who put some medicine on his hand to heal the wound. As a result of this medical treatment, he stopped biting. But as he stopped biting his hand, another symptom developed. Every now and then he would become very upset with some small moral problem.

For example, he had problems that went something like this: 'Should I wear my old tie, or should I wear one of these bright, beautiful new ties I recently bought? If I wear my new tie, I shall look good and will attract friends. But then it will be an embarrassment to my roommate who is poor.' He decided, 'I'd better wear one of my old ties; then I shall be harmonious with my roommate.' Every day some problem would crop up about whether he should do this or do that. If two friends were there, the problem was whether he should go with the one who belonged to a privileged circle or whether he should befriend the other fellow who was not so popular. There would be reasons for both, and he would not be able to come to any conclusion. You see how there was a transference of symptoms. Biting his hand stopped, yet another symptom developed. Then one day he unconsciously started biting the other hand. When he did this, the moral problems stopped, and he felt peaceful within himself.

As a result of some thorough analysis, the following facts came out: Sometime when he was very young, he thought he had committed a big sin. Whether his act was sinful or not is actually debatable. However, after a month or so he got the measles. As he lay in bed, his whole mind became occupied with a sense of guilt about the sin he had committed. From that time on he started biting his hand. Later he forgot the reason, but the habit continued. The guilt feelings had been driven underground into his unconscious mind, and biting his hand was the result of his suppressed guilt feelings. By continuing this habit of biting, he fulfilled his desire for self-punishment, thereby earning some peace of mind. Later, however, due to medical treatment, the biting stopped, but moral problems developed because the guilt feelings were not resolved. After he started biting his other hand, the moral problems subsided. This is how guilt feelings may operate. This is pathological guilt, guilt driven underground. This is what we mean by morbid guilt feelings and why so many of our irrational modes of behavior are prompted by feelings which are repressed and unconscious.

Let me give you another illustration. A young woman was competent and efficient in her job. But still, surprisingly enough, she had a submissive attitude in the office, and everyone seemed to take advantage of her goodness. She wanted to please everybody, but the result seemed to be the opposite. Occasionally she would be verbally abused by her supervisor. This produced a great problem in her mind, because she thought if she was innocent, she did not deserve all this humiliating treatment. It meant endless suffering for her. But in spite of this, she did not want to give up her job. Somehow she clung to that position.

This is also a common phenomenon. So often people complain about their suffering and about the injustice that other people are doing to them. But if somebody shows them a way out of all the suffering, he or she may be surprised to see their negative reaction. Often they will not take the advice. They do not want to escape from their suffering. This is a peculiar, paradoxical situation.

Let us go into the background of the case. We find through psychotherapeutic study that the woman had terrible guilt feelings. She was living with her old grandmother who happened to be wealthy. The young woman felt an unconscious death wish toward her grandmother because she would inherit all the wealth. But because she believed no civilized human being could conceivably entertain a death wish toward another, these feelings produced a great sense of guilt. Her submissiveness and acceptance of suffering fulfilled her desire to be punished. That is why she would not take a job in another office on better terms.

Some people cannot endure happiness. Some people reach the zenith of their happiness and then begin to fail. For example, some people find their difficulties begin when they get a good promotion. They become depressed and perhaps they sabotage their success. Why? Because of unconscious guilt feelings. They may think, 'I do not deserve all this success and happiness. I am no good. I deserve to be punished.'

In the same way, for some people, there is often a repetitious pattern of failure in marriage. A couple may be happily married with seemingly nothing lacking in their lives together. But one day the marriage breaks up. One of the individuals may then enter into another marriage which also proves to be successful and happy for some time. But for strange unknown reasons, that marriage also fails. This pattern may go on repeating itself — happiness and success followed by failure and negation of it. In these cases, we often find secret, unconscious guilt feelings operating. When a person is having a wonderful experience, he or she may suddenly feel, 'I don't deserve all this.' This is a dangerous human problem.

Not only do guilt feelings destroy our happiness and obstruct development, they also may incite people to commit crimes, of either a small or large nature, through a bribing of their super-ego. For example, a young girl had a strange habit. She was tremendously fond of candy. She would take a piece of candy, eat it and give herself a sharp slap. She would repeat this cycle until she finished the box of candy and then start in on another box.

We also find this same pattern in many adults. My wife and I were surprised to see a strange phenomenon in south India which I had never seen before. We were passing by a temple, and suddenly our attention was drawn to a man standing by the image of a deity. He was pulling his ears until he fell flat on the floor, and then he would stand up again. He continued that for a long time. What was he doing? He was confessing a sin and punishing himself. You might think this was good, that his self-punishment purified him, and he became all right. But after he came out of the temple, he evidently repeated the same crime for which he felt guilty — for we saw him again at the next temple punishing himself.

When we bribe our super-ego, we do something we know is wrong and our conscience bothers us. So then what do we do? We bribe our nagging conscience. We bribe our super-ego by punishing ourselves, and then our conscience is satisfied. After bribing our super-ego, we are released from our guilt feelings and then are in a position to do the wrong action again. This is why people sometimes are incited to commit crimes as a result of their unconscious guilt feelings. This is what has given rise to many neurotic criminals. Many criminals commit a crime, go to jail, serve a term of punishment, then come out of jail and commit the same crime and go to jail again. They are caught in a vicious circle.

This shows how dangerous these unconscious, morbid guilt feelings can become. We also learn how self-defeating it is to over-emphasize the sense of guilt or the sense of sin. It is unfortunate that so much of religious preaching harps upon people's sense of sin, for this can hurt the human personality. The true function of religion is to remind humans of their latent divinity, to draw their attention to the indwelling presence of the divine in our human nature. Yet instead, we find that so often religious preaching focuses on stimulating a sense of guilt. This can foster irreparable damage to the human psyche.

I am reminded of another story. One time an enthusiastic evangelist went to a rural village and preached fire and brimstone. After a few days, he casually inquired how the people liked his sermons. One of them said, 'Your preaching is mighty powerful. Before you came here, we did not know what sin was.' So in the minds of people we find that religion has been associated with sin, and this sin-consciousness borders sometimes on the pathological.

Let me tell you still another incident. A priest noted that one lady in the congregation had an interesting habit of bowing a little whenever he mentioned Satan during his sermons. One day he could not resist asking her why she did that. She said, 'It does not cost anything to be polite. And you can never tell when it might be useful to have a friend in a high place.'

Guilt is like a fire, and it can burn us badly. Therefore, leaders of society should use the consciousness of guilt judiciously and intelligently. Trying to exploit the consciousness of guilt in adults or in children in order to get some temporary advantage is wrong and irresponsible. A whole host of wrong ideas goes along with this exploitation of guilt feelings, but I shall mention just a few.

One idea concerns the devil, as I have hinted at already. Many people are obsessed with the idea of Satan and their religious consciousness often centers around this idea. Instead of being occupied with the love of God or with the thought of God, their mind is occupied with the devil, which is regressive. Most of what we call our evil tendencies proceed from our ignorance. The devil has nothing to do with it. There is no such thing as the devil in that sense. It is ignorance of the self, ignorance of our nature, ignorance of our relationship to society and to our creator which are responsible for criminal actions or wrongdoing. That is why Socrates was wise when he said, 'Know thy Self.' Instead of harboring destructive guilt feelings, we must know what are our main desires, our impulses, our ambitions and our strivings. What is our position in society and in relations with other people? The more we understand this, the better chance we have of acting in harmony with the transcendental order of goodness and truth.

Another wrong idea which contributes to guilt feelings is the idea that nature is evil. This comes from having a rigid distinction between the natural and the supernatural. The dualistic theological idea is that spirit is entirely different from nature, and that spirit is good and nature is bad. This is a dangerous idea, a wrong idea and a pernicious idea. This contributes to the growth of morbid guilt feelings.

Many people feel terribly guilty whenever they have a destructive wish or socially undesirable urge which comes into their mind. For example, say a man becomes aware of a destructive impulse within him to hit a person or to enter a house and commit vandalism. He is mature and brushes it aside. Still, he may have a terrible guilt feeling just on account of this wish. Or a young woman may have a sexual desire for her father in her mind. She brushes it aside, but still she may have guilt feelings: 'This is an awful desire; it is evil.' What is happening here? There is a failure to distinguish between impulses, desires, and feelings on the one hand and actual actions on the other. There is a failure to understand that a mental state is not the same as doing something.

Mere wishes and ideas are not to be equated with reality. All kinds of desires may arise in our minds because of our animal nature. Simply because some desire, even an undesirable one, may arise in your mind, you need not feel guilty. It depends upon whether you accept the desire and act upon it or whether you reject the desire on a rational basis. This will be your responsibility.

Many people suffer from guilt feelings over certain urges or desires because they think nature is evil. This is a wrong idea. Nature is not evil. There is a profound wisdom in nature. Most of the impulses and feelings that arise from nature have something to tell us. They have a purpose. Our job is to understand their meaning. Our main spiritual task of life is to organize intelligently the different impulses and desires that flow from our nature. Our job is not to negate or to spurn our nature, but to fulfill the constructive spiritual task of ordering, harmonizing, and organizing the different energies of our being in accordance with the central ideal of life. As we increasingly align all aspects of our nature with the spiritual destiny of existence, the more we shall fulfill our authentic function in life.

15

MAYA: THE ETERNAL FEMININE

The concept of *maya* in Indian philosophy is the eternal feminine principle in the structure of reality and represents the unfathomable mystery of life and existence.

Eastern philosophy espouses the view that ultimate reality is the unity of opposites, two most fundamental of which are the masculine and feminine principles. God is not conceived as predominantly masculine or feminine, either as God the father or the divine mother. God is the unity of these two opposites variously known as Shiva and Shakti, Yang and Yin, Yab and Yum, or Logos and Eros.

Here I want to examine from a practical standpoint the influence maya plays in our human relations. An interesting story in yoga philosophy tells how maya, the feminine principle, involves people in the affairs of life, and yet this same principle also helps us in getting out of our involvement. Maya is a beautiful dancing girl, and Purusha, the spirit, is the beholder, the witness, the onlooker. Maya comes in front of Purusha and begins to dance wonderfully, unfolding the charms and graces of her celestial form. The spirit beholds, bewitched and enchanted. So long as the beholder watches with great interest, Maya continues to dance. But she is very sensitive. The moment she realizes it has been enough, she immediately turns around and shrinks, withdrawing her dance form. Magically she is transformed from the dancing girl into the divine mother. This same power or energy now begins to help the beholder in attaining supreme liberation, which is the ultimate spiritual destiny of life. So Maya is the great enchantress whose power can bring supreme liberation to the individual self; for without divine grace, salvation is not possible.

One particular feature of this divine energy is the enchantment of role playing in society. Every one of us plays many roles. This is an important fact of our social existence. As we identify ourselves with a particular social or historical role, we become one with it, and it exerts tremendous power over our life, often unconsciously. Maya operates from the depth of the unconscious, and we frequently are not aware of it. It pulls the strings behind the scenes and that is why we can not do anything about it until we become more liberated.

What happens when we are under the magic spell of this self-identification which is called maya? All our life we identify with many things. First, we enact a religious role in our life. While this has abated in influence in modern times, this religious role was all-important in the Middle Ages. 'I am a Catholic.' 'I am a Protestant.' 'I am a Jew.' 'I am a Muslim.' 'I am a Hindu.' As soon as we identify, then what we identify with becomes the most important fact and we forget everything else. This can become such an overwhelming power in life that we may not hesitate to ignore the feelings of other fellow beings. If necessary, we might start a holy crusade and destroy thousands of people. In the name of God with whom we identify, we would violate the laws of God. In the name of love, we would practice hatred. In the name of peace, we would destroy. These things become possible because of this identification.

Then there is the racial role. When we identify with a particular race absolutely, it also can become a most controlling influence in our life. We say, 'I am white.' 'I am black.' 'I am brown.' 'I am yellow.' 'This is the essence of my being.' As each race develops its stories and myths of superiority and supremacy over others, this role identification can assume an all-pervasive influence.

Further, let us consider the role of the professional. Nearly everybody has to earn a living and choose some form of work. Then they put on the garment of that profession and become one with that role. They put on a mask and play a new role on the social stage, dictated by maya, the magic string-puller.

MAYA: THE ETERNAL FEMININE

You may have been acquainted with a person socially in one setting as one kind of person. But when you go to see him or her in a professional environment, you may be surprised to see an entirely different person. The same person whom you have found to be gentle and soft-hearted in a family environment, may become tough and ruthless in dealing with subordinates. When the professional mask is on, this person may treat other people as so many numbers to be used in so many different ways.

This is one of the tragedies of human life. This depersonalization of human relations is an essential ingredient of the present-day crisis. That is why in the midst of teeming millions of humans there are so many lonely people today. We meet and talk with people, but come across over and over again the same story of loneliness, of an unsatisfied hunger of the human soul. Often there is no knowing how to fulfill this hunger because even the cause is not recognized.

We go to factories and because of the role individuals are placed in, they are reduced to numbers. Also at big schools students often are not persons anymore; they, too, become anonymous numbers. This is true everywhere we go. Our sense of individuality feels crushed under the steamroller of these mass organizations, which constitute the main features of the human landscape today. This is an existential crisis. Most of the psychological problems today are a value crisis and a crisis of the spirit.

We can see how some of the great rulers of the world have become identified with the historical role of destiny. For example, Hitler identified with being a man of destiny. He felt impelled to accomplish certain things and was so identified with this particular role that he did not hesitate to ride roughshod over all other ethical, religious, or spiritual considerations. In the same way, many dictators identify with a particular role which actually blinds them to all other verities of life.

This kind of thing can happen under the hypnotic spell of a complete, exclusive identification with a particular role, no matter what that role might be. When a person becomes identified so completely with a destiny image it is powerful and potentially destructive because here the person may identify with God, with the divine will. Then he or she draws justification not only from human considerations, but from higher considerations as well.

In lesser ways, we all play the game of maya by being more or less identified with certain thought and value systems. Each of us is a philosopher. We all have certain views about the meaning of life, our position in the world and the nature of God. This identification can become so strong and enchanting that we close the door of our mind to other ways of thinking.

That is why we see the intellectual and political world flooded with all kinds of 'isms' and 'ologies.' All writers have their own theory which they carry in their mind. All have their own individual picture of the universe. Eventually these different pictures clash with one another. And often we find that when there is a debate or argument back and forth at cross purposes, pretty soon it may end up in a bitter fight which generates a lot of heat and smoke, but no light.

In the same way, each of us is involved with particular lifestyles and we often think that ours is the best, while others are inferior. Different lifestyles tend to have their day and there are many counter-movement lifestyles juxtaposed against the conventional establishment lifestyle. Further, there is the lifestyle of the scientist, the artist, the philosopher, and the ascetic. So just as each one of us picks up our own thought system and is identified with it, we each pick our own lifestyle and that becomes the only true one in the world.

Let me give you an example. Shankara, of the ninth century AD in India, was a brilliant intellect, metaphysician and ascetic. At an early age, he renounced the whole world in search of truth. He developed a philosophy in which he did not believe in the feminine principle. He rejected it because he had renounced women and was a loner entrenched in the consciousness of the absolute. Convinced that in his own life he could do without the feminine principle in the human sense of the word, he also had no need for it in the divine sense of the word. We tend to think of God in the image of our human nature, more or less, and this was his teaching — not accepting the need, power or value of the feminine. It was his mission to go throughout India spreading the message of pure consciousness without the reality of love energy.

One day after having discussions with other philosophers, he was coming back home. Because of the day's exertions, he was feeling terribly tired but he had still a few miles to travel. He felt so fatigued and thirsty that he desperately wished someone would appear to give him a glass of water. Just at that moment, he saw a beautiful pond nearby, but he was so tired that he could not take the remaining few steps to reach down to the water for a drink.

However, just then a beautiful young woman from the village appeared with a pitcher to fetch fresh drinking water from the pond. When Shankara saw her, he was delighted. He asked, 'Would you kindly bring me a glass of water? I am so thirsty!' She said, 'Certainly I will.' She filled her pitcher with water and came to him. After he drank his fill, he felt very good and took a second look at the woman. He saw she was so beautiful and charming that he fell in love. He was so much under the influence of this new-found love that he sprang to his feet and was about to embrace her. But she pulled back and said, 'Shankara, you don't believe in maya, do you? You don't believe in the feminine principle, do you?' Saying so, she disappeared.

This was Shankara's second conversion. His first conversion was his total faith in Brahman, pure consciousness and spirit, which has nothing to do with love. But the second conversion was belief in the reality of love energy. Nobody can ever completely overcome the power of love, so God had to teach him this lesson in the form of a young woman who appeared and then disappeared.

After that experience his life was changed. His heart mellowed, and he discovered a different dimension of life. He wrote some beautiful devotional songs addressed to the divine mother, which are now known to the world.

This gives us an idea of what maya is and why in Indian philosophy there is so much emphasis upon this fundamental truth of ultimate reality being the undivided unity of two equally real principles: the archetypal masculine principle, which is pure formless consciousness — and the archetypal feminine principle of love, joy, beauty, and creativity. The unity of the two makes life whole and gives us a holistic picture of God as the unity of opposites.

The most essential condition of happiness and fulfillment in human life is balance, harmony, and integration. This is the dharma. Dharma is the cosmic balance and the dharma of our life is psycho-spiritual balance. We can never live a meaningful life, a soul-satisfying life, if we lose our sense of these higher values and if we are alienated from our higher consciousness.

On the basis of this understanding, we have to think of the ideal goal of our life and the destiny of our human existence. An ideal human is one who has developed to the full both the masculine and feminine principles of his or her existence. Both of these principles are present in all of us, whether male or female. We potentially embody the principle of love and eros on the one hand, and the principle of knowledge and logos on the other — the principle of extroversion on the one hand, and introversion on the other. By harmonizing these into a dynamic and creative synthesis, we can blossom to the full and become perfect humans, authentic embodiments of an integral ideal.

16

HOW TO TRANSFORM THE EGO

Ego is a fundamental issue in our striving for spiritual growth. As all great teachers and masters have warned, the ego is the single stupendous stumbling block to the advancement of our spiritual potential.

I would like to clarify this, because we often draw wrong conclusions. Words are intended to communicate truth, but more often than not they lead to falsehood, partly because of the problem of linguistic communication. Language plays tricks upon the human mind. These are called the tricks of maya in Indian philosophy.

If a great truth is understood properly, it is a divine blessing; it can lift us immediately into a higher consciousness. However, if it is misunderstood, it can confuse us and steer us into dark bypaths and blind alleys. In ancient India, a teacher would never tell disciples the truth until he or she felt they were prepared. Were these teachers selfish? Why did they try to hold the truth to themselves?

The idea is that first we have to purify our minds. We must develop our cognitive apparatus, the ability to know, to understand and to apply truth properly. Until then, truth actually can hurt us. This is why there is the saying, 'Never cast pearls before the swine.' There has to be fitness and self-training to a proper receptivity before an individual is in a position to receive, to understand and to make constructive use of a great truth. This is the meaning of what is called *brahmacharya* in India — self-preparation through self-discipline and self-purification.

Until this is achieved, we cannot comprehend the truth and the ultimate meaning of life.

The principle of ego is particularly misunderstood. The concept of ego is a fundamental one which has great practical importance in our life. Many great teachers claim that one should overcome the ego by conquering and subduing it in order to realize the true self, the spirit in us, the indwelling divine presence in our hearts. From this many draw a negative conclusion that if ego is the arch-enemy of God, we need to destroy or kill it. This is a wrong conclusion.

It is not by destroying the ego, but by transforming it that we begin to solve our problem. This is the key. When we destroy the ego, exactly the opposite effect is produced. Destruction of the ego means destruction of the self. When the egos of individuals are destroyed, they enter mental hospitals. They become incapacitated for living in society, unable to live their own lives anymore. How can they live their own lives when the source of their sense of self is destroyed? We can see the absurdity of this. Ego is the seed of the true self in humans. In the interior of the ego, inside the husk, the kernel of a human's spiritual potential lies hidden. We are all familiar with the saying, 'God is the kingdom of heaven within.' This means God is present in every one of us.

Just as God's essential structure is a trinity, God in humans is also a trinity. From the psychological standpoint, what is the trinity of the indwelling divine presence in the human personality? It is the trinity of the ego, the super-ego and the fire. The Sanskrit names are *Manu, Indra,* and *Agni*. Agni means fire. Indra is the lord of the supernatural world, the super-ego. Manu is the middle principle, the mental ego, our normal ego.

Manu is the principle of mental self-consciousness which is a distinctive feature of humans. The self-consciousness makes humans what they are, because it is the reflection in us of the pure light of consciousness of the Supreme Being. Supreme Being is pure consciousness, the untellable master light that illuminates all other lights. That light is the essence of God or Being, the white radiance of eternity which shines as the light of all lights. The ego, Manu, the spark of self-consciousness in humans, is the reflection in imperfect human nature of that pure light and radiance of eternity. We should not destroy it; we need to cultivate it and transform it. This is a great principle of self-development.

In Eastern and Western mythology, the different kinds of manifestation of the ego have been described. We do not always recognize the lessons because they are in the form of stories, myths and legends. The ego principle is a divine-undivine principle, a god-demon principle. If we cultivate it properly, it becomes a divine power. If we do not understand what it is and abuse it, it becomes an undivine or demonic power. It is the hydra-headed dragon. It has many forms, good and bad.

Let us discuss some of these manifestations. Beginning with the lowest level, there is one called *tamasic ego* which is darkened with ignorance. People manifesting this form often say things such as, 'I am no good,' 'I am not able to do anything,' or 'My life is hopeless.' This is such a depressed, deflated ego that even when God appears in disguise to help, the person often refuses to receive it. The ego is so depressed that it closes the door to its own transformation. In yoga psychology, the dark ego has to be liberated with the sharp sword of the bright ego. We conquer or overcome something with its opposite. So when the ego is in a dark, deflated condition, it is good to think of the opposite possibilities of life. That is when one needs to think of uplifting goals and higher ambitions. This is when other people who want to help talk of the possibilities of enjoyment and prosperity. All these things become necessary to ferret out all the hidden desires of the human heart.

Inspirational books can help us too. Gandhi, in carrying on the freedom movement on a spiritual basis, used two books, the Bhagavad Gita and the Sermon on the Mount as main sources of inspiration to him. Another important spiritual book, which is not much known here, is called *Chandhi*. It is read in almost every great religious festival in India as it is such a positive and affirmative approach to life. *Chandhi* emphasizes the positive forces and desires in life which can be mobilized properly in order to lift people out of their stuck condition and to inspire them. There is mention of God in connection with prosperity, beauty, enjoyment, and harmony. The idea is that these things have great value in life and a proper function in our spiritual growth. It is recognition that everything we can find within ourselves is a divine gift of nature; therefore, everything has its place and function in the total scheme of self-development. It is foolish for us to take a negative attitude to the basic principles of life and try to destroy or suppress our ego. Suppression is dangerous and detrimental. This is one of the great discoveries in modern psychology.

Another form of manifestation is what is called *tapurich* ego, a fearful ego. Some people are full of constant fear and anxiety. Paul Tillich, the modern existential theologian, wrote a wonderful book called *The Courage to Be*. He talked about different kinds of anxiety people have and how these anxieties and fears make their lives miserable. Anxiety and fear are among the most pervasive problems of human life today. That is why this era has been described by some as the age of anxiety. The most important reason for this anxiety is the tremendous sense of insecurity in today's world. People are all too aware of nuclear weapons and the possibility of another world war. We hear of over-population, ecological crises, and other dire problems. No wonder people are anxious!

On top of all this there is what is called existential anxiety, which is more subtle. This is the secret anxiety of death and powerlessness. This feeling that we are finite, we are imperfect and we are helpless is always there, deep down in our hearts. Throughout previous ages, religious faith and the flame of spiritual aspiration helped us to conquer existential anxiety, but now that is gone. As a result of the technological structure of modern civilization, the spiritual means of subduing existential anxiety have all but evaporated. Therefore, our anxiety has become much exaggerated. That means we need to replace the ancient gods that have died with new gods. This is the great need of the present day. Martin Heidegger once said that at the close of every epoch of history and at the beginning of every age, new gods are reincarnated or incarnated. That is the kind of transition period we are going through today. Our old gods have died, and we are groping toward the discovery of new ones, the God of a new age. This alone can solve our basic problem of existential anxiety and serve as a new source of inspiration in human life.

Kuvaric ego is when we lose the sense of spiritual value of life. A main source of security becomes material possessions. The more we have different objects around us, the more we feel secure. This is an exploitative ego. We exploit and want to grab things. The more we succeed in grabbing, the happier we feel.

Similar to this is *gandharva* ego, hedonic ego. Such people claim, 'Eat, drink and be merry,' or 'Make hay while the sun shines.' When there is total absence of intrinsic spiritual joy, a vacuum, a void, an emptiness in the heart, we try to fill the emptiness more and more with pleasures we can accumulate from the outside. This becomes our lifestyle. When we overemphasize external pleasure, pretty soon we reach a saturation point and we become bored. When that happens, then what is the source of pleasure anymore? Drugs may become a source of pleasure. Destructiveness may become a source of pleasure. When we lose or close our inner sources of joy and happiness and peace, we become extroverted in our search for these things. Philosophers call this the paradox of hedonism. This means that if we always consciously search for pleasure, pleasure eludes our grasp. It is like a will of the wisp. You just do not experience it. You are always running after the horizon. You chase after butterflies, but they all fly away.

In actual fact, our keenest pleasures and joys are those that come unexpectedly. If you look back on your life, you will see that the deepest joys and pleasures came when you were not even striving for them. When you are striving for pleasure, you cannot have that kind of joy. Why? Because pleasure is not a positive content of the mind. This is a subtle psychological point. Pleasure is a by-product of the satisfaction or fulfillment of our goals.

Let us say we have a purpose or aim, some value in front of us that we appreciate. When we gain this objective, we have immense joy. We do not search for pleasure. We search for value, something good, something beautiful, something true. In proportion to our success and ability to achieve this goal, we have great joy. Joy is a by-product, not an objective or goal in life.

Then there is what is called *pishajic* ego. This is an idle, lethargic type of ego that is dominated by the law of inertia. Some people always seem to procrastinate. They try to shirk responsibility. They do not want to undertake anything which will mean responsibility. They do not want to exert themselves, even in their religious or spiritual life. They may accept a spiritual ideal of life and know that self-discipline, study, and meditation are good. They read in the scriptures that we are one with the Supreme. Yet because of this tendency to sink into inertia, they often draw a wrong conclusion. They deceive themselves that they are already one with God and do not need to go through all the fuss of meditation and self-discipline. They decide not to do anything.

There is a great divine, spiritual potential dormant in our human personality. Potentially we are one with the Supreme, but so long as we do nothing to actualize this potentiality, we cannot experience this union. We are both one with God and not one with God. It depends on how we understand it.

Let me share a little story. Two friends were notorious for their idleness and procrastination. One day they were resting and relaxing together in bed. Suddenly the house caught fire, but they were relaxing in great delight. One of them began to feel the fire on his back. A very idle person does not want to spend much energy by talking too much, so he just said, 'B.B.' That was shorthand for 'Back burns.' The other one replied laconically, 'T.A.' which means 'Turn around.' That was her solution.

Another form of ego is *rajasic*, the aggressive and destructive type. Here, one becomes antisocial, and destructive impulses come to the surface.

Then there is the *promethean* ego. Prometheus stole fire from heaven and so the gods were afraid. Possession of fire is good, because fire is a wonderful thing; but the gods were afraid because they did not know how humans were going to use fire. Fire is a great potential and a great blessing. The discovery of fire started human civilization, but this also was the beginning of wars which have killed thousands upon thousands of people. That which is a blessing also can become a curse because of human stupidity, ignorance and selfishness. Promethean types use their heroic strength and extraordinary ability to discover power. Modern Prometheans have discovered atomic energy. This is wonderful, but at the same time there has been created a great danger and threat to today's civilization.

Asuric egos are ideologically inflated. People with this type of ego discover spiritual, ideological ideas, great intellectual principles or systems, and think these are all that are needed to solve all problems. This has been an issue since the days of the Inquisition and religious warfare.

In a small way, all of us have this tendency when we find a good idea, a good ethical doctrine or a good religious creed. We think it will solve everything, and for a while we may absolutize it. We deify a particular principle or system of thought as the ultimate panacea of all evils. This is due to our human ignorance. Nothing can take the place of God. God alone is God. No idea or creed can take the place of God. This is why Martin Heidegger briefly summed it up by saying, 'The time has come for realizing that God is God.' He referred to God as Being with a capital 'B.' He said the time has come for us to realize Being is, period. This means we should not identify Being with anything else. Nothing can take its place. Being is. Being is Being. Do not indulge in a false identification. God is not to be identified with an idea, a creed, a scientific law, a system, or a machine. This is supreme spiritual wisdom, the realization that God knows no substitute. As Gandhi emphasized, truth alone is truth.

It is our task to cultivate, nourish, and bring to flowering what we may call the divine spark of self-consciousness within us, which is inside the shell of the ego. This has been called in Indian philosophy Vamana, the dwarf, the dwarfish light. Walt Whitman in *Leaves of Grass* referred to the word, *vaman*, dwarf. This is what St Paul called the imperishable spark of the divine in humans.

Let me tell you another story. A great king, Bali, was fabulously wealthy and immensely powerful. He was also very righteous. It is because he was righteous that he became wealthy and powerful, but even so, he did not believe in God. He was an atheist. He hated Vishnu, the god of love, who was worshipped by his people. He thought they should worship him and could not understand why they did not. Was he not the one who provided food and shelter for the kingdom? But he was compassionate, and he tried his best to help his subjects.

One time he gave a big social and religious festival. That is how the people thought of it; for the king, it was more a social and political festival. All were welcome, and whoever came would receive a gift from the king. Nobody would leave empty-handed. Many people came, high and mighty, rich and poor. Suddenly in the midst of the merriment, a small, dwarfish person appeared. His name was Vamana, and he was almost invisible in that vast gathering. At first, people did not pay any attention to him. But as they happened to have a closer look, they were taken aback, because he was a luminous figure. He did not pay attention to anything or anybody as he cut his way through the crowd and appeared in front of the king. The king was surprised at his audacity. But when he had a second look, he was also astonished at Vamana's radiating light. The king welcomed him, gave him a seat and said, 'What can I do for you?' In his exuberance he added, 'I shall be happy to give you whatever you wish. Just ask something of me.' Vamana said, 'My lord, I do not have much to ask. All I want is three narrow strips of land in your kingdom, land three steps wide.' The king was amazed. He said, 'What do you mean, three steps of land? Ask for a whole island or the whole province, and I shall give it to you.'

Just then the king's preceptor, Juspati, heard the conversation, and he understood the significance of what was going on. He turned to the king and said, 'You have made a blunder. What have you done? You have promised to give him three steps of land, but he will take everything you have. Nothing will be left to you, so immediately withdraw your promise.' The king said, 'No, I cannot do that, because I am a man of my word.'

The preceptor tried to convince the king that white lies are allowable in special circumstances. For example, in self-defense a person can tell a lie, he said, or in the defense of one's family or country. In order to preserve a love affair, a person also can tell a lie, he said. But the king was unconvinced. Turning to Vamana, he said, 'I have given you a promise. You may proceed to take your land.' In a twinkling of an eye, Vamana was expanded, and with one step he took the whole earth. With another step he took the whole heaven. Then he asked the king, 'Where shall I take my third step?' The king said, 'Please take your third step on my head.' Immediately he was transformed.

This is transformation. This is Vaman in the light, the divine spark that shines in the depth of our being which is capable of expansion. This is what spirituality is all about. Meditation, spirituality, and religion bring about the expansion of the imperishable spark of the divine that shines in the depth of us. This is how all hostile forces eventually are conquered. The king represents the big ego. Eventually the ego was conquered because the king overcame his hostility and antagonism. And this is the secret of transformation of the ego which is an essential condition of spiritual fulfillment.

17

INTEGRATING THE EXTREMES OF LIFE

Before we integrate all of the extremes in our personality, it is good to know what we are going to integrate. This is important. For instance, some people think that if we are to grow spiritually, we should go through delightful or happy experiences. Many psychotherapists have remarked that this is a defect in the character of contemporary American people. We do not want to hear about the negative or evil side of life. We do not want to hear about death. We turn a blind eye, which can be self-deluding.

Say, for example, a person has had a good peak experience. If he is under the impression that it is only by having more of this kind of experience that he is going to reach his spiritual goal, then what may happen? More and more he becomes withdrawn and avoids other situations in life. He may feel that if he gets drawn into social activity, he will lose his peak experience. This is one-sided.

In the past, meditation has been practised with a transcendentalist orientation toward ultimate liberation from the bonds of karma and samsara. This was part of the pattern of evolution. Especially in the Middle Ages there was a need to emphasize transcendental realization with all the force and strength of being.

But then life is not just peak experience. Life is also valley experience. Life is not only ontological experience; it is also existential experience. Life is a whole spectrum of experiences. At one extreme, there is the highest kind of ecstasy. On the other hand, we go through the abyss, the unfathomable depth, the bottom. Life is a whole spectrum of multicolored, infinitely diversified experiences. Our goal is to maintain a balance, to integrate, to organize this range of experiences into a whole, into a system, into an organized structure, which is a wonderful achievement. Only when we achieve this dynamic integration can we attain perfect equanimity and serenity.

That is what Buddha's picture in meditation is telling us. When we see Buddha in meditation we see no agitation, no perturbation. He has gone through all kinds of experiences. He has gone through the highest blissful state and also through rigid austerity and suffering, criticism and opposition.

It is the same when we study the life of any great person. We see they have gone through sacrifice, humiliation, defeat, frustration, and an encounter with death and nothingness — along with delightful and exciting experiences of an encounter with the divine, with the forces of light. In order to balance, it is good to recognize the role of abyss experiences in the development and strengthening of our character. If we do not, then one side of our life remains too soft and tender.

William James distinguished between two types of philosophers: the tough-minded and the tender-minded. Those who have seen only the good side of life are immature because they do not know what the seamy side of life is. Therefore, once they come into contact with the other side of life, they fall flat. People who have gone through all kinds of experience can take everything in their stride. Nothing can daunt them because they have gone through fire. In order to have that strength and maturity of character, one cannot be cowed by anything.

There are some wrestlers who may be very good and make a wonderful display of their strength. But once they go under, they are finished. They cannot take too much beating. However, others can take everything. Whenever they have the opportunity, they are on the offensive. They may get a good deal of trussing but they can take it. After a long period of sound thrashings, they come out of it and get a second wind. Therefore, they are the ones who win. They may become invincible and nothing can stop them. We may say they now have God's grace — the second wind is that.

It is important not only to think, feel and do well when things go well. You must also be able to have an inner strength even when life is giving you a good deal of trouble. Then as you come out of it, you are born with a new strength. Just as life showers upon us many blessings, it also confronts us with much challenge. We have both to learn how to accept the blessings and also how to stand the challenge. Just as in walking, we first place one foot down and then the opposite — that is how we go. It is by going through, assimilating, and digesting all experiences of life into the evolving, concrete texture of our psyche that we produce and develop something of sterling quality and everlasting value.

18

SECRETS OF SELF-CONTROL

As you know, human nature is a most paradoxical phenomenon because embedded within us are contradictory elements. For example, we have wise impulses in our nature which Schopenhauer called the unconscious will in humans. Some ancient thinkers called it the serpent power, a tremendous reservoir of energy latent within us. Modern psychology calls it libido, the elemental urges. This apparently limitless reservoir of energy is one aspect of human personality.

Looking to the other side of human nature, we find the rational side. There is conscience, the stern daughter of the voice of God. There is the human ability to hear the voice of God and enter into communion with the spiritual dimension and the eternal verities. The sense of higher values at the heart of human nature has an uplifting, ennobling influence on us, as a result of which we are never satisfied with what we are, with our embodied animal existence. We are perpetually looking for something, reaching out for something higher and greater and nobler, longing for perfection and infinity. As one philosopher put it, 'Man is finite, but he is always reaching out for the infinite.'

Herein lies the paradox. We have these contradictory elements intertwined in our human personality. The result of this paradox is that many possibilities are open to us. At one extreme we have the possibility to descend lower than a beast. At the other end we have a profound spiritual possibility in our nature, by virtue of which we can ascend even above angels. You may wonder how that is possible. Angels are the limit of perfection as we think of it, so how can humans rise above them? It is because angels have a fixed nature. They are archetypal. Each is a type. When you read mythology, each god is a fixed type. They are what they are.

But humans are involved in a process of infinitive evolution. We can break through all barriers, bonds, and limitations and rise up straight to the summit of perfection, entering into communion with the God above all gods, the supreme godhead beyond all angels. That is our possibility and prerogative, too, if we know how to finish up the unfinished process that humans are.

Another reason why humans can rise above angels is that angels belong to the ethereal kingdom. Therefore, they are ineffective in the material world. Without the cooperation of humans, they cannot do a thing in the physical world. Involved in a process of cosmic evolution, humans are charged by God with a mission to bring something of the glory and beauty, something of the perfume of the infinite into the realm of matter.

So we see within humans the possibility of descending lower than beasts or of rising higher than angels. What makes the difference? The answer is intelligent self-control and organized living. Much depends upon how we use the boundless energy at our disposal. Are we going to dissipate this energy or put it to destructive ends, or will we make positive, constructive use of it toward the fulfillment of higher ends and higher values? Everything depends upon this.

From the dawn of civilization, all the great ethical and religious teachers have in some form or other dwelt on this theme of self-control. In the Bible, God said to Adam and Eve, 'Thou shalt not eat from the tree of knowledge.' But as we look back in the light of modern knowledge, we find that if God really said that, God made a mistake. Why? Because human psychology tells us that as soon as you tell another human being, 'Thou shalt not,' he or she will do that very thing. As soon as God said, 'Thou shalt not,' Adam and Eve began to think how wonderful it would be to eat the apple. In the same way, as soon as we tell our children not to do something, we stimulate them to do that very thing.

We can see this in various other ways. Suppose, in trying to control little children, we scold them sternly and say, 'You are good for nothing!' Without knowing it, we are doing great damage to their growth impulse. The idea sticks in their minds, and an inferiority complex begins to develop inside them. Their inner striving for development may be blocked by that self-image.

Or suppose we tell them in anger they have done something wrong. 'You are idiots!' This is the same thing. Children take things seriously, often without our knowing it. Unconsciously they may become identified with that self-image and consequently act like idiots. For example, Jean-Paul Sartre described the situation of an orphan boy who felt unwanted and had no sense of identity. As often happens with people who are hungry for love and sympathy, he developed a habit of stealing. Stealing has a psychological value as it gets us something. It is a symbolic way of desiring and longing for love. However, one day the boy was caught red-handed in the act of stealing. There came the stern voice of discipline and control: 'You are a thief!' The man who said it did not know what great damage he did to the boy's personality. The boy said, 'Fine, I am a thief then.' He took up in earnest in this social role. He decided to be a good thief, because that was what he thought he was.

Another negative form toward self-control, that of self-suppression, has been disastrous in the history of human ethical and religious striving. We may take a stern, negative, punishment-inflicting attitude to the rest of our nature. To use Freudian terms, the super-ego becomes a great punisher and wants to control the rest of our personality with a whip in its hand. Throughout the history of religious search, humans have gone to great lengths inflicting punishment upon themselves in the name of higher development. They mortified the flesh to control the mind. They tried to suppress all impulses and desires and followed the path of extreme puritanism and asceticism. In doing so, it is true that they earned peace of mind to some extent, but it was the peace of negation or withdrawal and not the peace of positive fulfillment.

Today we know this is a wrong policy. As we practice such self-mortification, we set up within ourselves a civil war. Eventually this divides our nature to some degree into two personalities, a Dr Jekyll and Mr Hyde. The two parts of our nature are at loggerheads with one another and our human personality becomes a house divided against itself. In actuality, our total human personality is one indivisible, undivided whole. True holiness lies in realizing the wholeness of our being. Holiness is wholeness. We do not realize our potential by dividing our personality into warring and conflicting elements and by preserving the eternal tension between them. We realize our potential by understanding and bringing forth into manifestation the wholeness of our being. We understand how to press into service all our different elements — the higher and the lower, passion and reason, impulse and ethics. We have to bring these together into harmonious cooperation toward the fulfillment of the central goals of our life.

Having tried to disabuse our minds of some wrong ideas about self-control, I want to turn to some positive principles espoused by modern educators. In the past we controlled ourselves by saying, 'I must not do this or that.' Usually this does not work except as a temporary measure as inwardly a spirit of rebellion builds up. Instead of telling ourselves not to do something, we can present ourselves with other constructive experiences which will fascinate our minds. This produces a magical effect. Becoming engaged in doing something of interest imposes control upon our minds. Control comes from within; it is not imposed from without. The more we create interest in a healthy line of thinking or exploration of the outside world, the more we evoke a spirit of self-discipline.

When other individuals say something unkind to us, our natural reaction is to hurt back and we often get into a vicious circle. However, a positive approach is to keep quiet. If we preserve our silence, it is like a looking glass, and the harsh words uttered boomerang back to the source from which they came. When we over-react, we defeat our purpose. If we know how to control ourselves by keeping quiet, the tide can be turned in our favor.

Let me share an ancient story from the Upanishads about *brahmacharya*, intelligent self-control. A person was driving a chariot pulled by six horses. The chariot got stuck because the horses were pulling in different directions. The driver tried hard to bring them under control by whipping them, but they became more unmanageable and more wild. This is an illustration of the conflicts in our lives, or of the root conflict in human personality between passion and reason, the flesh and the spirit, or the libido and super-ego.

The driver may want to give up. He may cut loose the horses in order to regain peace of mind, but the purpose is defeated because he is immobilized. The destination cannot be reached. The real solution would be to approach the situation with tact and understanding. The driver has to inquire into the reason for the situation. Why are the horses behaving in that way? Maybe they are tired or thirsty or hungry. Maybe some insects are bothering them. So the driver takes time. He gives the horses some rest and looks after their needs. After a while he will find with amazement the horses are ready to run again until they reach their destination.

This simple analogy tells us a great deal about the secret of self-control. The horses are within us. They are our five outward senses along with one internal sense, *anthakarana*. Our chariot, our mind-body, is driven by these six horses, and behind these are different impulses. The wisest approach is intelligent, controlled fulfillment of the normal, healthy desires of human life. As we do so, higher and higher values emerge on our mental horizon, and we are on the road of evolution toward the fulfillment of the human destiny. That is *brahmacharya*.

We can have an image in our mind of our true self, of our best possibility, our deepest potentiality, what we want to be and what we should become. Then we cut out from our life all those things which interfere with the fulfillment or actualization of that self-image. We must let there be no straying away from this image, no wavering of the mind in regard to our positive goal. Much of our frustration and failure is due to a lack of knowing where we are going in life. However, once we have a positive sense of direction, other things fall into place.

Let me conclude by putting it this way. Let us call the two elements in our nature 'beauty and the beast.' The beauty in humans is called the soul in religion. Many people are not fond of the word 'soul' these days, so we may call it the deep spiritual potentiality, the inner sense which inspires us to respond to such values as truth, beauty, and goodness and to expand ourselves on the path of love and compassion.

This beauty often slumbers in us and has to be awakened. The secret of self-control, therefore, lies not for beauty to kill the beast and follow the path of asceticism, but in a happy, intelligent marriage between the two, as the fairy tale tells us. As a result of the magic touch of love, the beast is transformed into a beautiful prince because there is great energy and power in love. By understanding the purpose of life, our human personality blossoms into an image of the divine.

According to the great ancient sages of India, we can do two things every day to help us on our way. One is to have some practice of meditation because that deepens and sharpens our inner sense of values. Our mind wakes up and responds to the higher values of life, and we become increasingly aware of the purpose and destiny of our existence. Then meditation needs to be supplemented by loving action. True selfless action and harmonious interrelations establish with our fellow beings this inner sense of values, and a spirit of love gets expressed in the sphere of human dynamics. These are the two golden rules of intelligent self-control and self-development.

19

THE CONQUEST OF DEATH

One of the main objectives of our spiritual effort is the conquest of death. What do I mean when I say this? First, it means understanding fully the meaning of death. When we understand a thing, we are able to conquer it. Another implication is overcoming the fear of death. And a third implication is transcending the fact of death, the factual presence of death. We transcend the fact of death by discovering the reality of the spirit in life within us and by participating in the eternity of this spirit.

Death is perhaps the greatest challenge to us. If we do not understand the mystery of death to some extent, we do not have sufficient understanding of the meaning of life either. Life and death are complementary to each other. We cannot attain happiness, health and abundant life unless we understand life and death as a complementary pair of opposites.

In order to bring out the full meaning or significance of the phenomenon of death, let us discuss false and ignorant attitudes towards it. One attitude to death is to deny it. Those who try to solve their problems by denying them may turn a blind eye to the fact that death exists. But we do not solve a problem by just denying its existence. The best solution with regard to every problem is to face it, try to understand it, know it as it is, and then to put forth our best efforts to overcome it.

Others at the opposite extreme are constantly occupied with the thought of death. They are full of anxiety, worry, and fear that death may come at any moment. Hence, every moment they are dying. As Shakespeare knew, 'Cowards die many times before their deaths.' As a result of this constant fear, they cannot take risks in life. They cannot undertake any novel, daring action. They cannot take any bold step forward away from the beaten track of life. This then becomes a kind of living death. This attitude also is due to lack of understanding of the true meaning and significance of death.

Another attitude is a morbid attraction to death. Some have in their minds a peculiar fascination with death. They tend to run into the jaws of death. Such people are prone to accidents and when this tendency becomes more articulate, it may develop into suicidal or self-destructive tendencies. When it operates in a disguised form, we develop indifference to the rules of healthy living. We may not take care of our body. We may not eat the right kind of food. We may not get enough rest. This is an expression of an inclination toward death. Since this indifference is motivated by unconscious forces, we may tend to rationalize this way of living.

What is the true meaning of death? When we understand the meaning of death, we begin to realize that in ultimate analysis death is as natural as life. Both of these are parts of the whole scheme of nature, the whole scheme of fulfillment and development of life itself. Those who have lived their lives completely, with a sense of responsibility and with success, welcome death with peace of mind, understanding it to be a perfectly natural end to the process of living.

Further, death is a necessary supplement to life. It is as necessary as sleep is to the activities of the day. After all our daily activity, we welcome sleep because it is our opportunity for recuperation of lost energy. After the healing influence of sleep, the next day we arise refreshed. We are in a position to greet the dawn with renewed vigor, energy, and freshness of mind. Sleep fills the cup of life.

Similarly, death fills the cup of life. If we take a long-range view of the evolutionary career of the soul, we come to realize that we go through the storm and stress of a whole span of life. Like a wise dispensation of nature or of God, death comes like a healing power at the end of the road of life. If we understand and approach death from the standpoint of the inner self, the spirit which is beyond death, we find that it recuperates energy. By going through the portals of death, life is renewed and refreshed. We enter upon a new phase of evolution.

This brings us now to the deepest meaning of death. Rightly viewed, death does not mean total destruction or annihilation. It means a transitional phase in the long, evolutionary journey of the soul. It brings to a close a particular chapter of life and opens another chapter in our evolutionary development. Death is not destruction; it is a subtle form of existence or a transition to another phase of evolution. When we understand death in this way, our whole attitude to it is bound to change. We develop a broader perspective on life and a healthier attitude to both life and death.

Those who have spiritual enlightenment tell us that the basic cause of the fear of death is our metaphysical or spiritual ignorance, which lies in the identification of the spirit with the body. As long as we are not aware of our true spiritual essence, of the reality of the spirit or the true self within us, it is natural that we are subjected to this fear of death. The body is subject to the laws of nature. It is born, it grows, it attains maturity, it declines and it perishes. When we identify with this body and have no understanding of our spiritual essence, naturally we feel that decline and eventual disintegration of the body mean our decline and destruction. So in all religions, the great spiritual geniuses have declared unequivocally that the more we know of the true spiritual essence of our being, the more we overcome this fear of death. We take a deeper perspective. We realize destruction of the body does not involve destruction of our spiritual nature, which is immortal and imperishable in character. Therefore, it is evident that the best way to conquer and overcome this fear of death is to sharpen our spiritual understanding and experience.

Another cause of the fear of death is the tension of unfulfilled desires. When we have some unsatisfied, strong desires in our mind, we are afraid of dying. We cannot look at it or think of it because of a drive which is unfulfilled. But all of us have experienced a moment when a big desire of our life is fulfilled, and we have deep satisfaction. Some of us even say, 'Now I can die peacefully.' As we become integrated and at peace within ourselves, we can behold the phenomenon of death with perfect balance of mind and equanimity. We have no regrets.

Another cause of our fear of death is the fear of the unknown. As we think of death, it appears as a realm of darkness to us. It is unknown. We do not know what is going to happen. And this fear of the unknown is intensified if we have dark apprehensions in our minds. Whenever we are faced with the unknown, we unconsciously project these dark apprehensions on to that unknown, further escalating our fear.

That is why those people who suffer from guilt have a greater fear of death. Their sense of sin intensifies the fear of death. When they feel guilty, they project inner tortures on to that realm of the unknown which death represents. That is why criminals often have a far greater fear of death than those who come to terms with their true self and harmonize the different elements of their nature. Those who are perfectly at peace with themselves and with the world around them conquer the fear of death.

Throughout history, we find that contemplation of death has been the starting point of most daring philosophical speculation and spiritual pursuit. As we face our greatest challenge and begin to unravel its mystery, we begin to capture the kingdom of heaven. One historical illustration is the spiritual quest of Buddha.

Buddha was born in a royal family and was brought up in the arms of luxury. He had no unsatisfied desires, no wants. He had all the facilities of abundant and rich living. However, one day he went out of the royal palace with his attendant. As he went into the streets, suddenly he came upon a strange spectacle. He saw a coffin being carried by four people and accompanied by a procession of mourners. He had never seen the likes of this before. He asked his attendant, 'What is this I am seeing?' The attendant replied, 'That is the phenomenon of death. A person who died is being taken to the cremation grounds.' That was shocking news to Buddha. 'Death? What does that mean?' So the attendant tried to explain, saying, 'It is the natural end of every living being.' But this answer did not satisfy Buddha. Even though it is a familiar phenomenon to all of us, he did not want to accept it as a natural fact. He wanted to

THE CONQUEST OF DEATH

solve its mystery. So that day he could not go any farther. He hurried home to think about and to meditate on it. 'What is this phenomenon of death? Is that really the ultimate end of all existence? Or is there anything more to life? Is there anything greater in our existence?'

That was the beginning of his spiritual quest. Under the impulsion of the spiritual quest, he renounced his princely kingdom and went out into the world in search of spiritual truth in an attempt to solve the profound mystery of death.

As a result of Buddha's search, ultimately he succeeded in his efforts. The meaning of death was revealed to him through meditation. He discovered a way of rising above life and death and of participating in life eternal. This participation is known in Buddhism as *nirvana*, spiritual enlightenment, going above or beyond life and death.

In modern times, the existentialist philosophers especially have investigated death and have thrown light upon this matter. They have pointed out that facing death is a tremendous experience in life which can shake us to the depths of our being. It arouses the deepest creative forces within us and brings us into a profound vision of the truth of existence. It can have a wonderful sobering and balancing effect upon our psyche.

Let me tell you the story of a woman in the prime of her life who suddenly was found to have cancer. Doctors declared her case to be hopeless and gave her just a week to live. Imagine how she must have felt. That week was a period of death for her. But she did not die. By a miracle, she came out of the hospital recovered.

Imagine her mental condition after that week when she came out of the hospital. She shook hands with death and then death left her. She experienced a profound change in her psychological outlook. She said, 'As a result of this strange experience, I feel a profound depth to my emotional life, a maturity of which I had no idea before.' Before she had cancer, she frequently quarrelled with her husband over petty affairs, and she would spank her daughter for arguing. If she lost a dollar or broke a glass in the kitchen, she would be terribly upset.

After this brush with death, she was totally changed. She began to realize how silly her outbursts of temper were. She saw the stupidity and the vanity of her upsets. She realized they were the result of great emotional immaturity and lack of perspective in life. All her harshness of attitude was replaced by a kind and loving attitude to everybody.

Another consequence of having a direct contact with death is a realization of the immeasurable value and preciousness of life. So long as we are just living, we do not realize its value. Once we have a taste of death, a direct awareness of death, we begin to appreciate the preciousness of life in a profound manner. This also brings about a great change in our life.

In India, especially in the Tantric spiritual tradition, devotees meditate alone at night on the cremation grounds. Among the things which are used in this spiritual practice is the skull. It is said in Tantra that only heroic souls can do this. Those who do it successfully can capture the kingdom of heaven by storm. They must overcome all their fears and come face to face with death itself.

After the devotees overcome their fear, profound thoughts begin to surge up in their minds. They look at life from a deep perspective. They begin to realize the vanity, the stupidity and the ephemeral character of much of our ordinary living. They develop a timeless perspective and begin to understand the meaning of happiness in life from the standpoint of eternity. As the great philosopher Spinoza said, the essence of spiritual wisdom is to be able to behold life under the aspect of eternity. Since these devotees see death as the great leveller, they accept the quality of all living beings. In the face of death, there is no distinction of high and low or rich and poor. All are equal there. So in this way, Tantra says, people can be moved profoundly to the depths of their consciousness, and the flight of the soul toward the infinite can be speeded up.

20

MEDITATION AS THE ART OF ALL ARTS

Meditation in its pure spiritual essence is a supreme art, the art of all arts. This is true for two important reasons. First, meditation is the art of all arts because it is the inspirational root of all original creations in art. Whether in poetry or painting, music or song, sculpture or architecture, at the source of all creative expression lies the act of meditative communion with Being. Through such communion, new values are revealed; new significant forms are disclosed; new peaks of emotion are attained. New dimensions of existence are unveiled. Art at its best is a spontaneous expression of new forms and values, but it owes its inspiration to meditation.

Secondly, meditation is the art of all arts because it lays the foundation for the highest of all arts, namely, the art of living in tune with the eternal. Life at its best is the art of expressing in action and human relations such eternal values as truth, beauty, righteousness, and love. Meditation is the technique of communion with the realm of eternal value. It is the source of inspiration for creative living.

Let me elaborate further this concept of meditation as the inspirational root of both creative art and creative living. In an ancient Hindu scripture, there is a beautiful legend about creation. After the dissolution of the previous order of existence, Brahma, the cosmic creator, was assigned by the Supreme Being to create a new world order. Brahma was wondering how he should proceed to fashion this. As he was pondering his great assignment, he heard an inner voice which declared,

'Meditate, meditate, meditate. Enter the depths of your being, mobilize the resources of your personality and then create.' Following this ethereal instruction, Brahma created a wonderful new world.

No new creation of value is possible without prior communion with the spirit of existence. Broadly speaking, meditation assumes three forms: objective, subjective, and radical. In each form, it brings forth into manifestation certain pleasures of the spirit.

Meditation in its objective form may be called contemplation. Artists who are lovers of nature go into the heart of nature, relax there, and drink in the surrounding beauty. Having left behind all mundane concerns, they enter into silent communion with the spirit of nature. They contemplate the majestic grandeur of the lofty mountain peaks or the lovely texture of a flower that is in full bloom. They watch in fascination the starry heavens above or listen in rapture to the joyful outpouring of a little bird sitting on a tree top. Whatever it is that captivates their attention, as they contemplate this beauty, they gradually lose themselves in their aesthetic appreciation. Through meditation they enter into communion with the spirit of a landscape. They bridge the gulf of separation between subject and object, between themselves as observers and nature as the object of observation. They become one with the spirit of the landscape. Or expressing the same experience in another way, the spirit of the landscape enters their soul and permeates their inner being. This experience of oneness is the moment of supreme inspiration in creative art.

After the inspiration of this experience, artists proceed to create. If they are poets, they write poems about the landscape. If they are painters, they paint the landscape on canvas. Whatever the medium is, as artists try to bring forth their inward inspiration, they feel that the creative act flows from a level of consciousness beyond themselves. It flows from a level of consciousness where their inner spirit becomes one with the spirit of nature beyond their ego. In the process of inspiration and self-expression, they feel as if it is not them but the landscape itself which is getting manifested through this medium. In giving expression to the loveliness of a flower, they feel as

MEDITATION AS THE ART OF ALL ARTS

if the spirit of the flower enters their soul and utters itself forth through their artistic medium.

Art at its best is neither an imitator nor mere representation. As mere imitation of the hidden object of nature, art is of little value. It is a mere shadow of a shadow, as Plato criticized art in his *Republic*. Objects of nature are in Plato's view mere shadows of eternal value, eternal ideas which are archetypal modes for perfection. As an imitation of change, art is condemned to imitating imitation. There is not much point in representing, reproducing or duplicating the outward appearances of things existing in nature. Art becomes meaningful when it aims to express unique values. When the human mind enters into meditative communion with the spirit of nature, new values emerge as an offspringing of the union of mind and nature. Art at its best is the creative expression of such emergent process.

The image of Buddha in meditation is one of the finest creations of Eastern art, but the master poets, painters, and sculptors of the East were not very concerned with the outward physical features of the historical Buddha. They would contemplate the spirit of Buddha, his message, his acts of self-giving to humankind. They would meditate upon the meaning of Nirvana as the unity of wisdom, peace, and compassion — Nirvana as the spiritual destiny of humans. During meditation, the essence of Buddhahood would illuminate their consciousness. They would try to express his inward illumination in art form, and that would be a new creative source of inspiration to thousands of people.

Besides object-oriented meditation, there is meditation in its subjective form. Subjective meditation begins with the withdrawal of attention from the outside world. One closes the eyes and focuses upon one's authentic self, upon the center of one's inner being, or upon the spiritual essence of one's own existence. Or having closed the eyes, one relaxes and lets the mind go and observes with detachment the free flow of ideas, feelings, emotions, impulses and memories. As the meditator continues on the path of self-observation, deeper and deeper levels of the conscious mind are activated. We gain access to the archetypal images buried in what Dr C.G. Jung called 'the collective unconscious.' The treasures of accumulated wisdom of the entire human race are hidden in the collective unconscious. Archetypal images like the serpent and the bird, the eternal child and the grand old man, the heavenly father or the heavenly mother, are symbols of humans' eternal quest for mature growth and self-realization. These archetypes represent the latent power and dynamic potentiality of the human psyche. When artists express themselves in songs of such archetypal images, their effort to speak is like having a golden tongue. They make an eloquent appeal to the universal mind of humans, transcending the boundaries of race and nationality, of space and time. Modern expressionistic art owes its inspiration to such a deep self-awareness.

Meditation increasingly deepens self-awareness. In expressing the inner self, artists may express different levels of their psyche. They may express inner frustration, anger, hatred, and violence. Of course, in the very process of recognizing and expressing such negative emotions, they often largely transcend them. As they advance farther in meditative self-awareness, they begin to grasp the inmost purifying center of their being. A new higher self, the divine child within them, is born on the inmost level of their consciousness. At this point their art expression also undergoes a profound transformation. What they create acquires a new quality. It carries the power to kindle the light of awareness in the heart of others. As a symbol of the artists' inward illumination, their art inspires others.

Art is of paramount importance in the sphere of education. Education in the West has been predominantly intellectual. As a result, the power of imagination, which is one of the greatest gifts of God, gets atrophied. Imagination is, as William Blake claimed, our human ability to commune with the gods. Unfettered imagination is indeed a sure sign of the flexibility of the mind. We can use our artistic insight into the manifold possibilities of life and to enrich our vision of higher planes. It prevents the mind from ossification and fixation in rigid stereotypes. Art can play a vital role in keeping alive and unfolding the power of imagination in humans. Toward the end of enriching imagination, art goes hand in hand with meditation. A simple exercise in free art expression is this: instead of giving a model to people from which to paint, first ask them to close their eyes for several moments. Then have them express in painting or clay or writing whatever images or emotions come into the mind from their inner being. From this process, the creative and spontaneous functioning of the mind begins to get a chance to come into its own. Meditation deepens this process of the free flowering of individuality. This can bring to the average person salvation from his or her unthinking conformity, mediocrity, or crowd mentality.

Having discussed meditation in its objective and subjective form, let us now turn to meditation in its most fundamental or radical form. Meditation in its full fruition brings humans face to face with Being, the ultimate ground of all existence. This is the ultimate goal of meditation. As spiritual seekers encounter Being, the meaning of life and evolution is fully revealed. Seekers gain unerring insights into the purpose of their own existence in the world. They become aware of their own personal mission and destiny.

Being, while transcending both nature and the self, unifies them in its creative essence. Being manifests itself as nature on the outside and as the self on the inside. It is not to be equated with either exclusively. Nature and self are the objective and subjective poles of the Supreme Being. They are inseparably interrelated manifestations of the Supreme.

When meditation reaches its crowning fulfillment in unveiling the essence of Being, life in the world takes on a divine meaning and significance. The entire universe stands transfigured, shining with the light of Being. As the mind beholds the cosmic spectacle, it is aware of the Self as the creative center of Being. The great master minds of history such as Buddha and Christ, Krishna and Lao-Tzu, Moses and Mohammad, Ramakrishna and Aurobindo, were masters of meditation. As an all-out search for Being, meditation led them to luminous contact with Being. At the heart of their enlightenment was an awareness of that historic mission. Each of them performed his mission to perfection as an illumined center of Being.

These observations bring us now to the concept of meditation as the art of living. It is indeed the highest of all arts, the art of living in harmony with the light of Being. There was a famous sculptor who made an exquisitely beautiful statue of an elephant. The king of the country was profoundly impressed and gave the sculptor a handsome reward. The king wanted to know the secret of the sculptor's art. The sculptor said, 'As soon as I came across a huge slab of white marble, I saw the image of a beautiful elephant there. The secret of my art lay in chipping off whatever marble did not look like an elephant.' It is the image, the inward vision of form, which imposes order upon chaos and fashions out of raw material a thing of beauty and joy.

Meaningful living in the light of Being is the loftiest art imaginable. The spirit in humans is a creative spark, the spark of the light of Being. The human soul is an artist, the artist of divine light. Human nature, with its instincts and impulses, emotions and desires, tendencies and potentialities, is the raw material for the creative work: it is like clay in the hands of the potter, like stone or rock in the hands of the sculptor, like canvas in the hands of the painter, like language in the hands of a poet. Through meditation, individuals are restored to their authentic self. They discover their spiritual identity.

This self-discovery holds within itself an image of beauty and perfection. Self-awareness unfolds an inspired image of latent development because humans are an image of God. By revealing the image of the self in its profoundest potentiality, meditation lays the foundation for perfect living. Following the lead of the self-image, one now organizes the affairs of life in the spirit of balance and harmony. One re-channels one's psychic energy toward the fulfillment of goals which are in harmony with the spiritual self-image. With tact and patience, one also weeds out negative tendencies and those distractions which threaten to interfere with the fulfillment of these goals. Creative self-fulfillment will transform the chaotic mass of natural impulses and desires into an aesthetic whole of life divine.

Art has two interrelated aspects — discipline and inspiration. Every artist has to put in hours of rigorous practice on a regular basis in order to master the techniques of his or her art. Painters, for example, have to acquire skills through sustained training in the use of brush and ink or oil and color. They have to develop their sense of proportion and perspective and cultivate imagination for the interweaving of design. Assiduous study of other master painters is essential to this end. They have to acquire through long discipline mastery in their own field, but technical mastery alone is only one aspect of the secret of master artists. The secret of secrets lies in the moment of inspiration. It is the depth of inspiration that imparts the moving soul quality to a great art work.

In the same way, meditation as a supreme act also has the two aspects of discipline and inspiration. As a mode of self-discipline, meditation is the organization of one's whole pattern of living geared to the spiritual ideal, namely the idea of knowing and living in the light of Being. With this end in view, many old habits may have to change, and one may have to move from old to new associations. One has to exercise caution in choosing the right kind of job and a place of residence. One has to put into practice the spirit of moderation in order to keep the body in top form. It is desirable to set apart every day an hour or two for open-minded study of spiritually inspired books and from an half an hour to an hour for regular practice of meditation. This will set in motion an inner process of spiritual growth overcoming bodily inertia. Otherwise, one would feel every now and then tempted to get away from it on a flimsy pretext.

But discipline and regular practice constitute only the outward side of meditation. It is helpful but not enough. Overemphasized, meditation may degenerate into a rigid, mechanical affair. That would kill the inner spirit of meditation. The soul of meditation transcends all discipline and regulation. Meditation in its spiritual essence is joyful communion with Being, resulting in illumination. All self-discipline is only a preparation for that moment of inspiration and illumination that can transform life into a sacred poem of divine delight. Discipline devoid of illumination is an empty shell. Illumination without discipline lacks the resources for effective communication. If, for instance, an individual has not adequately prepared himself or herself in terms of body strength and purity, emotional maturity and intellectual clarity, when the moment of inspiration comes, he or she will be unprepared to function as an effective channel of expression for the in-streaming light of truth. Meditation may, therefore, be defined as the discipline of self-preparation for integrated and creative living in luminous union with Being.

21

ASPECTS OF SPIRITUAL UNFOLDING

Many stories in spiritual literature tell us that in achieving illumination or spiritual understanding, we have to go beyond the realm of verbalized expression — the realm of concepts, notions, categories, and images — and enter into the transcendental realm of silence, which is ultimate truth. The idea which has been emphasized in the Upanishads is that when we attain this goal and experience oneness with the divine in the depth of silence of our being, we achieve the power of transmitting this light, love, and joy to others in a non-verbal way.

There are two ways of understanding this transmission. One is that the actual knowledge or power of consciousness is transmitted from one individual to another. But others think that the transmission of energy awakens the power within us. Every individual has this spiritual potential for wisdom and for knowledge of the supreme. What a teacher does is to communicate or transmit energy vibrations, which awaken our spiritual potential. It is only through the awakening or actualization of our own spiritual energy that we can know truth. The light of truth cannot be transferred. It has to flower from within an individual. A teacher can only help us to activate our own spiritual potential.

In Western thought, a holistic outlook is coming more and more to the fore. Yet if we go back to the Upanishads, 1500 BC, there is also emphasis upon wholeness. The Sanskrit name for it is *purna advaita*. *Purna* means whole. *Advaita* means nondual. Nondualism undivided, indivisible, nondichotomous.

A beautiful passage in the Upanishads says, 'Fullness above, fullness below, fullness everywhere. Fullness is derived from fullness.' Wherever there is any creation or activity, fullness is derived from fullness. The very characteristic of fullness is such that even when you take away fullness from fullness, what remains is fullness. When you take away infinite from infinite, what remains is infinite. This is what is called a logic of the infinite, which is essentially different from a logic of the finite. We are dealing with non-Aristotelian logic here.

Aristotelian logic says that A is A and B is B. Therefore, the part cannot be one with the whole. According to Aristotelian logic, the law of identity, law of contradiction, and law of excluded middle, everything is what it is in a static, fixed manner. The law of finite numbers in arithmetic says the part can never be the same as the whole.

We come across a contradictory idea here. Fullness taken away from fullness leaves fullness. When we understand it, we will find this is right. This has been demonstrated with the idea of mathmatics of the infinite. According to this, when we deal with infinite numbers, the part is equal to the whole, which is contradictory to the law of finite numbers.

Those of you who want to have some philosophical understanding of this principle may read Josiah Royce where he discusses how modern mathematics is a demonstration of the spiritual truth of the Upanishads, of Vedanta — '*Ta twam asi*' — 'Thou art that,' that the individual spirit is one with the infinite spirit.

From the standpoint of the mathematics of the finite, of Aristotelian logic, we would say this is self-contradictory and meaningless. How can the part be one with the whole? It has been discovered that the laws that hold for finite things do not apply to the infinite. Laws which are true of the finite numbers, finite things and objects, do not apply to the subject, to the spirit. A different law holds true there. You cannot expect this analogy to be a hundred percent the same kind of thing, but as far as it goes, you will find that this is demonstrable.

In mathematics, what is the meaning of oneness, equality? There is a mathematical definition of equality. Two structures are equal when there is a one-to-one correspondence between

ASPECTS OF SPIRITUAL UNFOLDING

the two systems. Structurally, for example, a map is equal to the territory of which it is the map. Or let us take two classes of students. If the same number of students is in both classes, they are equal classes. Corresponding to every student here, there is a student there.

As I mentioned, Josiah Royce showed that in the light of modern mathematics, we can understand the truth that every individual being as a spiritual being is identical with the infinite. Before modern mathematics, philosophers did not have any positive definition of the infinite. They defined it negatively. In other words, the infinite is that which is not finite, which is a negative definition. But in science, negative definitions are not allowed. One must have a positive definition. However, philosophers could not come up with one.

What is the positive definition which has been developed in modern mathematics? It is that the true infinite is a self-representative system. In other words, if you come across a system which can go on representing itself with its parts, it is an infinite system. We may call it a self-representative or self-imaging system, that which can reproduce itself in an endless number of images within itself. That is what absolute is. The absolute can go on reproducing itself endlessly within itself, within its own images. This is why every human soul is an image of God. God is an all-encompassing, all-embracing, self-imaging system. Therefore, as a self-imaging, infinite system, the absolute spirit can go on reproducing itself in an infinite number of images.

We are essentially finite-infinite beings. The human is not just finite. If you say, 'I am only finite,' then you are committing a mistake. If you say, 'I am finite and God is infinite,' you are making a dichotomy. You are placing God outside of yourself. In that way God ceases to be infinite. This is a logical fallacy.

This has been the trouble with Western theology. In Aristotelian logic we have a tendency to separate the finite and infinite. The result is that when you think of yourself as an individual, as finite, then you think of God as outside of you, infinite. But what happens in this way is that God ceases to be infinite. God becomes finite, too, because you are left outside of God. God becomes finite, and you become infinite. Because if God can be finite, then why can you, outside of God, not be infinite?

This gets you involved in a logically fallacious situation and is the result of dualistic thinking. We think of God as 'out there' because God is infinite, and we think of ourselves as finite. We are making God finite by postulating the existence of this world outside of God. If God can be infinite outside of the world, why should not the world be infinite? This is why science rejected God — because if God is infinite, the world is infinite, too.

Why not just say that the world is a self-supporting system? By thinking this way, we make God unnecessary. God has no real job to fulfill. God went out of employment as soon as the world was created. Since that moment of creation in the remote past, the world has been functioning according to its own laws. Science has said God is of no use anymore. We can explain everything in terms of its own laws.

Instead of that, we could say the true infinite is all-embracing, all-encompassing. When we say infinite and all-encompassing, this is the positive significance of the infinite — that the infinite has the ability to reproduce itself endlessly within itself. This is why we can understand that ultimately God is the cosmic, infinite medium in which we all live and move and have our being. This is why there is endless self-reproduction occuring within itself.

Much change has taken place in modern science. Many revolutionary changes in modern thought have involved the rejection of the old scientific principles of atomistic concepts or mechanistic theory. The methodology which has developed in modern science is what is called the systems view. Previously atoms were seen as individual entities, particles of matter which are indivisible, the ultimate constituents of the material world.

Prior to the development of the systems view, science had a dichotomous view. Descartes, who is regarded as the father of modern European philosophy, believed our personality is composed of two absolutely antagonistic actors, our mind and our body. Body is material which is unconscious, and mind is immaterial, which is characterized by consciousness. This is a dualistic view of personality.

Immanuel Kant, the German philosopher, further developed this idea. He said we are rational beings; the mind is rational, yet the body and our impulses, passions and desires are irrational. He thought the ultimate goal of life should be to live a life of pure reason and to exterminate from our nature impulses, desires and passions.

This gave rise to the puritanical tradition. Many psychological problems stem from this dualistic conception that the human personality is composed of the natural and the supernatural. Rationalistic philosophy espouses a dualistic conception of body and mind. This became a fertile cause of many of our distorted ideals and distorted visions of self-development. In order to grow, to be happy and to achieve real perfection, we had to negate or repress or eliminate our physical desires, impulses, passions. However, as psychology has discovered in its investigation of mental problems, this is the wrong approach. It was based upon a wrong philosophical view.

Look at the change that is taking place among some of the philosophers of this country who are developing a nondualistic outlook. Is it not wonderful that we now have the conceptual resources to express linguistically a nondualistic vision of truth? Our human knowledge has been advancing at such a rate and to such a height that we are mastering the ability to express profound spiritual truths, which is a remarkable achievement. We are gaining the ability and resources truly to help ourselves and others in a new way.

Not long ago, nondualistic truth would have been unintelligible to people, but now we can begin to understand. By thinking and talking together we can make each other understand. The human being is a natural thinking animal. Thought is the forerunner in our life. First, thought has to grasp something. Then changes begin to take place.

More than we realize, many of our actions and motivations are determined unconsciously by ideas at the back of our mind that we imbibe from our environment. We are not always aware of these ideas. This is why Buddha's first principle of the eightfold path was 'right understanding.' Buddha knew that the human is a thinking animal, and unless our thinking is straightened out with the right ideas, we can never straighten out our life.

However, since ideas play such an important role in our

behavior patterns, how is it that spiritual teachers talk about going beyond the mental level or intellectual level in order to experience 'no-mind' as the way to full enlightenment? What is happening here? 'No-mind' implies that the mind cannot grasp the truth.

All spiritual truth is paradoxical. When we go beyond the mind, we become more united with the mind. As we go beyond the mind, we are able to know the mind better. So 'no-mind' is also perfect mind. This is why, again, there also is the philosophy of 'mind-alone' in Mahayana Buddhism. On the one hand, we say 'no-mind,' and on the other hand, we say 'mind-alone' is reality. This is a paradoxical situation. If we read any spiritual philosophy, we frequently come across paradoxical statements like this. So we can understand these kinds of things, it is important to discipline and sharpen our minds.

When we go beyond mind, we do not mean to go beyond consciousness or pure reason. We go beyond the normal mind with which we operate in so many ignorant ways. From childhood we go through much socio-cultural conditioning, and the mind with which we usually live, think, and function is heavily encrusted. We imbibe many ideas unconsiously from our environment and our childhood, which later we find are limited. We absorb many prejudices, biases, strong conceptions and a narrowness of outlook.

When a spiritual teacher says, 'Go beyond mind,' he or she is saying, 'Go beyond your narrow, socio-culturally conditioned mind.' This is 'no-mind.' Going beyond your mind is not losing your mind or going back to the condition of a stone. When your go beyond the socially conditioned mind, you discover a larger, cosmic mind, a more luminous mind, which is the divine mind.

This is the paradox. We negate our mind, and we gain our mind. Christ said, 'It is by losing your life that you gain your life.' We enter into life everlasting by losing our life. In the same way, by transcending the limits of our narrow mind, we become one with our higher mind. By transcending the limits of the prejudiced mind, our consciousness comes to its own, and the light of consciousness begins to shine far and wide. Finally, we begin to see things just as they are.

22

MEDITATION AND SELF-DISCIPLINE

Meditation as the art of attaining self-realization and enlightenment is essentially the same in all systems of self-discipline, especially in the final phase of spiritual unfoldment. But people who practice meditation may get confused as they become exposed to various techniques from different systems because there are some differences in approach and emphasis. I have had people tell me they practiced a particular form of Hindu meditation and also have been exposed to Buddhist practice. Then they encountered Sufi teachings and learned an entirely different version of meditation. After all of these experiences they are confused and wonder what is the right path.

There is an element of relativity here as in all other human matters. For example, a person cannot just be guided by advertisements to start using a medicine. That is dangerous. In the same way, a specific technique or spiritual discipline that is good for an individual depends on one's character structure, world view, one's social, cultural, spiritual or religious background and one's state of evolution. No standardized description for everyone can be made if a person wants to gain higher states of spiritual growth. That is why individualized guidance and counselling is fundamentally important.

Keeping this in mind, let us consider some differences in approach and formulation which have caused confusion in many people who sincerely are seeking spiritual truth and growth.

One basic problem is that some teachers hold meditation to be a spiritual discipline. We cannot advance without discipline and self-organization, the restructuring of our lifestyle in accordance with our chosen goals of life. Other teachers tell us that in meditation no discipline is necessary. All that is needed is just to relax, let go, and everything will be fine. It all depends on how we understand these guidelines. There is a semantic problem and there is also a deeper problem.

Let me clarify the semantic problem. When we talk about opposites such as discipline or no discipline, you must understand that this is a relative difference, not an actual distinction. No human distinction is absolute. Relativity is the essential structure of human life and knowledge. Sometimes we get into difficulty because we tend to understand a distinction in an absolute sense.

When we say no discipline is needed in meditation, you may think absolutely no discipline. That is wrong, because nothing great can be achieved in life without application and mobilization of available energy. Just study the life of any great teacher. You will see that much of their time has been taken in tremendous one-pointed concentration or focus of energy on a chosen goal of life. No concentration, no achievement.

It has been said that even God created this world by an act of sacrifice and discipline. Whitehead, the great American philosopher, said that at the beginning of creation God, the infinite, surveyed the endless possibilities of creation. But if God just rested content with this envisioning of infinite possibilities, nothing would have been possible. No creation happens that way. Creation begins with an act of concentration, then selection and translation or discipline. First God surveyed the infinite possibilities of existence. Then God focused attention upon a combination of possibilities and selected. There was an act of divine will. Then God said, 'Let there be light' — and there was light. This is also sacrifice, because God sacrificed other possibilities. All possibilities are part of divine nature, but God selected a particular combination. This involves disciplining of consciousness. Then God precipitated into the space-time continuum the selected possibilities. This is creation.

In the same way, suppose some bright students enter college. All the courses being offered are wonderful. They take courses in literature, science, art, psychology, and education to acquaint themselves with the range of possibilities. If throughout their whole educational career they just pick and choose randomly, nothing will come of their college experience. They will end up being jacks of all trades and masters of none. Their minds will be wasted because they will just be floating. That is fine for a time, but finally they have to make decisions and commitments. They may wish they could continue taking all the courses they wanted, but they cannot because they have a limited amount of psycho-physical energy at their disposal. So they make decisions about their goals and concentrate on special courses to acquire proficiency in their selected fields. That means concentration, selection, and discipline.

Teilhard de Chardin once said that whenever something new is born in human consciousness, it is born upon internal heat. Creation occurs when consciousness turns in upon itself. As long as our consciousness always flows outward, we are spending our energy, enjoying or expressing ourselves. But to take a new step forward in spiritual unfoldment, consciousness has to turn inward. Then we achieve a vision of truth and beauty from a new direction. Chardin gave an example of boiling water. You put water into a kettle that will hold it. You limit it. Then you put it on the stove and heat it. Something new is created. As you boil it to a certain point, water gets transformed into steam and rises up. This is what heat does. It is the result of mystic fire which is a transforming power.

In the same way, this is what we do in meditation. Water is a wonderful symbol of consciousness. It spreads out, just as our consciousness is always floating from one object to another. We have fleeting interests, flying from thing to thing, idea to idea. If you want to do something creative, you withdraw your attention. Whatever your enterprise, whether it is business, politics, art, or science, if you have a job you want to do seriously and well, you close yourself in a room. You withdraw your consciousness from outside. You focus your attention upon your goal, shutting out all outside distractions. Then a divinely inspired idea flashes forth in your mind. That is when you can create or discover something new. Everyone who is doing something seriously is meditating without knowing it. Serious endeavors involve concentration, focus, and discipline, without which nothing can happen.

So what is the true meaning of no discipline in meditation? It is not absence of all discipline, which is misleading. This gives people a wrong impression. No discipline means no externally imposed discipline. It does not mean all negation of discipline. It means a new kind of meaningful discipline, an internal discipline.

Along the same lines some unthinkingly talk about it in this way. They think that God is already within us, so all we have to do is to be quiet and the kingdom of heaven will shine out. That sounds reasonable. Some spiritual teachers say that we are all children of God, that the divine inheritance is within us. Even so, we have to spend years of preparation and discipline to bring this forth. It calls for a lot of effort, which is what we call meditation. Life's great fortune is there in the inmost sanctuary of our soul, but we have to possess it fully and understand it. So long as the veil of ignorance separates us from that richest treasure of the spirit in our own being, we are not enjoying it. It may as well be a thousand miles away.

Meditation and self-discipline help to cut away the veil of ignorance. In this case, action has a negative function, not the positive action of producing the truth, but the negative function of lifting the veil of ignorance from our eyes. This is the view of traditional mysticism.

But according to modern mysticism and integral yoga, truth, beauty, and perfection are not already there as finished products within us. They are there as potentialities. Therefore, meditation is a creative act. It does not serve the negative function of lifting the veil and seeing the finished product. Our job through spiritual discipline and meditation is to actualize that potential.

The human soul or spirit is like a creative artist. Our body, mind, impulses, desires, emotions, determinations are our canvas, our marble, our raw material that nature has given us. A potential of divinity is engrained is this material, but that does not mean it is already there as a finished product. That is our job. Our soul is the creative spark. We must examine our material with all its different functions and attributes with great care and love, insight and vision from day to day. We have

MEDITATION AND SELF-DISCIPLINE

to organize and structure ourselves, cutting out something here, focusing on something there, according to our self-image and our inner vision of how we could be as an image of God. This is a creative process.

That is why as we enter into meditation, we make clear in our mind the image of our own true self. We take stock of our inner potentials. In the depths of meditation we transform our life with all its assets and liabilities, its shadow side and bright talents, into a transparent image of the Supreme.

23

SAMATTVA — EVENNESS OF MIND

Subjectively, *samattva* means equality of mind, equilibrium, psychic balance. It is the ability to experience tranquility and serenity in the course of our living and through all kinds of vicissitudes of fortune. No matter what, we are able to maintain an undisturbed calmness within ourselves.

Objectively speaking, *samattva* means equal-minded vision, the ability to see all as equal. Just as in the eye of God all living creatures and human beings are equal, so are they in the mind of a spiritually illuminated person.

How come? We see all kinds of differences between creatures and humans, so in what respect are they equal? From the spiritual standpoint, it means that one sees the presence of God in all. God is the principle of equality. In divine presence there is no degree. God is not a quantity that can be divided into parts. God is indivisible unity. Divine essence knows no fragmentation. If we believe that God is present in all human beings, then we have to understand that God is *equally* present in all.

Just as when we see the moon reflected on the water a thousand-fold, it is present in every image as a whole, not partially. One part of the moon is not here and another part of it there. The whole moon is reflected in all of these images. Therefore all human beings, in spite of all their phenomenal, characterological or psychic differences, have the same spiritual potential. This is how we truly can understand *samattva*.

24

DIALECTICS OF SPIRITUAL GROWTH

All great processes in evolution and unfolding are dialectical processes. A great discovery in both Eastern and Western wisdom is that all developmental processes have a triadic rhythm, a dialectical rhythm, which is a movement forward through a triadic process of thesis, antithesis, synthesis — affirmation, negation, reconciliation.

This is the formula of all growth and progress. This method of human understanding is also the method of nature. It is the method of human understanding because it is the method of nature. Our understanding is a wonderful development of the creativity of nature, so therefore this method reflects the dynamics of nature's own growth process.

What does this mean? What is the significance of this dialectical process of growth? In some essential respects it is different from the traditional approach to religion and spirituality. Some important differences constitute the essential characteristics of a modern spiritual idea: an integral experience of spiritual development, an integrated approach, a balanced growth of a multidimensional personality. Balanced growth of our human nature is multidimensional richness and fullness of being. In order to achieve this fullness of being, it is important to pursue a dialectical process of development.

Let me explain this technique of self-unfoldment. In our self-development, all of us start with what we may call the bodily self-image. It is natural to feel, 'I am this body. I am one with this body.' You ask someone, 'Who are you?' She points to her body because that is what she is. Yet, as we grow to higher levels of self-awareness and self-realization, we experience changing phases of our self-image.

An important principle of nature and growth is consolidation. Everything has a part to play in the scheme of self-development. Since a body self-image is important, nature allows us to consolidate it. But it is also part of the methodology of nature's growth process that as we accept something or affirm something as true, good and valuable, we tend to carry it to the extreme. This is human nature.

We start with the bodily image, and then we carry it to the extreme. We fall in love with our body. This is what happened to Narcissus. Narcissus was a handsome young man. He fell so in love with his own beauty that he was not interested in anything or anybody else. When he was in the radiance and splendor of his youth, hundreds of young women used to come to him. But he was not interested because he was too much in love with himself.

One time, the Greek legend says, he went to bring water from a pond which was crystal clear. As he looked into the pond, he saw his beautiful image created on the water. He was so enraptured in admiration and contemplation of himself that he could not take his eyes away from his own image. That is how he perished. The magic of the enchantment consumed all the energy of his life. He died gazing at the beauty of his image.

Let me give you another illustration. A beautiful young girl entered her mother's bedroom and saw a huge mirror. She stood there admiring her beauty when her mother entered the room. The girl asked, 'Mommy, who created my father?' Her mother said, 'God created your father.' Then she said, 'Did God create you also?' 'Certainly.' 'Did God create me also?' 'Oh, yes. God is the creator of all.' Then the girl said, 'You know, Mommy, God has been creating much better these days.'

This is narcissistic excess, and it is natural at a certain age. Yet as we grow up and begin to discover other realities and values of life, we go beyond. We transcend. There are many mechanisms in our life by which we transcend this narcissism.

For example, as a young boy grows up, he discovers a wonderful friend, a pal. When the friendship develops and deepens, he is brought out of his narcissistic love. Love here is a mechanism for transcendence of egoism. It is a powerful vehicle for self-transcendence. Another kind of love begins to flourish. Instead of ego love, we begin to discover other people, other values. Gradually this becomes a powerful mechanism in the growth process.

The boy transcends his exclusive identification with his body. He gets his first lesson in the meaning of life, his first lesson in self-transcendence. How? In the case of adolescent development, he is so in love with a friend that he is willing to sacrifice personal comfort for the sake of his friend. He has some beautiful things he wants to share. Sometimes he is willing to make sacrifices, embracing inconvenience, discomfort, and suffering for the happiness of his friend. He realizes, 'I am not just this body. I am also something more than the body.' This is an expansion of consciousness beyond the limits of physical existence.

This is dialectics. First you say, 'I am the body,' and you are in love with yourself. Then you discover other realities beyond your body. As you begin to appreciate these realities of life with which you are connected organically, you transcend your bodily self. You sacrifice the comforts of the body and pleasures of the flesh for the sake of another person in your life. This is what Martin Buber has called an 'I-Thou' relationship as the first important lesson in self-expansion.

It is the same concerning expansion toward a global image. Both Teilhard de Chardin and Henri Bergson said we begin to expand our self-image in this way. 'I am not just this body. I am also my friend. She is a part of me.' Then you may come to a point when you say, 'I am this community in which I live; that is part of my being.' You may go farther and say, 'I am this country,' and reflect patriotic or nationalistic love. If you expand a little farther on the frontiers of your self-image, you say, 'I am the whole of humanity,' which has been called 'species consciousness.' 'My being is co-extensive with the entire human race.' That is when a person becomes a philanthropist and an internationalist.

Let us come back to the meaning of dialectics. Each of us starts with the belief of self as the body. Then comes the antithesis. We discover some realities and values beyond the ego. We say, 'I am more than the body,' because we are willing to sacrifice our bodily comfort for the sake of somebody or something else.

But again, as I said, running to the extreme is the greatest weakness of human nature. Having discovered something or someone else, we carry it to an extreme. Some people identify with the community, their country or a party or organization to which they belong. They carry it to such an extreme that they do not entertain any thought about personal development and integration, or self-actualization. These people get so absorbed in doing things for a cause that they become totally indifferent to the potentials of their own self. This is excessive altruism.

Altruism, basically a good thing, can become bad. When you carry a virtue to an excess, it becomes a vice. Balance is the order of life. By carrying a virtue to its extreme, it will reach its opposite. This is the law of dialectics, and it is important.

We see this dynamic when we carry freedom to an extreme. Some young people crave freedom, but what is the concept of freedom to the immature mind? In the immature mind, freedom is 'to do as you please.' However, doing as one pleases may be destroying somebody else's property, or a public park, or committing vandalism. In the process of exercising freedom, one may become a slave of one's passions and desires and live no longer free. You can see how a virtue can be converted to a vice.

This is an important law of dialectics. It is illustrated over and over again in the development of nations and peoples. Over and over again we move from one extreme to another and then to still another extreme. If we are wise, we realize the folly of that other extreme, too. We discover the opposite also has its limiting characteristics.

This has been illustrated abundantly in the Middle Ages both in the West and in the East. The Middle Ages was the period when people were eager to go beyond the self, the ego, to something absolutely beyond. There was emphasis on forgetting the self. There was complete absorption in the pursuit of God, in doing the will of God, which is a wonderful thing.

DIALECTICS OF SPIRITUAL GROWTH

But as I said, as soon as we carry something to an extreme, it ceases to be good. In the Middle Ages, people turned their back on self-image and tried to develop the love of God as opposite of the self or ego. They practiced extreme mortification of the flesh, for example, or went through painful austerities, such as self-deprivation, sensory deprivation and starving the body of essential nutrients. In pursuing God through extreme self-mortification and cruel ascetic practices, they often became victims of hallucinations and thought this was wonderful, or ended up with other psychological problems.

This is the dialectic again. We stand today on the vantage ground of the twentieth century. As we look back on history, we can learn so much if we keep an open mind. We can see clearly that both extremes are inadequate, insufficient, and can become hindrances to the full flowering of our spiritual potential.

On the one hand, we see that ego love is a hindrance. Why? Extreme ego love means that you are shut up within yourself, that you are not growing. You are living within a small shell of your being. This is the path of self-destruction which happened to Narcissus. This is one dynamic.

Yet when you go to the other extreme and completely deny the self, your potentials, your balance, your possibilities, and get absorbed in helping others or whatever you consider to be better, you lose your ability to help.

The best thing you can give is the mature fruit of your self-actualization. This is what you are destined to give to the world. If you destroy your own potential, you have nothing to give. What can an inwardly poor person give to others? You have to be rich in order to give. Self-actualization is the method of self-enrichment, so you can share riches with other people.

This is the meaning of dialectic — thesis and antithesis. As we look back on our life, we will find this is always what happens. We discover a truth, and we are all excited. For some time we are absorbed in this truth, which is good. But then, human nature being as it is, we tend to close our mind and be completely smug and satisfied. We begin to think this single truth is the whole truth and there is no other. This is the thesis here.

We become dogmatic and fanatical, and in this way we violate the very law and light of truth, because truth is infinite and boundless. Nobody can have a monopoly on it. Truth is like the boundless light of the sun that shines eternally upon all. The closed mind is the greatest enemy of progress, of growth.

Then suppose you realize your view is not entirely right. You may go to the other extreme and begin to fly from idea to idea, from system to system, not wanting to settle in any one place. In an effort to expand, you end up with what is called spiritual window shopping. You just look at the wonderful treasures of the spirit and intellect in the windows of differing systems, but you do not care deeply for any. This other extreme involves dissipation of energy and not accumulation, not profiting from the truths and experiences.

The right method is that as we broaden our mental horizons and discover different truths, we try to bring them together in a systematic whole, always keeping an open mind. Whatever the truth you discover, try to profit from it; try to incorporate it into your broadening mental outlook.

Let me give you some other illustrations so you understand the meaning of this dialectical process of growth. Some people, by virtue of their temperament and psychical makeup, identify completely and exclusively with what is called 'the will to power.' The power trance becomes the essence. 'I am power.' As the person grows and thinks and acts, entrenched in the sense of power, he or she becomes more and more intoxicated with it.

Alexander the Great, for example, was intoxicated by power. He felt his own power potential and identified himself with it. Dreams of conquering the world began to unfold. Forgetting everything else in his life, he launched upon the adventure of conquest, conquering territory after territory. He died at the age of 33. At the last moment of his life, he called the best physicians in the country to his bedside. He begged them to add a few more breaths to his life so he could see his mother once more. Whoever could add a few breaths to his life was promised half the kingdom Alexander had acquired. However, the doctors said that even if he gave the whole kingdom, there was nothing they could do. That was a shocking realization of truth to Alexander. He said, 'Had I known the breath was so precious that not even a whole kingdom can buy it, I would not have wasted my breath in trying to conquer the world.'

This is where we see the value of meditation, of breathing, which is designed to conserve energy. In our ordinary life, we dissipate energy unthinkingly. We do all kinds of things which are not useful or meaningful. In that way we waste our breath, because activities which are performed in an extroverted manner, especially when performed without any sense of purpose or value in life, follow what is called in physics 'the law of entropy.' 'Entropy' leads to the dissipation of energy and order.

The whole art of spiritual self-development — meditation, prayer, communion — is the art of conserving energy, anti-entropy. It is the art of arresting the dissipative process of energy. True spiritual practice is anti-entropic, a process of focusing our energy on the highest destiny in life.

This is an important existential situation for us to contemplate and to profit by. It is important and necessary in our lives to have a synthesis. First of all, we do things to achieve goals such as success, power, position, and wealth, but we dissipate a lot of energy. All these activities are subject, more or less, to the law of entropy. This means there is also a need for anti-entropy.

Nature, of course, has made provision for this. However busy you are, however ambitious you may be, nature compels you to sleep. This is anti-entropy. But especially in these days, this does not seem to be sufficient. Some people cannot sleep, even when they go to bed. It is important that there is sufficient conservation of energy and a rechanneling of energy to the higher goals of life, which is the true meaning of meditation. Here again you can see an important illustration of the process of thesis, antithesis, and synthesis.

Some people identify completely with their intellectual nature. 'I am my reasoning power.' Intellect is very good and is an important aspect of human personality. But here again if we identify with the intellect entirely, some people become intoxicated with it. They become what are called 'intellectual eggheads.' Another kind of ego love is an ethical self-love which is self-righteous. Patanjali, the celebrated teacher of yoga, made an interesting and elaborate analysis of these different forms in which the ego manifests in our life. This is why in ancient mythology ego is known as the hydra-headed monster. It has many heads. You chop off one head and another pops up.

The intellectual self is fine, if people realize there is much more to life than intellect. For example, an illustration is that of a king who was very bright. When he renounced his kingdom, he thought that by intellectual development he could know the supreme truth. He went to some of the most celebrated scholars and mastered all the existing knowledge of the time.

Since he had a deep seeking and an open mind, he soon realized this was not enough. He thought, 'Truth is far larger and vaster than intellect can ever comprehend.' He began to practice meditation, because meditation is the art of the leap beyond the limits of the intellect.

But here again there is the danger of going to the extreme. Some meditators renounce intellect. Being disillusioned with the omnipotence of the intellect, they go to the other extreme of intuition. They want to bypass the intellect, forgetting that it also is an important aspect of human nature. However sincere and good people may be, however well intentioned and however much they may develop their intuition, if their intellect is not developed adequately, there will be a lot of confusion in their minds. Confusion is darkness, a fog in the mind, and a great hindrance to full growth.

I am reminded of a bright young woman who came to one of my talks. Afterward she came up to me and said, 'You know, Dr Chaudhuri, when I came today I was in a confused state of mind. And now after listening to you, I am still confused, but on a higher level.'

Confusion can be a terrible thing. Some people have a lot of intuition, but they get confused when they are exposed to important ideas about intellectual and spiritual development. Different experiences, impressions and ideas can be of no use to you unless you transform them into a self-coherent system of truth. Left disorganized, they will produce confusion. If you are confused, you cannot mobilize all of your energies. There can be no meaningful self-expression.

To come back again to the dialectical method, one must

develop the intellect. But then one has to be aware of its limitations and develop the intuitive powers of the psyche, without being carried off in that direction. The final goal is an integration of intellect and intuition which alone can help us develop an integrated personality, a total self. The integrated self alone can give us the total truth shining upon our life. This is a most important truth about the dialectics of spiritual development. If you remember this and try to regulate your spiritual striving in light of this, your effort will be successful.

25

METAPHYSICS OF DREAMS

The metaphysics of dreams is an interesting approach to dream work. Metaphysics, in a nutshell, is the theory of Being, existence, or reality. Broadly speaking, we mean three principal factors when we talk about existence. One is the universe in which we live, the world around us. Second are humans. Third is the Supreme Creator, the ground or foundation of all existence, including the universe or nature, and humans. So, by 'Being' we mean these three things: nature, humans, and God, to put it in common language.

When we analyze the fundamental question — what is the nature of existence? — we find it resolves into three basic questions. What is the nature of the universe in which we live? What is the nature of the self? And, what is the nature of ultimate reality? When we obtain answers and insights into these fundamental human problems, we have some idea about the meaning of life, which is the ultimate issue for all of us. But an answer to this question about the meaning of life is dependent upon some spiritual or metaphysical knowledge about these three questions.

In order to acquire an adequate and balanced view of the nature of existence, we must question and study the total human experience. Dreams are a significant form of human involvement, but too many thinkers ignore this area. Mystical, dream and waking experiences each throw a flood of light upon the nature of the self and the nature of human psychic existence. Through inquiry into these realms we gain profound insights into the meaning and destiny of life. A metaphysical truth is that dreams reveal the structure of our own being. Let us consider some of the different types of dreams which do this.

Some dreams reveal what has been called in psychology the subconscious strata of the human mind. Let us take the case of a woman who is a qualified surgeon. Living in California, she is tied up with heavy responsibilities in her field. She is making a name for herself, and her patients are increasing. Day after day she is absorbed in making examinations and going over the same stories of pain and agony in connection with this or that disease. More and more she is getting a little fed up.

With this feeling comes an increase in dreams. She is traveling in her dreams, exploring New York or Paris or the Grand Canyon. As she examines her dreams, she finds she has a strong desire to go places and to see beautiful things. She has been suppressing this desire because of preoccupations with her career.

Wishes that we ignore or neglect because of pressure from our activities in society are not vanquished from our minds. They continue to exist even though they are driven underground. Once in a while they invade the kingdom of our rational minds by surfacing in dreams. That is their best opportunity. There are so many other things of this nature which we try to suppress. However, if we persist in ignoring or suppressing them, they create a great deal of trouble.

If we are adamant and ignore the writing on the wall which dreams are revealing, increasingly we may lose interest in life. We may enter into deepening depression because life starts to lose its warmth and color. That is a great price to pay. Suppressed desires and unconscious forces dwell in this instinctual aspect of our life with which we must come to terms. We cannot afford to ignore them.

If this woman takes into account her dreams, she will say, 'This is another area of my life. As a result of my pressure of work in the medical profession, I must not ignore this desire of mine to travel. I must do something about it. It's time for me to take a sufficient vacation so I can release some of these desires in a reasonable way.' She is guided by these dreams, and so she can help herself to a more fulfilling life. Her psychological balance will be restored, and her interest in life will be renewed.

Other dreams direct our attention to another area of our psychic existence. Suppose throughout the day you have been preoccupied with a problem. You have been racking your brain for a solution, but you do not see any answer. You seem to be groping in darkness. You go to sleep and dream. The language of dreams is symbolical and may be indirect, but you have a dream which seems to be associated with your problem. By examining that dream you get a solution.

This wisdom comes from a deep source of your own psyche, of your unconscious mind. You come to realize that there is a deeper power within your mind, a creative power which seems to know better than your rational mind. It offers a revelation about your life which you did not know before.

All of us have many dreams of this nature. People who are creative in temperament suddenly may arise in the middle of the night all excited. A poem, a solution to a problem, or a new idea has come into their minds through a dream. Where did that vision come from? It came from a deep source inside of us. As we examine that source, we find that this is an autonomous function of the human psyche which is creative in its stability and which can be cultivated. This particular area has been called by some the subliminal mind.

Let us turn to a variation of the same theme. Let us take the case of a woman living in Chicago whose son is in London where he is working. One night she has a nightmare in which her son is in grave trouble. She is anxious and worried when she awakens. The same day she receives a telephone call from London telling her that her son has been hospitalized as a result of an accident. What do we make of this? This may seem miraculous, but such dreams have often been recorded. This is called telepathic transmission.

Dreams of this nature also furnish us with a different channel into the realm of the spirit. It may be mysterious to us because we do not know much about it, but there is proof of a close connection between spirit and spirit, between mind and mind. Vibrations flow between these in the inner world. We know in the physical world that vibrations flow, as a result of

METAPHYSICS OF DREAMS

which we have telephone communications from one part of the world to another. When the human psyche is receptive it can capture spiritual vibrations. In the daytime our rational mind is often too busy. It has neither the time nor the training to pay attention to subtle vibrations because of its almost exclusive preoccupation with the practical affairs of life. In sleep the rational mind is put to rest, and somewhere deep in our psyche we are ready to receive some of these subtle vibrations coming from other parts of the world.

Some other types of dreams are still more significant. These are in the nature of predictions. These are events casting their shadow beforehand in our dreams. Sometimes we seem to visualize or precognize future events. These miraculous happenings direct our attention to another great power of the unconscious psyche and are called prophetic dreams.

One example is of a man I knew in India who was a talented teacher. One night he dreamed that his guru, who had died several years before, appeared before him and said, 'Why are you wasting your life in this profession? Teaching is not for you. You have a great mission to fulfill in your life. An ancient Ayurvedic medicine has almost been lost, and it is your mission to revive it.' The guru indicated in the dream what books he should find and study. Later on the teacher found those ancient scriptures and did wonderful pioneer work in this field all over India.

The more people are in communication with the depths of their being, increasingly destiny may speak to them in different ways, often through dreams. A queen in India once had a strange dream in which the divine mother Kali told her to build a temple in a certain spot, place an image of Kali in it, and dedicate it to her. The queen acted accordingly, and from that temple a new spiritual renaissance started in India in the nineteenth century with the great sage, Sri Ramakrishna. It all started with a prophetic dream which spoke not of the destiny of an individual but of an entire nation.

Sometimes people who have had profound mystical experiences say that life is like a dream. They feel they have entered a deeper reality, by contrast with which waking reality seems dream-like. One man had a fantastic dream in which he went to Egypt for an appointment with the ruler. The next night his dream started up where it had left off the night before. That night he traveled more in Egypt and then was about to leave it. The third night the dream continued again. After several nights of these successive dreams, he began to wonder: When am I actually dreaming? Am I dreaming when I am asleep or when I am awake?

Many people have speculated about this. When you dream, your waking experience is shut out. Dreams become your reality. When you wake up, dream experiences are shut out. Waking becomes your reality. But there may come a time when you begin to wonder. What is the criterion by which to decide which is true and which is not?

If a person goes on dreaming night after night consistently, suddenly he or she has reason to believe that perhaps that reality may be the one true reality and not this waking reality. Whatever the answer, one fact emerges: the truth about the relativity of what is real. In dreams you experience many things, and during the dreams you believe your experiences are real. You have a sense of reality. You experience joy and sorrow, sadness and exaltation. In waking life you do the same thing. We begin to see the relativity of subjects and objects. Objects now in some sense are relative to consciousness, and consciousness seems to have a creative function. What you see is in large measure dependent upon the way you see, your angle of vision, your type of consciousness.

Similarly, one day you may wake up to a different type of reality. Just as you wake up from a dream, one day you wake up to a reality in which the waking experience of the material world appears to be a dream. Mystics tell us life is like a dream. A metaphysical truth about it is that objectivity of the material world is relative to the subjectivity of consciousness which is present within us.

Let me share one more example: A man had a long dream in which he went with a lot of companions to various places around the world. At one point he found himself alone in a big jungle in South America, confronted by a terrible monster of gigantic proportions. Soon he was in the monster's jaws and then in the monster's belly. He tried his best to get out, but eventually he gave up all hope, certain he would die. Just at that moment the dream ended. He awoke with great relief to find out it was all a dream.

I want to direct your attention to a point here which has spiritual significance. He found himself in the monster's belly, struggling to solve his great problem. What is the nature of that effort? Just as being in the belly of the monster is a dream, so, too, is his effort to solve his dilemma a dream. The whole problem is solved, not by tearing the monster's belly, but by waking up and realizing that he was having a dream.

When people awaken and have what we call spiritual enlightenment or God-realization, they understand that they have attained this realization not as a result of their efforts. They may have gone through much suffering and effort to know God. But when they attain enlightenment, they find that their efforts were just like a dream, and so were their problems.

This bring out the idea of grace. When great spiritual thinkers tell us about grace, they mean that it is not through our efforts that we attain enlightenment. Our egoistic effort is as much a part of the dream as our problems. True spiritual enlightenment comes through the grace of God. When we are told to relax about our problems, give them over to God, and that in a mysterious way they will be solved — this means through the grace of God. By letting the power of God that is present within us operate, someday we may find ourselves waking up from a dream with the most basic problems we have been struggling with now solved.

26

EXISTENCE, CONSCIOUSNESS, AND JOY

Consciousness is co-extensive with existence. There is no level of existence which is absolutely devoid of consciousness. Every level of existence has its appropriate level of consciousness. One of the essential points in Teilhard de Chardin's theory of evolution is that as evolution marches forward, there is greater and greater complexity and complication of structure and function. The more the complexity, the more the intensity or temperature of consciousness rises.

This is similar to the ancient theories of the sages. That is why there is the expression in Hindu philosophy '*Satchitananda.*' *Sat* means existence. Existence is a structural principle of reality. Nothing is real without having an existence aspect, a being aspect. *Chit* is consciousness. Consciousness is not something static; it is not passive. It is a dynamic energy. That is why the more consciousness we have, the more dynamic our world. It is a fact of life. The more we are aware of things, aware of what is happening, the more we are dynamic. Then *ananda* means joy. Wherever there is existence and consciousness there is also an appropriate kind of joy. For example, a blooming flower has existence, its own kind of consciousness and its own kind of joy. Wherever we see something beautiful or glorious in nature we feel there is a joy there. If we open our heart, if we open the door of our consciousness, we can feel that joy and love in life everywhere.

27

THE POWER OF SILENCE

Silence is the ultimate source of power and energy. The ancient sages declared that God is the great silence. The true secret of spiritual living lies in accumulating an illuminative power, a creative power of silence.

Today, as we look around, we find little realization among people about this power of silence. The fact is just the opposite. People are trying to kill silence in all possible ways. Noise is all around us, in the streets below and the skies above. However, we are not satisfied with this much noise, so we carry noise around in our pockets as well, in the form of pocket radios and tape players. People may go to the park or to the beach for relaxation, but even so, they are not ready to cultivate silence. Instead, they talk and play radios and make all kinds of noises.

This is an unfortunate symptom of the growing rise of materialism and technological civilization, and it is all the more reason why we should be mindful of the importance of silence. There are some areas in life in which we can enter into communion with the ultimate ground of existence, with the ultimate source of life, which is silence.

There are different aspects of the power of silence. First of all, silence is illuminative; it is the source of illumination. To explain this point, I shall tell you a story from the Upanishads. The title of the chapter is 'Mounam Brahman,' which means 'God is Silence.'

Four young people were friendly with each other and were inspired by the same spiritual ideal. They decided they should find a great teacher and attempt to gain some authentic understanding of the nature of supreme truth or Brahman. Brahman is the Sanskrit word for ultimate reality, the infinite. The name of the greatest teacher of the time in the country came to their mind, and they decided to go to him for spiritual instruction.

After traveling a long distance, they reverently sat down in the teacher's presence, and one of them said to him, 'We have come a long distance to see you. Would you kindly instruct us on the nature of Brahman?' The master was silent. No answer. No talk. After a while they repeated the question, but the teacher remained silent.

After they repeated the same question for the third time with all their eagerness and earnestness, the master said, 'I have already replied to your question, because God is the great silence — Mounam Brahman. It is by entering into the depth of silence of your being that you can realize God.'

When we study the lives of some of the greatest thinkers and leaders of humanitarian action, we find they had an understanding of this fact. For example, I think you know that Mahatma Gandhi was a man of great action. He was in the political field and at the same time was an illuminated soul, a saint. Every now and then we find in his life that local, national, and international political problems pressed in upon him. First he listened to all of the different points of view. Then before coming to a decision himself, he would make a point of retiring into silence, allowing all these different outlooks to be absorbed in the unconscious. After a period of silent contemplation of the various problems, wonderfully enough, some inner light began to shine on them.

In every single one of us, the light is there. You may call it the light of the infinite, the light of the eternal, the light of God which dwells in your heart. In whatever way you understand the inner light or inner guidance, it is there. If we know how to enter into the silence of our being, the inner light shines in us, throwing light upon some of the most pressing problems of our life.

We all know how silence can be tremendously recuperative. Nature has embedded a method of silence in our lives so that we can recuperate from the stresses of the day. Nature gives us the silence of sleep. All day you work hard, dealing with many things and meeting many people. Sometimes conflicting forces pour into your mind so that maybe you become fatigued, tired, and depressed. You go to bed, fall asleep, and there is a wonderful miracle of cure. In the morning you find yourself refreshed, revitalized, a newborn individual ready to start the day again with renewed vigor and energy. Is this not a miracle?

All creative action takes place in silence. It is when the mind falls absolutely silent, when we let go and relax, when our little rational mind is not chattering too much; it is at the moment of complete silence and relaxation that some of our most creative ideas flash forth. This is why we find all creative thinkers, philosophers, scientists, and artists have to retire into the depth of silence. Otherwise, authentic creation and original thinking is not possible. This is why the scientist must have silence in the laboratory, the artist must have silence in the studio, and the mystic must have silence in his or her retreat. Silence is a 'must' for all creative activity.

Let me tell you a story about the great American thinker, writer, and novelist, Ernest Hemingway, to portray another aspect of the value of silence. A press correspondent once asked Hemingway, 'What book are you writing now?' Hemingway said, 'I don't want to discuss it. I don't know the reason, but it is my feeling that when I discuss with anybody my plans before a book is published, something goes wrong. I cannot explain it, but this has been my experience. It is my practice now that I never discuss my writing with anybody before I am finished and the work is ready to go to press.'

This is called *mantragupti*, a Sanskrit expression meaning the secret silence in all serious endeavors. It is a good principle. When you undertake something noble, something serious, something original, something creative, it is a sound principle not to talk about it with people who cannot help you in any way with the project. You can talk with those who are working along with you, who will understand or whose help you need in some way. This is different. But otherwise, it is better not to discuss it.

Suppose you have made a plan about your spiritual growth.

You are going to meditate or study on a regular basis. Or suppose you plan to write a book. If you talk about it, you dissipate some of your energy. The less you talk, the better, because in this way you preserve energy. This energy then is channeled constructively and wholeheartedly toward your chosen endeavor.

Another aspect is that an element of egotism often comes into our talking without our knowing about it. This is bad, too. The more there is a display through talking or an element of bragging, the more we undermine our main activity.

So for various reasons it is desirable to follow this principle. First finish the job, whatever you have in mind. Then let your deed speak for itself. Our actions and deeds are more eloquent than our words. Similarly, we may let our own life speak for itself. What is the use of talking about what we have done or what we are going to do? Let our life and its actions speak for themselves.

One time a man went to Mahatma Gandhi and asked, 'What is your final message to the world now that you are at the evening of your life?' Gandhi at once replied, 'My life is my message.' This response was wonderful. This is what everybody should have in mind. Our life has to be our message in the world.

When by living right, thinking right and cultivating the power of silence we accumulate creative energy within us, we can communicate this to others and share it in a silent way. This is another mysterious fact. We find it illustrated in the lives of all great sages. We find they instructed others more by the power of silence than any other way. People come from different places with a great hunger in their soul and all kinds of questions. As a result of sitting silently in the presence of a true teacher, automatically some of the questions and problems seem to be solved from within. They receive something. This is silent communication. When you have the power within you, you can communicate it spontaneously in a silent way, just as a lamp radiates light. The sun shines and the flower gives out its perfume spontaneously, silently. So an illuminated soul radiates light and peace and joy in silence. Those who come into the orbit of its influence, automatically receive this power, something of the perfume of spiritual illumination.

Let me tell you an incident about Paul Brunton, a famous American journalist and writer. He went to India in search of spiritual truth. One day walking along the streets of Bombay he met a holy man. The holy man told Brunton: 'You have come to India, but perhaps you don't know what your true mission is here. Apparently you also don't know who is going to help you in obtaining what you are seeking.' Then he said, 'You have come to India to meet the great saint Ramana Maharshi, so you have to go to him.'

Paul Brunton said, 'Why? I haven't even heard his name. I cannot do that. I am going to Agra to see the Taj Mahal. I have already made my reservations.'

The *sadhu* or holy man told him, 'I understand. But I tell you that your main purpose here is to contact Ramana Maharshi. You will have to go to him, so think about it. Tomorrow I shall come to see if you have changed your mind.'

That night he seriously contemplated the issue. He thought, 'What a strange man! He says he knows the mission of my life, which I don't even know.' The next day, when the *sadhu* came to see him again, he said, 'You have certainly scored your point. I am going with you to see Ramana Maharshi.'

So they made a long and uncomfortable journey to Madras, and then to a remote village where Ramana Maharshi lived. Many things that occurred appeared very strange to Brunton. First of all, his ego was a little hurt. He thought there would be a royal reception because he had come all the way from the United States. Instead, everyone was going his or her own way. Then he was led to the meditation hall where Ramana Maharshi was seated. It was a big hall and people were sitting on the floor meditating. There was no talk, no noise, nothing.

As he entered the hall, he thought the master would now pay some attention to him. But, no. The master was not paying attention to anybody. Maharshi was just sitting there in silence, wrapped up within himself, his gaze fixed into eternity.

Brunton was puzzled. He sat there and tried his best to draw the attention of the sage without any successs. So following the custom of the place, he also tried to meditate, to absorb the silence of the atmosphere. Then, as he testified, after a period of time, it seemed a veil was lifted from his mind. A new dimension of existence opened up to him and he began to be aware of himself on a deeper level of being.

That was a big change, a turning point in his life. It was his first experience of a new value of life and of a new dimension of existence. How did he have it? Just by sitting in that silent atmosphere. The atmosphere was surcharged with the illuminative power of silence of the great sage. This is silent communication, which is a fact, not fiction.

I can tell you about my own experience in Pondicherry, with the great master Sri Aurobindo. There were only four days throughout the whole year when people were able to have the *darshan* of Sri Aurobindo. The rest of the year they could not see him. He spent his time in his house engaged in meditation, spiritual work, study, and writing.

On these four occasions, when people had a chance to have his *darshan*, a thousand or more people would form a long line. One after another they would go into his room, stand in his presence, pay their respects and come out quietly. It was an absolutely silent affair.

Not only from my own experience, but from what I know of the experiences of others, this was a miraculous event. That half minute had a tremendous impact on the life of many, many people. In that brief moment, there was a silent communication between two pure souls. The dynamic contact of the two souls in silence was a wonderful experience.

The truth is that when we accumulate the power of silence, which is a creative, illuminative power within us, we can share it with others. We can enter into a mysterious silent communication with others on a deeper level of consciousness. This is a fact, but many people are not aware of it.

Now I shall tell you about some of the inevitable stages of mind in our spiritual search as we develop the power of silence in our life.

Patanjali, a great teacher, tells us the first condition is what is called *vikshepa*, a diffused, scattered condition. We cannot concentrate on anything for long. Our mind is like a monkey jumping from branch to branch on the tree of life, now eating of this fruit, now eating of that fruit. Some fruits are sour and some of them are sweet, but we often cannot settle down anywhere and concentrate on anything for a good length of time. This condition is the opposite of silence.

Then there is *dhrithshepa*. In this stage, we can concentrate for a while. For example, at this stage you can take a book and read perhaps several paragraphs, but then you mind goes to a television program or perhaps to a friend. Your mind likes to wander and it takes a little time to bring it back again.

The next condition is *ekagrata*, which is a single-minded power of concentration. From our childhood on, as we go through different developmental stages, we learn how to concentrate in doing a project and in achieving something. The more we learn how to focus our mental energy in a particular field, the more we can mobilize the resources of our mind. We begin to feel and apply great mental power. In other words, concentration is the mobilization of the powers of the mind, and that gives us great strength.

In the practice of meditation, we can develop this power in different ways. You may begin by concentrating upon some particular thing. Say, for example, you take an image of a vast ocean. You visualize the ocean and concentrate on it. Or perhaps you are a lover of mountains, so you fix in your mind the image of a beautiful, majestic mountain. Or if you are especially religious-minded, you can concentrate on a particular religious figure. With these different ways, we develop the mind into *ekegrata*. This is a big, important step in developing the power of silence.

In *ekagrata* you are putting forth effort. As a result, there is an intensification of your consciousness. This is like converting an ordinary lamp into a searchlight. In an ordinary lamp, the rays of light are diffused in all directions so there is illumination but no penetration. In a searchlight, the rays of light are focused in one direction, so the light has a deep penetrating power.

In *udashin*, the next step, you let go of your mind and body and completely relax. You do not concentrate on anything in particular. Because it is difficult to bring the mind under control, the mind has also been compared to a serpent. It moves in a serpentine way, mischievous and treacherous. You want it to do one thing, but every now and then it does just the opposite. What do you do? In *udashin* the technique is to give this monkey mind a long rope with which to hang itself. Let go. Do not fight with it. The more you interfere with it, the more it thinks it is fun, and it can hit you back. As you allow it to freely run its full course, eventually it exhausts itself and comes automatically under your control. Think of whatever you want, but keep an eye open and observe it. You observe in a detached way, without being identified with any of the activities of the mind.

A great Indian master once said that meditation is like a snake charmer charming a snake. He brings a big snake out of his basket and lets it go. He gives it free play but keeps a constant, vigilant watch. He is watching the eyes of the snake and by watching while not being identified, he controls it. This is *udashin*.

As you go through these practices, you achieve inner quiet, calmness, peace, and silence. Quietness implies an elimination of restlessness from the mind. However, this is only the beginning of silence. Even though the native restlessness is eliminated, the mind is still likely to be disturbed from within or without. A little disturbance outside may break this quiet. But disturbance may come from inside also. You are quiet, and suddenly a particular memory comes from your unconscious mind and disturbs your restful state.

In a state of calmness, distractions and conflicts are eliminated. When you attain calmness, you may hear a noise outside, but it will no longer disturb you. Silence is becoming solidified within you. Similarly, some disturbing thought may come from inside, but you are able to look at it with dispassion. Then all of a sudden it vanishes.

As a result of this freedom from conflict, distraction and disturbance, you attain an awareness of the inner self, which is the unifying and harmonizing principle of your existence. As a result of calmness, you discover peace because you become aware of a deeper level and inner harmony of your being.

After this is silence. In peace you have the awareness of your innermost spiritual reality, which is harmonizing and unifying. Through this, your Self becomes an avenue to God, to ultimate reality. As you know your Self, you enter into communion with the divine. When the inner channel of communication is open, you gain a new, profound experience of the inner flow of indescribable joy. Your whole being is flooded with the light and love of the infinite. You feel you are in the loving embrace of God.

This silence can be of two types: static and dynamic. Static silence means you enter into communion with the infinite more and more deeply. You want to abide permanently in the incomprehensible, transcendental peace of the absolute. However, dynamic silence is a more balanced spiritual achievement.

In dynamic silence, you also enter into silent communion with the infinite. Yet, you offer your whole being, your mind, your emotions, your senses, and your body as a channel of expression of the creative energy of the absolute. Inwardly you enter into silent communion with the infinite, while outwardly you allow the creative power of God to flow freely through you. Your whole being becomes dynamic and creative. It is not exclusive of living in the world. It is inclusive of the whole of life.

As a result, you come out of meditation and look at the world with new eyes. You deal with people; you go to work; you carry on your thinking and feeling as a transmuted instrument in the hands of God. Inwardly there is profound silence. Outwardly there is the performance of activities as an instrument of the divine. The activities of life do not disburb your inner silence, for all your activities are performed for the glory of God.

28

INTUITION

As we evolve spiritually, our intuition also develops, because this is one of the prerogatives of the human psyche. In the past, many people emphasized reason, the rational faculty, as the greatest human ability. However, besides this rational faculty we also have some deeper cognitive powers. One of them is intuition, which we have on different levels of our being.

As a general definition, intuition is the power of immediate awareness or immediate cognition of something, whereas reason means to mediate knowledge, to know something on the basis of something else. For example, at a distance we may see smoke coming from the top of a mountain. Then we say there must be fire inside the mountain. This is reason. However, intuition is immediate knowledge, a direct grasp of the essence of something.

In most of our educational systems, it is reason which has been emphasized and over-emphasized. But educators and others are recognizing that intuition is a precious faculty of the human mind which needs to be cultivated more and more. As a matter of fact, when we emphasize the need for spiritual exercises such as meditation, the precise goal is to cultivate this intuitive power of the mind.

The great French philosopher Henri Bergson talked about instinctual intuition, intuition in the form of instinctual knowledge which we find in animals. For example, when a lion strikes a lamb, the lion instinctively knows which is the weakest part of the lamb. Throughout nature we find illustrations of this unerring cognitive power. However, according to Bergson, as humans evolved out of the matrix of animal consciousness, the instinctive-intuitive power was driven underground and took second place. Reason or the rational faculty became the primary faculty of humans because it was pragmatically more useful. Bergson said reason emerged in the course of evolution because intellect is a tool which helps us to organize the affairs of life. It is an organ of manipulation. It is an organ to structure the affairs of society and human relations. William James also shared this view that reason or intellect is a pragmatic tool which evolved out of necessity in the course of our growth.

But in order to have metaphysical knowledge, knowledge of things as they are, knowledge of their essence, we must also develop our latent intuitive power. We need intuitive powers if we want to go into the innermost essence of things and people.

By exercising our rational faculty, we can only go round and round an object or person, discovering and analyzing the relation in which it stands to other things and people. For example, if I work with you, by reason, all I can see is how you behave in the office, how you relate to others, how you relate to your family members and how you relate to God. I analyze all of these relations with the help of my intellect, seeing patterns of behaviour in different situations as you relate to the world. With my intellect, I encircle you, but I can never penetrate your innermost essence. What is the inmost thing which inspires you? What are the conditions from within which govern all these behaviour patterns in relation to the different things of the world? Only my intuition can discover these things.

As human beings we are imperfect, and so our functions naturally are also imperfect. This is all the more reason why we should cultivate our different abilities and continually integrate one with another. Mahatma Gandhi often emphasized this point. He believed many yogis and swamis emphasized intuition too much. Gandhi took his stand in saying that both intuition and reason are complementary to each other and that we should check one with the other on an ongoing basis.

Let us look at some of the implications of intuition on different levels of experience. On the level of sense experience, there is a kind of intuition which we may call sensory intuition. For example, on the level of sense experience we somehow experience or know space and time, and we may say that both are infinite. This can never be known by reason. Infinite space or infinite time are not objects of reason, because reason can grasp only finite, limited things. That means that infinite space and infinite time somehow are intuited. We have an intuitive apprehension of the infinite space in which things exist and the infinite time in which events happen. It is a matter of intuition, not a matter of perception, reasoning or inference.

Samuel Alexander developed this view in his book *Space, Time and Deity*. He pointed out that space and time are not just intellectual constructions; they are the basic realities of this universe. But we intuitively apprehend these realities; we do not imagine or rationally construct them.

When we think about it, it is fascinating that we have this ability to intuit infinite space and infinite time in which all the endless things of the world exist and happen. Children have a vague intuition of space and time, and this becomes more clear and definite as they advance intellectually. Through language and conceptual development, they begin to give definite structure to space and time. Just as at the beginning, I see you from a distance as a human being, as I come closer and observe you at short range, I begin to see your distinctive features.

We also have intuition on the intellectual level. When we function on the intellectual level, there usually is an element of intuition, without which we cannot do too much. For example, scientists work in their laboratories to try to throw light on some phenomenon. Intuition plays an important role in this process of investigation. After they gather all the necessary data and information, they make a hypothesis with the help of their intuition which will fit all the facts together in an organized structure. For example, Einstein said before his law of relativity was established as a fact, he first glimpsed relativity with the power of his intuition. Many others also have attested to this same kind of experience.

We also may talk about intuition on the unconscious levels

of the psyche. For example, intuition can be in the form of ESP powers, including telepathy, clairvoyance, clairaudience or precognition. These wonderful cognitive powers of the human mind lie buried in the unconscious awaiting to be developed. In the course of spiritual practice, some of these latent intuitive powers come to the front. However, those who have this intuitive power also need to have a deep sense of values, or their abilities may be misused.

Some profound spiritual realities can be known only by intuition, even, for example, knowledge of our own self. We know our self by intuition. We know our self by being our self. This is called knowledge by being. This is immediate cognition. We know our own self not inferentially nor by reasoning. Self-knowledge is direct knowledge, as is knowledge of the ultimate ground of our existence. If we take the word 'God' as the ultimate ground of our being, we come to know God through intuitive apprehension.

As we become integrated and harmonious in our living and practice love in human relations, our intuitive power increasingly grows within us. There is a vital relationship between the intuitive faculty of consciousness and love. The more we develop and practice love, the more the intuitive faculty is cultivated. That is because the attitude of love or empathy brings about an attunement of our consciousness to a particular person or thing. We tune in to its direct vibrations.

Another important way to develop greater intuition is to foster the dissolution of our inner conflicts and dichotomies through psychological work on oneself, contemplation and the regular practice of meditation. The more our inner being is divided, the more intuition is shut out. However, as our whole personality and inner consciousness become integrated, our intuitive power begins to flower.

Finally, meditation results in the highest form of intuition — the cognitive power of an integrated personality. When we cultivate ourselves so that our total being becomes harmonized, we begin to experience the highest power of intuition possible in human life.

29

INTEGRAL THEORY OF IMMORTALITY

When we try to understand the implications of the theory of reincarnation, we find this doctrine is the outcome of the application of the concept of evolution to the human soul. Just as in nature there is a process of evolution, as a result of which we see a perpetual offspringing of ever new forms, qualities, and values — in the same way, the human soul is involved in a process of evolution. Our spiritual pilgrimage is ultimately destined for union with the infinite. According to the theory of reincarnation, our present life is one chapter in the checkered evolutionary growth of our human soul. According to the cosmic plan of God, many other opportunities also exist for the growth and further evolution of the individual soul. This view is based upon the idea that every human soul is essentially a spark of the divine. Since by its very nature, every human soul is imperishable and indestructible, therefore, sooner or later, it is sure to attain the ultimate goal — namely, immortality or blissful union with the divine.

I want to discuss what may be called an integral theory of immortality. That is, immortality here and now in the flesh, in the body. This has been called diamond immortality or material immortality. First, there is the concept of immortality of the spirit. The spirit is in essence immortal because the spirit or the soul is essentially a spark of the divine. As a spark of the divine it partakes of the life eternal of God. It is imperishable.

In other words, by its very nature the spirit in humans, the soul, is beyond the destructive fury of the elements of nature. All the great mystics the world over from different countries have testified that there is this spiritual essence of human nature — the spirit in us, the soul in us which is essentially immortal. By realizing the soul, the spirit, the Atman, we can partake of the life eternal of God.

An important implication of this immortality of the spirit is that we do not have to wait until after death to experience it. The immortality of the spirit is not to be equated with what is called heaven in the popular imagination — of going to a higher plane of consciousness, a land of all wish fulfillment after death. Immortality of the spirit is something we can attain here and now in this very world living in the body, in the flesh. The moment we realize God, attain enlightenment, realize the spiritual essence of our being, we obtain that master key with which to open the door of immortality so that we can participate in the life everlasting of the Supreme. The moment we have that transformation of our consciousness resulting in wisdom and enlightenment, we attain that.

An integral theory of immortality implies yet an even greater achievement. This means that our total being — body, mind, soul — can partake of the life eternal of God. Not only the soul but our total being, our total existence, our total personality can be transformed into an immortal image of the divine.

I want you to grasp the distinction between the immortality of the soul, which is transcendental immortality, and diamond immortality, the total immortality of our total being. This is also called by some material immortality. That is to say, first we realize immortality on the highest spiritual plane, by contacting the divine on a spiritual plane. Then we bring down the light and power and love of the divine into our physical existence, our mental existence. Thereby we transform our total physical existence into an immortal image of the divine.

Buddhists talk of the diamond body. In the course of our spiritual unfoldment we can attain a state where we not only glimpse the immortality of the spirit, but we also bring something of that into our physical existence. As a result of our contact with supreme reality, we acquire a new diamond body which is imperishable.

This idea is also found in Hindu mysticism and Taoism. For example, *The Secret of the Golden Flower* talks of diamond immortality. Taoists believe that in human personality, there are two apparently opposite forces, Yang and Yin. Yang is the masculine principle. Yin is the feminine principle. Yang is the power of light. Yin is the power of darkness. Yang is the rational mind. Yin is the intuitive domain. These are the two constituent elements of human personality. We are often torn in our nature and being. As long as there is conflict, a disharmony between our conscious mind and the unconscious psyche — the masculine and feminine principle within us — we suffer from inner dichotomy and we are short-lived. According to *The Secret of the Golden Flower*, through meditation and harmonious living, by following intelligently the way and spirit of nature, these two principles can be harmonized and integrated.

The gulf that exists today between the conscious and the unconscious in our nature can be bridged. Our conscious living and thinking can be brought into perfect harmony with the profound depth of our unconscious being, so that we can function in a unitary fashion with an undivided strength of our personality. When this happens, we attain immortality; we attain the diamond body. Lao Tzu and Taoism hold forth this concept of attaining immortality in our existence, with emphasis on an individual scale. This is an individual possibility. An individual human being with his or her spiritual potential can attain this goal.

We find in Hindu Tantra the identical idea of attaining immortality in our total being. Instead of Yang and Yin, they say Shiva and Shakti. Shiva is the masculine priniciple, and Shakti is the feminine principle. Shiva is the principle of pure consciousness. Shakti is the principle of pure energy. There is a little difference in concept here. Shakti is pure energy, and with this energy goes emotion, love. Love is energy. Emotion is energy. Shiva is pure consciousness, pure intelligence. These two principles of logos and eros are within us.

In our daily living there is often a disparity between these two constituent elements of our personality. Our energy is not in harmony with our understanding. We put forth our energy in many activities which do not make sense. There is a discord

INTEGRAL THEORY OF IMMORTALITY

between the two, and so we suffer. According to Tantra, the secret of spiritual unfoldment is the gradual harmonization, integration of pure intelligence and pure energy. This is the secret of higher living. When these two are brought together in perfect harmony, we attain the diamond body, a body which is imperishable, which becomes a perfect vehicle of the spirit, which is transformed into a perfect image of the divine.

Scientists are working with an idea of material immortality. They believe that by following the laws of science, the laws of good living, intelligent living, we can enormously increase our life span. A Russian scientist predicted that by the end of the century, science will be able to increase the average longevity up to three hundred years. But his thinking was purely in terms of longevity. This is what we may call a quantitative theory of immortality, thinking in terms of increasing the life span. But as we have noted in the spiritual theory of immortality, it is not just a question of quantitative increase of the life span. There is a qualitative aspect, the enormous enrichment of our being, our participation in higher consciousness, wisdom, and love, the timeless dimension of Being.

This idea of diamond immortality also is found in alchemy. The alchemists had the same idea of total, material, diamond immortality, establishing the immortality of the spirit on the physical plane. The hermetic philosophers and alchemists expressed it in a symbolic way. Their goal was to transform base metal into gold. The gold stands for material immortality — spiritual gold. The base metal is our nature and impulses, passions and desires. They saw the vision of the profound potentiality of human nature, of transforming the lower passions, impulses, and desires into pure spiritual gold. They used three ingredients: sulphur, salt, and mercury. By mixing these together the mixture goes through stages indicated by different colors. In the course of these mixtures we attain black, white, then red.

The mystical interpretation of this is that the three ingredients of sulphur, salt, and mercury are the three constituent elements of human personality. Sulphur is the body, the physical organism. Salt is the mind, intelligence. Mercury is the spirit, the pure soul which is the divine principle of life, the creative spark of the divine. The vessel in which these are blended together is the human being. The idea is that harmonizing these three elements is the way of higher unfoldment. As a result of intelligent living in harmony with the transcendental order, we go through three phases, black, white, and red. These colors correspond to three well known stages of mystic growth.

First is black. When we begin to live in a higher way, there is a pressure, there is an upsurge of the elements of the lower nature to the fore. This always happens, just as in the story that when the churning of the ocean begins, poison begins to surface. First we live in an ordinary way without much thinking, following the natural impulses and instincts of our nature, following the drift or following the crowd. That is called the inauthentic way of living, following the conventional way of living. The conventional way of living is the line of least resistance. We do not have to use our brains too much. The moment we make a break with convention, and within our own inner soul we catch a glimpse of a higher ideal, of a standard of perfection, and decide to live up to our vision of that supreme ideal, a great change takes place within us. This change and determination put a pressure upon our lower nature. For so long, while we were following the drift, there was a compromise with our lower nature. But as soon as we make a stand, many of the desires and impulses of the lower nature feel threatened. Their merry-go-round way of living is going to be disturbed, so the lower nature offers great resistance. This is black, the upsurge of the poisons to the surface. This is what is called in mystical language the period of purgation, purgatory. A great turmoil takes place within us. This is a critical phase of our self-development. The goal of this catharsis is the purification of our inner nature. As we go through this purgation and catharsis, the mechanism is there for a gradual purification.

As we successfully come out of this ordeal, the next color is white. This is illumination. We have a deeper understanding and wisdom based upon our insights into the meaning of life and the nature of existence, the true nature of the soul. It has been said that the pure in heart will enter into the kingdom of heaven, which is illumination and wisdom. In the terminology of Christian mysticism, purgation is followed by illumination.

The next color is red, which means unitive consciousness. Purgation, illumination, union. Union with the divine. This is the higher trinity of Self-realization.

The main emphasis in alchemy or hermetic philosophy is that these three have to be blended into spiritual goals. In our normal living, body and spirit are separate. That is why when we are determined to live the higher life, we begin to feel the conflict between flesh and spirit. But as we successfully come out of the turmoil and our dark tunnel and see the light of the transcendental truth, the power of that light helps us in uniting body and soul. Mind or intelligence mediates between the two. This is the view of alchemist philosophers when it is properly interpreted. Alchemy has been interpreted in a crude way to mean that metal can be turned into gold so we can make more money. It has been interpreted as a materialistic pursuit. But no, behind these symbols was great spiritual significance.

Jungian psychologists also have investigated this symbolism and have found 'archetypes' that are indicative of the deeper potential of human nature. This deep potential implies our possibility, our power to integrate our total nature and to establish immortality of the spirit in our physical existence.

This is what Sri Aurobindo called the ideal of an integral theory of immortality, the ideal of total transformation of human nature. This is transforming our whole being into a perfect imperishable image of the divine. Sri Aurobindo has given this idea a cosmic and evolutionary significance. From his standpoint it is not just the case of an individual human being attaining total immortality. This is the profound potentiality of collective humanity as it is advancing through evolution over the centuries toward the fulfillment of its ultimate destiny — namely the establishment of the kingdom of heaven in human society, in the world. In *The Life Divine* and *The Synthesis of Yoga*, he discussed this philosophically, and in *Savitri* he presented it in poetic form and beautifully elaborated this drama.

The first step of total transformation is the individual. Everything in the life of society is the outcome of efforts of individuals. Society is an organism of individuals. It is a super-organism. Society is the unity of different individuals. In order that something can be established in society, first it has to be realized and established in the heart of individuals. It begins with you and me. A great individual realizes a great idea in his or her own life and transmits it to other individuals. Through the collective effort of many, a new value is created in human society. Therefore, this total transformation of human personality has to be attained within individuals who are eager to realize the ideal within their own lives. Through their concerted effort, society can be transformed into a new world order.

There are three stages to achieve this: psychic transformation, spiritual transformation and supramental transformation. When we have psychic realization, we establish a unique relationship between ourself and God through love and devotion in our heart. When our whole being is transformed by the light of this realization, we see God everywhere in the outside world, in all beings and in all objects. This is a sign of psychic transformation. Our contact with and experience of God are brought down into even the cells of our body. Our whole body is attuned to the divine consciousness. The cells of our body are saturated with a new sense of values.

Let me give you an illustration of how our physical body can be affected by higher consciousness. It has been said that Ramakrishna's whole being was so committed to God that he could not endure the presence of persons who thought or talked on a low level about social success or how to make more money. His inner being would revolt. One day somebody wanted to test him. Without letting anybody know, a person put a rupee under Ramakrishna's pillow. Ramakrishna went to bed. He did not know what happened, but he felt uncomfortable and could not sleep. The person who did it watched to see how genuine Ramakrishna was in his profession. Finally, Ramakrishna got up and called his attendant. He said 'Something must be wrong here as I cannot sleep.' Then the fellow pulled out a rupee from under the pillow. This is an indication of how the cells of the body become saturated with a sense of higher values when a transformation takes place. Mystics say that when the consciousness of God is brought into our lower being, even our blood and cells are filled by the touch of the divine.

The next step is spiritual transformation. A chief characteristic of realization of the spirit is attainment of authentic freedom, peace, serenity, and calmness. Spiritual transformation means these things are established even in our body. Normally our body is restless, sometimes nervous. But when a spiritual transformation takes place, the body becomes a perfect image of peace and serenity. It radiates joy. It becomes a spiritual dynamo.

Finally is supramental transformation. The supermind is the highest creative power of God. When we succeed in transforming our body, mind, and life by the light and power of the supermind, this is called supramental transformation. Many of you have heard of Swami Vivekananda, a disciple of Ramakrishna. He was a brilliant young man. One day Ramakrishna told some of his other disciples, 'Vivekananda has been born to carry the method of the highest spiritual life to the world, but he will be working so long as he has not attained full realization. As soon as he fully realizes his divine essence, he will give up his body.' And that is what happened. He accomplished a lot in his life and died very young.

We find similar statements in the writings and sayings of many mystics. They work with and live in this body so long as there is a little ignorance. For them, the body is like a prison house, a tomb of the spirit. So they discard it and become completely free from the shackles of the prison. Even Plato has said the body is basically a prison for the soul, which is absolutely free.

Sri Aurobindo began to think about it. Was there really such a disparity between the body and the spirit that we have to discard the body? The answer that came to him was no, there is no ultimate dualism or disparity between the body and the spirit, because in ultimate analysis even the body is the temple of the spirit or an instrument in the hands of the spirit. There is no absolute necessity that we have to discard the body after we realize the spirit. On the contrary, it is our task to transform the body into a perfect instrument and abode of the spirit, or a medium of expression of the spirit. This is supramental transformation. Aurobindo says it is well within our power as humans to bring down the higher creative power of God, the spirit, into physical consciousness and to transform the whole physical organism. After a full Self-realization, we do not feel the body is a prison to be discarded. It is a wonderful instrument with which to serve God, to do God's work and to transform the power and light and love of God into society.

30

MYSTICISM AND DEPTH PSYCHOLOGY

According to both Hindu and Buddhist Tantric mysticism, when we reach the summit of spiritual experience there is a complete harmonization of the masculine and feminine principles in the human personality. This harmonization is a major goal in modern depth psychology also, as these two fundamental principles are constituent elements of personality.

In Indian mysticism, Purusha and Shiva are the masculine principle, and Prakriti and Shakti are the feminine principle. From the metaphysical and spiritual standpoint, these are not to be understood as male-female distinctions. Here, 'masculine' does not mean male and 'feminine' does not mean female. It is not a sex differentiation — it is a psychological and metaphysical distinction. These principles are found in all human beings, male and female.

As Carl Jung and other psychologists have claimed, the difference between male and female is a difference of degree and not an essential difference. The masculine or logos principle is the intellectual or knowing aspect of personality. In the masculine nature what predominates is knowledge, consciousness, thought, and reason. Logos is present in both male and female as thinking and knowing in different degrees. Shakti, the feminine principle, is eros, the emotional and energetic aspect. In Indian thought, these two have been combined and equated; emotion is energy and energy is emotion.

With the full blossoming of the human personality, there is a perfect union, a real harmonization of the masculine and feminine principles of human nature, resulting in a perfect union of wisdom and love, knowledge and emotion. As we unfold spiritually, we also attain a perfect balance between the individual soul and the universal spirit. We enter into a balanced relation with the divine. It is an equality, a harmony between ourselves and God.

Dr Jung pointed out that people belong to different psychological types, which inevitably control their attitudes and actions. In this respect, as a person approaches God, he or she may adopt one or another attitude. Some people, both male and female, in approaching God are predominantly feminine in their attitude. Others are predominantly masculine in their approach. Even in our relation to God we need to move toward establishing a harmony between the masculine and feminine elements of our nature. This is the perfectly balanced attitude to God.

Let us explore this a little further. First, we may adopt a feminine approach. In some mystical writings we come across the idea that many mystics and spiritual seekers look upon God as the bridegroom and the human soul as the bride. We approach God in this spirit, with complete surrender, with total devotion and self-offering, a self-giving without reservation. From this standpoint, union with God is conceived as a mystic marriage between the human soul and the supreme spirit. The idea is that in relation to God all human beings are feminine because their attitude to God is one of self-giving and self-surrender.

Let me share a story which brings out this point. In medieval India, there was a famous spiritual leader and devotee whose name was Mirabai. She is still known today as a highly evolved being and a great mystic, and her songs and devotional poems are sung frequently. At that same time in Benares, which was the religious capital of India, there lived a great mystic and philosopher whose name was Sanatan. Sanatan was given to self-discipline and austere practices. His fame travelled far and wide and Mirabai became eager to meet him. She set out on her journey toward Benares. On entering the city, she met a disciple of Sanatan who carried the news to the master that Mirabai wanted to see him. Sanatan had taken a vow of austerity and silence, and one of his vows during this period was not to see any women. Accordingly, Sanatan's disciple told Mirabai he would not see her. Mirabai was surprised. She exclaimed, 'What do you mean he will not see any women? In this city, which is so devoted to Lord Krishna, all devotees are female! What does he mean? Is he not female too?' When Sanatan heard this, he was greatly impressed. Immediately he felt that here was a great soul. He set aside his vow, and the result was a historical meeting of two remarkable devotees.

Thus, we can approach God with the attitude of total self-offering, and from this standpoint every individual soul is feminine. God alone is the masculine power. All individual souls can approach the divine in the spirit of total dedication, love, and self-surrender.

However, an extreme development of this approach can be complete self-absorption in the spirit. One's self-offering may be carried to such length that one feels completely lost and absorbed in God with nothing left for oneself or others. This attitude is found in some devotional mystics, especially in Sufism, Hinduism and Christianity.

Just as some mystics and spiritual seekers approach God with a feminine attitude, others approach God with a masculine attitude. A masculine approach is an attitude of self-affirmation and taking, not an attitude of self-surrender and giving. A spiritual seeker thinks of God as a vast, rich treasure and reaches to possess the treasure. Or she or he thinks of God as an ocean of honey, an ocean of love and joy, and says, 'I want to partake and enjoy it.'

Iqbal, a Sufi mystic, wrote some poems reflecting this approach. He described love as a flashing sword. The sword is a symbol of masculine power, of conquering the kingdom of heaven by storm with a sword of love and appropriating its treasures. Some have approached God in this way and have attained spiritual realization from this attitude. But, just as the extreme form of the feminine approach is total self-annihilation, so there are also extreme forms of the masculine approach. One such extreme occurs when people try to use God to achieve their own goals. For example, some religious groups today claim that people can become millionaires by using the power of God.

Using God for one's own purposes is an unspiritual form of the masculine attitude. In history we sometimes find this attitude in political leaders. God can easily become a kind of divine henchman. Dictators such as Kaiser Wilhelm, Hitler, and Mussolini seemingly felt the higher power of God and misused it. The solar plexus was opened and activated in these men, and what we call *kundalini* energy was partially awakened, but not directed properly. When power and ambition are stimulated without further spiritual insight, there is a chance of this power going to one's head. An individual who is intoxicated with power strays from a true spiritual path.

If we evolve along the right lines in our inner growth, we will experience a balanced relationship between our soul and the universal spirit. The ultimate goal is not to be annihilated but to be enriched with divine power and wisdom. Both self-annihilation and self-exaltation are extremes to be avoided. Our true aim is to realize ourself, our soul just as it is, in its true nature and to understand it in its true proportions.

What does it mean to realize our soul, our authentic self, as a dynamic center of divine action? On the one hand we have love, devotion, dedication, and self-offering to the divine because we are nothing apart from it. We have an attitude of self-surrender. The other side is an affirmation of our self as the center of the divine. We are aware that we have a spiritual purpose in our life and that it is our job to fulfill this purpose, not to lose our self, but to enrich and strengthen our self as a channel of divine activity. This is how the balance is maintained. We have to draw upon the power of God. We are intended to do this, but we must draw upon the power of God toward the fulfillment of a higher purpose, as an instrument in the hands of God and not for self-glorification.

Finally, we may enter into still another experience of supramental consciousness. In moving toward this, we rise above embodied existence. This is realizing Being on a very lofty level of consciousness, on the supramental level.

What is the practical bearing of this achievement? In our spiritual search, in our exploration of higher levels of consciousness, we can realize God on different levels and in different aspects. For example, we find in the history of the human religious experience some who have realized God on an intellectual level. They have been the great mystic philosophers and contemplatives. They have emphasized God as wisdom and knowledge, as did Sankara, Plato, and Plotinus. On this level God is realized as infinite consciousness, as wisdom and knowledge. God can also be experienced on the emotional level, as absolute love. And according to some, God can be realized on the physical-vital level as in hatha yoga or in some forms of Tantric yoga. Here God is experienced as energy and infinite power, the *élan vital*, the universal life force. God can also be realized on an ethical level, the level of action, the volitional plane of our personality. When we realize God on this level, we realize God as did Mahatma Gandhi and Albert Schweitzer.

When we realize God on the supramental level, we know God as the perfect unity of love and wisdom and energy, where none is higher or superior to another. There is a perfect balance between these values. This is one meaning of supramental realization — the perfect balance of wisdom, power, and love in one personality.

Another implication is when we enter into union with the divine, we realize God as the timeless reality, as the great silence, the great beyond, the unfathomable mystery. Many mystics have been intoxicated or 'drunk' with the vision of the transcendental order, to use the words of Plato. As a result of their intoxication, often they have felt withdrawn from the flux of time and evolution. As we study the history of mysticism, we find an element of 'other worldliness' because of overwhelming transcendental experiences. However, when we rise beyond and experience God on a supramental level, we attain an integral experience of Being.

What does an integral experience of Being mean? With our full opening, we have an overwhelming experience of Being in its timeless transcendence. From the supramental level, we experience Being in its integral fullness as both a timeless reality and as the power of destiny operating in time and history. We experience God in the flux of time, in the process of nature, in the march of civilization, and in the growth and advance of history as the power of destiny operating in the world. Seeing this we develop an integral outlook. Much of ancient mysticism has been static, transcendental mysticism, but as a result of supramental realization we develop evolutionary mysticism.

Buddha said our life is like a river. On this side of the river is the ordinary life we live. It is a life of *samsara*, the cycle of death and rebirth, empirical existence, social development, economic growth, the march of history and civilization. On the other side of the river is timeless reality, the kingdom of heaven in the transcendental sense of the word. Some people through their spiritual development cross the river, experience transcendental reality and come back to tell their fellow beings about the other shore and to help them get there. Still others cross the river, experience the treasures of transcendental reality, and discover that both shores are interconnected and interdependent. There is no dualism, no complete separation. These people come back armed with the power of the divine and with a clear understanding of the purpose of ultimate reality. They understand the ultimate purpose is to develop something on this shore. They come back to inspire others to build a divine kingdom on this shore, transforming human society into the perfect image of the transcendental reality. This becomes their purpose and is the true goal of evolutionary mysticism. It is the balanced spiritual ideal: attaining mystical experience and also having an evolutionary perspective regarding life. Through this we grow true to the kindred points of eternity and time, of heaven and earth.

31

PSYCHOLOGY OF ENERGY CENTERS

There are two important phases in our personality growth and spiritual development. The first one is psychological house-cleaning. In the course of living in this world, as we grapple with problems of psycho-social existence, we tend to develop inner, emotional conflicts which hinder our growth. It is important to try to eliminate, as much as possible, these unresolved inner conflicts. They are hindrances to the free and full flowering of our spiritual potential. Spiritual self-healing helps us to lay a good, firm foundation for further constructive and creative development.

The goal of much of psychotherapy is psychological house-cleaning. Ancient sages call this initial phase self-purification. After this has been achieved, we go forward without any back pull, without unconscious obstruction or hindrance toward the fulfillment of our highest potential. This is the second phase of spiritual house-building.

The Tantric theory of energy centers of the human body is both an ancient and an eternally new spiritual technology. It is a practice based upon self-healing, self-development, and self-fulfillment. This concept of energy centers existed in a rudimentary form in India even before the Aryans came in the Indus Valley civilization. It developed more and more as a result of interaction between the Aryan and the Dravidian cultures and is a mature flower and fruit springing from this historical interaction between these two ancient civilizations.

Let me give you an idea of the energy centers of the body,

although here I can only scratch the surface. The essential precondition of health, harmony, happiness, and fulfillment is the coordination and harmonious functioning of our different energy centers. Harmony is the essence of constructive and creative health. We repeatedly forget how important harmony is. Often a fundamental impulse and tendency of human nature is to violate this law of harmony. All of us are extremists in some measure, and this tendency unconsciously prompts us to go to the extreme in this or that direction. Although intellectually we may understand that harmony and balance are good, in actual practice we often forget. Much of the time something within us leads us too far over in one direction to the neglect of other aspects and dimensions of life.

It is extremely difficult to maintain an active rhythm, a broad, balanced perspective in life. But this is the essence of spiritual growth. Spirit is harmony, nothing else. Spirit in its inmost essence is the principle of harmonious growth within us. Harmonious functioning of the energy centers of the body is the most essential condition of all growth and self-fulfillment.

The reason we are prone to disturb the balance of our life is that at the center of our human nature there is a duality, a polarity of opposite tendencies and impulses. Because of this polarized energy tendency, we are unconsciously inclined to an extreme and lose sight of balance. From this standpoint, therefore, we may say that the dynamic harmony of opposite impulses is the essential condition of health, growth, and self-actualization.

Most of you are somewhat familiar with these different energy centers, which are called *chakras*. There are seven major centers of the cerebrospinal structure of human personality, and every center has an important function. They are not there for nothing. When we understand the significance of all the different energy centers, we will understand why it is important to maintain balance. Within human nature we may have an overly active or deficient functioning in any one of these centers. When an energy center is not vibrating in tune with the other centers, something inevitably goes wrong. The whole arrangement that nature ideally has made is like a wonderful orchestra. All of these energy centers are different musical instruments. Only when there is an orchestrated functioning of all the energy centers of the body can life become what it should be — a symphony of joy, love, and beauty.

The root center is at the base of the spinal cord and gives us the feeling of being grounded in our body, the foundation of our life. It also gives us the feeling of rootedness in the material world which is also our foundation. So long as we feel comfortably situated in our body and in the world, we have a sense of stability, inner strength, and firmness. When it is shaky, we feel disoriented and disturbed. When there is an earthquake, for example, we all tend to get disturbed, whether directly affected or not.

When the root center is insufficiently active or neglected, we feel alienated from the body. It is a problem in which many hermits, ascetics, and mystics have been trapped. They have believed, 'This is not my body. I am somewhere else, something else.' Sometimes this may give us a nice feeling, but it is basically unhealthy.

Psychiatrists come across this kind of phenomenon frequently. They see people who have been torn out of their body consciousness. Their sense of stability is gone, and they may feel like they are floating on clouds. In such cases this root center needs to be strengthened, reinforced and properly stimulated. The mind has to be brought down into the body so it can function constructively and intelligently.

There also can be the opposite danger. When the root center is overactive and out of proportion to the level of operation of the other energy centers, a person becomes too bodily-minded. They may be gross, crude, and without refinement. Throughout the ages, the function of spirituality has been to help human beings become what they truly are -- essentially instruments of the divine. Inner refinement is necessary in order to strengthen our foundation. We cannot find happiness when we are so body-conscious or materialistically minded that we cannot live higher values. Then we are suppressing our higher potential. Any kind of suppression produces psychological or physical illness, because we are not being what we essentially are.

The next center is the abdomen energy center. This is what

Freud called the domain of libidinous impulses, the primordial, elemental passions and desires of our human life — such as the desire for food, sex, and creature comforts. These are basic instinctual drives.

If the abdomen center is over-active, we may become very passionate. We can even become animalistic, which naturally creates real problems in life. This is what also gives rise to a hedonistic lifestyle. When we accept undisciplined gratification of our instinctual drives as the ultimate goal of life, we may think, 'If this is what gives me happiness, then what is wrong?' But the point is, it does not really make us happy.

If the abdomen center is over-active, one tends toward licentiousness. This is called in spiritual philosophy 'the paradox of hedonism.' It we deliberately set before ourselves the goal of pleasure primarily through instinctual gratification, we do not obtain happiness in life at all. The more we run after pleasure, the more it eludes our grasp, and like receding horizons it fades away. The keenest pleasures and joys of life come unexpectedly, when we are not searching for them. Why? Because, psychologically speaking, experiences of joy and pleasure are by-products of the fulfillment of our true nature and of being in tune with the cosmic whole. This is when we feel true happiness. Real pleasure is not a goal, but a by-product of self-actualization.

The other side of the picture is that we may contract many psychosomatic ailments if the abdomen center is insufficiently active. This happens when a person is extremely puritanical or ascetic in orientation. Such a person thinks instinctual drives have no value and that one has to practice rigid austerity to come close to the attainment of perfection. When this is the idea, the abdomen center becomes very subdued. This paves the road for a split personality between two halves — a wonderful, exalted self and a lower, bestial self.

As we get acquainted with our different impulses, it is important for us to organize them intelligently. We need to ask: 'What is my ultimate goal? What is it that I expect from life?' As we set a goal on the basis of a realistic self-estimation, we organize the healthy desires of our psyche and move forward.

Working with our instinctual impulses may be seen as training the horses within us. Horses are often seen as our different powerful desires. If we kill our horses, we are finished. But if we completely submit to our horses, this is dangerous, too. Both extremes have to be avoided. The ancient sages of India visualized our body as a chariot. The mind with the help of reason and intellect drives it forward. The inner spirit, the true self, is the head for whose happiness and fulfillment the mind is driving it.

Then we come to the navel center, which is the center of power. It is customary with many spiritual and religious leaders to denounce ambition and to encourage people to suppress or eliminate it. This is also unhealthy. We have to accept our total nature with all its potentials and powers and properly guide and regulate it toward the fulfillment of our ultimate goal. This is our job, as a principle of intelligence.

Freud thought the sex drive is the most powerful, but according to Nietzsche and others, the will to power is even more potent than sex. At a certain stage of life the sex drive is most predominant, but as we enter into adulthood our urge to succeed in business, politics, or in other areas often places the sexual drive in the back seat. Power comes to the fore. Position, name, and fame become more important than sex. So the navel center is then in the dominating position.

We can see that whatever is a great potential can also be a great danger. This is where intelligence is necessary and balance is so important. If, for example, this center becomes overactive, then all the other values of life are subordinated; they fade away. One becomes power-crazy, which is extremely detrimental to full spiritual growth. Power is not the ultimate goal. It is a means to the attainment of a higher goal. If we lose our sense of the ultimate goal, what good is power? It will just make us crazy. We need to learn the proper handling of this center. We do not want to destroy it. If we destroy our power center, we cannot achieve our goals, our ideals and our wonderful dreams. So what good is dreaming?

There has to be a balance between love and power and wisdom. For example, in the early days of Christianity some Christians became sentimental in their pursuit of love. In reaction to this, Nietzsche wrote about the 'Superman' to point out that one-sided pursuit of love leads to a sentimental, toothless love. We have to put teeth into our love. In other words, power is necessary. With this power we can express the spirit of love and compassion in life and in human relations. Otherwise, it all evaporates into empty sentimentalism.

However, we also need to remember that power has to be used as the means toward the constructive fulfillment of higher values such as truth, beauty, goodness, peace, freedom, and justice. Even in spiritual life, I have seen some people get sidetracked as they become interested in meditation and spiritual growth. They lose sight of the ultimate — the unity of wisdom, love, and power. They become preoccupied with power. They may become preoccupied with powers of extrasensory perception or other supernormal powers.

Next is the *anahata*, the love center, the heart center, center of the psyche. The technique of meditation on the heart center is prescribed because it is the 'royal road' for the majority of people. Our heart leads us in most of the affairs of life. Here also there can be too much or too little. When there is an excess, we do not progress further. We may not want to cultivate knowledge, for example. We may get caught there and spend the rest of life in a kind of rapturous, motionless way of living. Holy Rollers, for example, show this pattern. There are many devotional equivalents of this attitude displayed in people whose spiritual life and energy are spent in emotional outbursts and excessive expressions of inner sentiment. It is necessary to grow further.

The next center is the *visuddha*, the throat center. Its main function is the ability to see things as they are — everything in its suchness; every human being as he or she is; every individual thing, whether it is a flower or a mountain or an ocean or a star, just as it is. This is tremendously important. When this center is somehow malfunctioning, we begin to see things in a distorted fashion. We live in a world of illusions and hallucinations. We fail to make the distinction between fact and fancy, between imagination and reality. When we lose this ability, we suffer serious illness.

Seeing things properly is called in Sanskrit *tathata*. This requires a lot of development. We may think, 'Everybody can do that,' but such is not the case. However, many of us may have had this kind of experience. For example, just near your home there may be a park or a tree, or every day as you get up you may look at the sun or simply know it is there. Day after day, you are familiar with these things, and you may not give them any thought. Yet one day as you get up in the morning, open your windows and look at the sun, suddenly you see it in all its glory, as you have never seen it before. Or one day, you look at a tree and suddenly see indescribable beauty, which you never noticed before. Or you go to the garden and look at a flower and see something uniquely valuable and beautiful in that flower which you have not noticed because you have been too preoccupied with the affairs of life to notice things in their suchness.

This is what Aldous Huxley discussed elaborately in his books *Heaven and Hell* and also *The Doors of Perception*. This is a great gift of the human mind which we do not always cultivate. In the absence of it or when it is malfunctioning, we more or less live in a world of subjective fancy. If it gets worse, we begin to live in a cloud-cuckoo land of subjective imagination, which means hallucination.

The quality of the forehead center is a great potential of human beings. It is the ability to see things in their wholeness. The previous quality is the ability to see things in their suchness, to see and to know people in their unique personalities. From this develops the ability to see life steady and whole, to envision the universe in its cosmic wholeness, which is a broad perspective we are capable of attaining. Everybody has this ability to some extent, but it needs to be cultivated. When we lose this perspective, we go through emotional fluctuations and, when it is extremely disturbed, we frequently lose our tempers, creating tempests in a teapot. Every little thing that goes contrary to our wishes disturbs us. To rectify this condition, it is important that we succeed in unfolding a broad perspective on life. This is one of the goals of spiritual growth. This gives us wisdom. When we have this perspective, we can take things in our stride. Nothing disturbs us too much. We can preserve our mental equilibrium and harmony. This is the significance of the lotus, which is used as a symbol in Eastern spiritual symbolism. When we have this perspective, we are *in* society but not *of* it. Even though involved in different activities of life, we can preserve inner peace and self-poise, which is wonderful. Immediately, this gives us protection against all kinds of ailments and disturbances in life.

Finally there is the highest center, the *sahasrara*. What can there be beyond the broad perspective of the universe? Sometimes we can have a broad, comprehensive, intellectual perspective of life. We can be knowledgeable people, but still experience much suffering. Something may seem to be missing, and inwardly we may be unhappy and have unresolved conflicts. What is the cause? The great sages who developed this scheme of energy centers and spiritual experiences point out that even people with broad knowledge and great perspectives may be too emotionally involved and attached to the world. This bond of emotional attachment detracts from our inner spiritual perfection.

When we are liberated from the last bond of attachment to this world, we become perfect. This is spiritual perfection. This perfection and liberation was expressed by Jesus when he said, 'I have overcome the world.' The last bond of attachment may be snapped, but this does not mean, however, that we go away from the world. It just means that we participate in the Being of the world, in the evolutionary process of this world, in a spirit of non-attachment. This is the highest health and harmony we can attain, because we are *in* the world but not *of* the world. This is when we can act in the most unselfish manner and express the spirit of love in our hearts in the most unegotistical fashion. It is this which is the essence of human perfection.

32

META-THERAPY

We are all familiar with the saying, 'Physician, heal thyself.' If healers do not heal themselves, their acts of healing cannot be complete. In addition, they eventually may become victims of the problems of their clients, which often happens. As a matter of fact, statistics tell us the greatest rate of suicide in the United States is among psychiatrists and therapists. Why? Because of a lack of certain necessary precautionary measures.

We all have desires to render help and healing to those for whom we care. This wish to help friends and fellow beings is a good and natural human impulse. But if we do not know how to render this healing with a psycho-spiritual approach, it can have a harmful effect upon us, because suffering is contagious. Negativity in any form is contagious. If we do not know how to protect ourselves against the negativity and suffering of others, we also end up being influenced adversely.

Many people feel that physicians or psychotherapists simply act upon and give help to others. The patients may have their suffering alleviated, and that ends the whole matter. But this is not completely true. Every human relation has a circular movement. There is mutuality and reciprocity in all human relationships. We human beings are not simply machines, so that I as a machine say something to you, and you as a machine automatically receive it. We are all organic beings. Whenever we engage in a relationship, it has a mutual and reciprocal significance.

To some extent, all of us are therapists in dealing with our family and friends. When our friends have problems, naturally we want to help them. It is good, therefore, to know how to help others, not in a haphazard, ignorant manner, but in an effective, intelligent and integrated way. One of the techniques which therapists can use to protect themselves is what I call 'meta-therapy.' What is meant by it? 'Meta' means beyond, so the word literally means 'therapy beyond therapy' or 'therapy of all therapy.' When we analyze it, we find a profound significance in this expression.

Meta-therapy helps healers to heal themselves and also to offer effective, radical healing to other people without themselves being adversely affected. The philosophy and techniques of meta-therapy are based upon the recognition that we human beings can function to the best of our ability, enter into fruitful relations with other fellow beings, and help each other if we adopt some of the techniques of meditation. Throughout the centuries, the best healers have been masterminds of spiritual enlightenment. What was their secret? Simply stated, spiritual therapy or meta-therapy.

Any great sage or saint spontaneously is a marvelous therapist. But often we do not think about it or try to understand the mystery and secret of this situation. In recent times, Ramakrishna, Ramana Maharshi and Sri Aurobindo were master healers. Why? Because they knew the secret of total, radical healing and not just partial treatment of symptoms with the help of drugs or pills. Radical healing goes to the root cause of a problem and eradicates those root causes so genuine healing can take place.

Ordinary healers consider only a specific ailment or problem — a pain in the neck or stomach or whatever it is. They give patients something to remove the symptom and the discomfort of the moment. After a while, the problem resurfaces and the healers then must give another pill or drug. They only provide temporary, provisional symptomatic treatment. After the pain or symptoms are gone, the healer's job is considered to be over.

True psycho-spiritual healers have a greater concern and ability. After the temporary discomfort has been removed, they try to bring about further development. This is called developmental healing. It is not just healing in the ordinary sense of the word. Psycho-spiritual healers activate the growth dynamics of our spirit and the developmental potential of our inner soul.

Humans have tremendous growth potential and the possibility of infinite perfectibility within them. This wholeness is the essence of the human soul because the seed of perfection is present, lying dormant in our human psyche. This is what we mean when we say that God is present in all of us.

Everybody, on the basis of proper understanding and application, can heal themselves and spiritually evolve. In proportion to our own success in doing so, we can also offer effective help to others. We can tackle many of the existential problems of life on a spiritual basis by applying some of the techniques of self-communion, nature-communion and God-communion. According to integral philosophy, body-mind-soul-spirit go together. They are interrelated aspects of our total being which is indivisible.

Let us consider some of the principles of meta-therapy, both in self-healing and in healing others. The design of nature is such that as we begin to employ some good principles and attitudes of living, they immediately have a double effect. The result is an inspiring, stimulating, revitalizing effect upon ourselves and a corresponding influence upon others.

One such principle is non-attachment. I hesitate even to mention the word, because today it has become so hackneyed. Non-attachment is a profound principle, but often we do not know what it really means. Unless we clarify our thinking with regard to its proper significance, we do not know what practical bearing it has.

Many people think non-attachment is an intellectual concept and practice it as a principle of existential discipline. In other words, many people practice it as a kind of physical withdrawal from others. Some people practice meditation and spiritual development in this way. They understand non-attachment as if it were a physical movement away from other people, when it is not a physical movement but rather a spiritual understanding and attitude.

Further complicating the whole situation is the psychological fact that we tend to understand things in the light of our own wishes and desires. We misunderstand so often because we want to understand. We distort reality in the light of our own unconscious wishes, and hence we understand non-attachment in a negative way. Why? Because we wish to escape from life and society.

This is what Krishna brought out in the teaching of the Bhagavad Gita in a story about Arjuna. Arjuna was a brilliant young man of his time. He was placed in the forefront, in the middle of the battlefield of life. Suddenly he collapsed and said, 'I don't want to participate in battle. I would rather go away. I would rather find some solitude so that I can spend the rest of my life in contemplation of the eternal verities of existence.' Arjuna told Krishna, 'You have brought me here to fight, but I tell you, I have a spiritual desire now. Following this, I want to withdraw.' What was the divine teacher's response to this? Sharply, Krishna rebuked him. 'You are rationalizing, Arjuna. You are being victimized by fear. You are talking like a wise man, but you are acting like a fool. See how your hands are shaking and your lips are trembling. Your body is a much better index to your inner state than your mind. You are in the grip of anxiety, and so you want to run away. You want to rationalize your escapist tendencies by saying, "I want to know God."'

This is not non-attachment. When we are confronted with a critical issue of life, a crisis, we may tremble and shake and want to run away. Then we might rationalize any say, 'This is pursuit of the path of God — this is non-attachment.'

Non-attachment does not mean withdrawal. When we are too disturbed or too surrounded with problems, temporarily we can go into solitude, of course. But this is entirely different from withdrawal as a lifestyle. Temporary withdrawal is a strategic retreat, as even soldiers in the battlefield do. Strategic retreat for recuperation is important, but this is not retreat or withdrawal as a way of living. There is a world of difference between these two.

When, in meditation, we withdraw into our private, quiet, solitary room and further withdraw into the silence of our inner being, this is our strategic withdrawal. We have a higher goal in mind. We withdraw into the depth of silence of our being in order to renew our spirit through communion with the divine. Then we can come back with renewed vigor and a fresh mind as an instrument of the divine. This is non-attachment.

Non-attachment is retreat into the silence of one's own being, not the silence of a cave. Some people may need to go on a retreat temporarily, so they can enter into the silence of their own being. But this is provisional so that they can come back revitalized, resuscitated, and recuperated. This is the kind of non-attachment which gives us tremendous inner strength and divine protection. This is when we are able to deal with many things without being adversely affected. The true purpose of non-attachment is a positive goal. It is the art of spiritual revitalization so that we can participate in life more intelligently and constructively.

Other principles can help us as well. Suppose we have some knowledge about therapy, healing, meditation, and spiritual growth. Suppose we try to comfort friends. Suppose we successfully render help to another person and he or she benefits from it. Immediately, our ego may become a little inflated. We begin to talk about it and to brag about it. This can spoil our help. This leads to a loss of spiritual protection, because the divine withdraws from where the ego is inflated.

This we find illustrated in the lives of many great mystics and seers. For example, there is the well known story of Radha, an Indian woman with an intense love and devotion to Krishna. After a long search, defying the criticism of family and society, going through hardships and hazards, she finally had the great fortune of discovering Krishna and coming into his immediate presence. She was rapturous about her dream coming true. As a result of her coming into the glorious presence of her divine love, her ego became inflated. This is a part of human nature. At a moment of success and rapture, the ego has a tendency to get blown up. We often begin to feel a 'holier than thou' attitude.

However, at the moment of Radha's inflation, Krishna disappeared, and she plunged immediately into a deep darkness of the soul. Christian, Hindu, and Sufi mystics have all discussed how in the process of increasing self-perfection, human beings go through alternating periods of light and darkness, now united with God, now separated from God. As soon as the ego is inflated, God disappears. So again we have to be self-cultivating and set our psychological household in order before God can appear again.

As a means of resolving this problem, there is another principle, which is one of self-opening to the divine. Some spiritual healers feel that when they heal, they have not done it actually, but that God has done it. This is a good and valuable attitude. When we feel we are not really healing others but are a medium or channel, we open ourselves so that the divine power can work through us and give us some help. This gives us protection and keeps our ego in its proper place. This further enforces the principle of non-attachment. By keeping alive this attitude of self-opening to a higher power, we do not become obsessed with ego-glorification or ego-exaltation.

Another principle of meta-therapy is that of the middle path. Our human mind has an automatic tendency to run to an extreme, either this way or that way. Some people in their desire to heal others may become more and more emotionally involved. But as they become too involved, they begin to lose perspective. They lose the kind of psychic distance which is necessary for maintaining a balanced outlook. And as soon as this happens, they succeed in opening the door to dark forces.

There are many examples of sincere people who, in their desire to help, take on the problems or diseases of others. In doing so, they allow their own lives to be cut short. If we become too emotionally involved in helping another person, we are going to be more and more affected and will not be able to help them heal authentically. In fact, we may do some harm. An over-concerned doctor or therapist spoils a client, just as an over-protective parent spoils a child or an over-eager teacher spoils a student. Instead of developing inner strength and power, the client may become increasingly dependent and emotionally crippled. He or she may lose the power of independent functioning in life. As a result of too much emotional involvement, we harm ourselves and we harm others.

Freud had a vivid awareness of the bad effects of emotional involvement, so he went to the other extreme and adopted more of an impersonal attitude. He would not even sit face-to-face with the client for fear of too much interpersonal contact. He asked questions and the client answered, but the client did not even see him. However, modern therapists have come to realize that this type of approach to healing is another extreme. After all, personal care and warmth really do have a healing power. When a client is deprived of personal warmth, care, and love, he or she is robbed of an important, effective therapeutic agency. In truth, love is actually the greatest healer of all.

Teachers and therapists can and should show love and concern, because this is human. They can show love, but the secret is also to maintain a psychic distance. In healing another, there is a need to combine love and respect. Respect helps to preserve the distance needed. When there is too much intimacy without the proper respect, rest assured that psychic damage will be the result.

Love combined with psychic distance and respect combined with warmth of heart can produce miraculous effects, not only between therapist and client, but in all human relations. When we succeed in applying genuine warmth along with objectivity, or love with non-attachment, we provide a fertile soil for the emergence of experiences which foster authentic and permanent healing and growth.

33

REFLECTIONS ON *THE TIBETAN BOOK OF THE DEAD*

Introduction

The Tibetan Book of the Dead is not a light book; it is difficult and profound. We have to do some digging in order to penetrate to its essential spiritual core, which has a powerful and provocative message.

The title may convey the suggestion that it is an otherworldly book, concerned with death and after-death. For a long time many people took it that way. Much of traditional religion, as you know, has been distinctly other-worldly. Orientation to life beyond the grave has been the primary concern of many religious and virtuous people. But when you look between the lines to find the underlying deep significance of this book, you will make a great discovery.

The discovery is that it embodies the art of living as well as the art of dying, and the two are inseparable. Only a person who lives well and successfully can die bravely and gracefully. Only the person who embraces death fearlessly can be guaranteed a higher mode of existence. Death is an essential ingredient of living, and this is true in more than one sense.

The book's essential significance is that it portrays the art of dying in such a way that death can be a passage to life everlasting. It also shows the art of living the life of immortality, rising above death and duality. As Hindus and Buddhists put it, we now live the life of *samsara*. However, the book shows the way of living the life of immortal existence here and now in the flesh, in this world. A great philosophical message of Mahayana Buddhism, on which this book is based, is that samsara is nirvana—which means that when we are illumined, heaven is not beyond or outside of us. Heaven is within us if we know the secret of heaven. So we are talking here of the art of living the life of heaven in the midst of this world in the full flood of activity that is samsara.

As an introduction, let me also clarify another point. There are two broad interpretations of the message of this book, which are not incompatible. They represent different aspects of the same total truth. The traditional interpretation is concerned with our mode of existence after death. What kind of existence is the soul that departs from the body likely to have after death? What are the different experiences and phases through which the departed soul goes in its postmortem journey? What can be done so that the soul can go right through the different phases of experience and achieve liberation instead of falling downward? The book is like a traveler's guide to the dying. They have to remember certain things which will help them and stand them in good stead in their journey in the other world through various planes of existence and consciousness, so that they can go straight to the ultimate destiny, the spiritual destiny of the human soul.

But there is another meaning of death in the figurative sense, which from the spiritual standpoint is even more important. Death also means death of the life of ignorance, egotism and suffering. To use the expression of this book, death is the death of the life of samsara. Out of the ruins of the death of the ego, an individual can be born on a higher plane of consciousness while living in this body—which is the life of nirvana, an illuminated condition. This interpretation is not concerned with the physical death of the body. The moment we die our ignorant life, we find ourself reborn on a higher plane of consciousness and begin to partake of the life eternal of the spirit.

Background

Tibetan mysticism, as it was developed by Padmasambhava, the great Buddhist teacher and philosopher in the eighth century AD, is based upon Mahayana Buddhism. Buddhism has two major wings. One is called Hinayana, the smaller vehicle, and the other, Mahayana, meaning the larger vehicle, the wider path. Evidently this expression 'Hinayana' is a little derogatory and was given to that particular school by the followers of Mahayana. Its proper name is Theravada, meaning the path or doctrine of the elders.

Each of these two schools is based upon a great statement of the master Buddha. Before his departure, Buddha turned to his disciples and gave them a precious piece of advice. He said, *'Atma dipa bhava.'* which means, 'Be a light unto yourself,' because the light of truth dwells within each one of us. So shine as a light, as a lamp unto yourself. Hinayana Buddhism stressed this precious piece of advice, interpreted it in a particular way and developed a philosophy which is called Theravada. Its central tenet is that every individual has to work out his own or her own salvation because nobody else can do it. This doctrine of spiritual self-help and self-development emphasizes the spiritual potential in everyone. Buddha dwells in the heart of all. So the fundamental spiritual task of every individual is to actualize this dormant potential and shine like a light.

This doctrine became a little aristocratic, because not all people are capable of self-help. The majority of people need help; we need to depend on others. Mahayana Buddhism looked to another great saying of the master, *'Karuna citta bhava,'* which means, 'Have compassion, love for others.' Both statements complement each other. The main point is that as you develop, as you attain spiritual experience, as you partake of the life eternal, do not keep it to yourself. This wonderful treasure of the spirit is something of which we ordinarily are completely unaware. So as you gradually attain spiritual awareness, share it. Spread the message to the whole world.

Each school has its merit. Theravada has the outstanding merit of purity. It wanted to preserve the original message of the Buddha. Mahayana wanted to help the masses of people in different countries. The difference is analogous to the distinction between a mountain stream and a big river. The mountain stream goes on leaping in the mountain ranges. The water is pure and crystal clear. No mud is there. But it is narrow, and it is not accessible to the people. Only the mountaineers who climb the mountains can drink from the stream. This is Theravada.

But a big river majestically flows from the high mountains through the plains. The waters become muddy, but the river is of immense service to the masses of people. This is Mahayana. It acquires some impurities in its course through different countries. Some of the original doctrines become diluted, but this is good for the people. In that sense, spiritual truth is sometimes like a very strong medicine. You have to dilute it to some extent so it can be useful to ordinary people.

The followers of Mahayana took their inspiration from the example set by the great master himself, Lord Buddha. Buddha attained enlightenment, *bodhi,* which is also nirvana, emancipation, liberation. Later on his biography says he was brought to the doorstep of *paranirvana*, the highest heaven, abode of supreme joy and transcendental bliss. Buddha paused, retraced his steps and said, 'No, I am not going to enter into this realm. If I do so, I shall attain the highest bliss for myself, but for all practical purposes I shall be lost to humanity.' Instead of entering, he took what is known as the *bodhisattva vow*. He said, 'Instead of entering into nirvana, I vow to dedicate myself to the service of humanity and all living creation. I shall not stop working until and unless all living beings are brought to the path of light, love and joy.'

This bodhisattva vow is known as *maha karuna* or universal compassion. As we evolve and discover the treasures of the spirit, the spirit of compassion dictates we share our experience with fellow beings. This is a basic tenet of Buddhism upon which *The Tibetan Book of the Dead* is based.

Another important tenet of Mahayana Buddhism is what I call a democratic conception of immortality. Universal compassion—*maha karuna*—is linked up logically with the democratic conception of immortality, which means that Buddha dwells in the heart of every human being. This implies that every human being has the potential of attaining salvation or entering into union with the Supreme, discovering ultimate reality and making an immediate encounter with Being, as an individual alone, face to face with the alone.

As Buddhism puts it, *bodhicitta*, the enlightened mind, is present in each one of us, and this ties up with the concept of universal compassion. Buddha was eager to make people aware of this inner spiritual potential of all human beings. This doctrine of *bodhicitta* goes back to the teaching of the great sages of the Upanishads. They proclaimed to the whole world this message of democratic immortality. There is an oft-quoted and memorable passage in the Upanishads in which a great sage is addressing the whole of humanity: 'Listen, please, oh mankind; you are in essence children of immortality; you belong to the kingdom of heaven. Beyond the realm of darkness there is one supreme truth which is self-shining like the sun.' That is the great message. All human beings as spiritual entities are children of immortality. This is their essence. Therefore, the fundamental spiritual task of life is to be what we essentially are. It is becoming what we are in Being. That is it. Not becoming something different. Not reaching out for something which is foreign to us; that is not spirituality. In spiritual striving, we discover our own true identity. That is the whole meaning and purpose of our spiritual search.

This is what I call the democratic theory of immortality. As you can see, it is the repudiation of the ordinary religious or theological doctrine of eternal damnation, or what I call the conditional theory of immortality. The view is that some people are destined to be immortal, to attain salvation, and some people are destined for other directions. If you fulfill certain conditions and accept certain creeds and doctrines, you go to heaven and attain salvation; if not, you are doomed.

Another tenet of Mahayana Buddhism, which is common to the Hindu-Buddhist tradition, is that the ultimate goal of our spiritual search is nirvana. Etymologically, nirvana means the blowing out or blown-out condition, the extinction of the four-fold fire in which we live our life of bondage. This four-fold fire of ignorance, passion, conflict, and agony is our normal existence. We suffer because we have forgotten the true essence of our being; we have forgotten what we essentially are. This loss of identity is at the root of our suffering. That is why all spiritual seeking begins with the questions, 'Who am I? Where did I come from? Where am I going? What is the true essence of my being?'

Negative emotions such as greed, envy, jealousy, hatred, and selfishness are conflicts within us. We have all kinds of inner conflicts—a desire conflict, a conflict of emotions, a conflict of impulses. From these we suffer pain, agony, anguish of the soul, and anxiety. Nirvana means the extinction of this fourfold fire. It does not refer to any supernatural place somewhere out of this material world. It refers to the loftiest level of consciousness known to humanity. Nirvana means wisdom, enlightenment, knowledge of our true self.

As soon as you know your true self and your position and function in the total scheme of existence, what happens? Your whole being is filled with the spirit of universal love because you know yourself as part and parcel of the whole, as one with others. You experience the oneness of all existence, the interdependence of all in the medium of the One. As the result of this experience, the spirit of love floods into your being. So wisdom, love, compassion, and peace that passes understanding are the characteristics of nirvana. It must be evident from what I have said that nirvana is something you can attain here and now in this life, in this world, living in this body. The moment you attain enlightenment, you attain nirvana and liberation.

This contrasts with the super-naturalistic conception of emancipation or liberation. In theology, the ordinary view of liberation is supernaturalistic. That is, if an individual lives right in this world, following certain creeds, after death he or she attains salvation and goes to a supernatural kingdom. But the doctrine of nirvana tells us the moment we experience inner illumination, here and now in this world, we attain liberation or salvation.

According to Hindu and Buddhist teaching, liberation is like awakening from a dream, suddenly discovering a new transcendental plane of consciousness. You wake up on that higher plane of consciousness and a veil of ignorance is lifted from your eyes. Nirvana is an experience beyond all dualities. The Sanskrit word for duality is '*dvaita.*' So long as we live in a state of ignorance, we are torn between dualities. In religion we have the dualities of heaven and hell, of gods and demons. In ethics we have the duality of right and wrong, of good and bad. Our mind is often torn between these. Nondualistic experience reveals the fundamental unity of existence, beyond all of these polarities.

Let me give you an illustration. A man dreams he has gone to Egypt and has fallen in love with a beautiful woman. He is in a palace having a wonderful time. Suddenly the scene changes, and he is lost in a dense forest. As he tries to grope out of the dark forest, he finds himself surrounded by ferocious beasts and serpents. He sees no way out. Just at the moment when he screams at the top of his voice, he wakes up and finds himself comfortably, securely lying on his bed. He experiences serenity and profound peace.

Ordinarily, our life is one of bondage. It is the life of mental polarities, of being torn between right and wrong, good and bad, heaven and hell, god and devil, love and hatred, life and death. In our ignorance we are oblivious to our true identity. When we experience illumination, we realize we have not become something different. Rather, we have become what we are, our true self.

Let me give you another analogy. Suppose you are looking for your glasses. You look in all the usual places, on your shelf, in your drawer, but nowhere do you find them. After a desperate search, suddenly you discover them. Where? On your eyes. You have already put them on. Sometimes we look, look, look for something, and suddenly we find it is already there; we just forgot. This is the experience of enlightenment. We are looking for God, searching for the truth, going everywhere desperately knocking at different doors. When we find it, we realize it always has been at the center of our being, as the consciousness of our consciousness.

Bardo Thodol

The Tibetan name of the book is *Bardo Thodol*. '*Bar*' means between, and '*do*' means two. So 'Bardo' means intermediate, in between two. '*Thodol*' comes from '*thos*' meaning hearing. Therefore, the book deals with the intermediate experiences. What are the intermediate experiences? Attaining salvation by hearing on the intermediate plane, on the bardo plane.

The obvious meaning of 'intermediate experiences' is between death and rebirth, so the book is concerned with giving instructions to the dying person. If a person hears these precious instructions given at the death bed, and remembers them, he or she will be helped through many different kinds of intermediate experiences and attain salvation and liberation. This is one interpretation. It is the art of dying right, so one can attain liberation through properly interpreting and evaluating the bardo plane experiences which take place after death and before rebirth. This is the exoteric meaning.

The esoteric meaning involves the 'intermediate experiences' which come after we transcend physical consciousness through meditation. If we meditate right and deeply, we transcend the limitations of the mental plane and rational mind. As we leave the rational mind behind and transcend our physical consciousness, we enter higher, deeper regions of consciousness, or the unconscious. From this standpoint the two mean the same thing. The higher ranges of consciousness in a sense are unconscious because we ordinarily are not conscious of them.

When we go into deep meditation, exceptional experiences may happen to us. These are bardo experiences, unusual transcendental and mystical experiences. If we understand them and evaluate them properly, it is good. If we are swept off our feet misinterpreting these mystical experiences, we get entangled and the prospect of liberation recedes farther from us. We come back again into the realm of ignorance or samsara. These intermediate experiences happen after individuals transcend physical consciousness and before they attain liberation or come back to physical consciousness, whether these experiences take place as a result of the time-tested method of meditation or as a result of taking drugs.

In this connection the word 'rebirth' can have several meanings. This is how to distinguish it from the word 'reincarnation.' Rebirth has a wider denotation. It means reincarnation and it may mean other things as well.

Reincarnation means that after death the soul departs from the body, goes through different experiences and then comes back again and takes another body. It is reborn on the material plane. It is reincarnated in the flesh.

Rebirth may have two other additional meanings. By the grace of God, instead of coming back to the material plane, the soul may continue to dwell on some subtle plane of consciousness, on some other domain of the spirit. It is reborn there and begins to function on a subtle, higher plane of awareness.

Further, rebirth means being reborn on a higher plane of consciousness and becoming illuminated while living in the body. You no longer live and function on the lower material, physical consciousness. Of course, you still live in the body. Inwardly you have a vast expansion of consciousness, and enlarged and enriched awareness. You are a new person.

Now let me take up the meaning of 'thos,' because hearing plays an important part in our spiritual growth, according to *The Tibetan Book of the Dead*. The Sanskrit word for hearing is *sravana,* and this doctrine also has been discussed elaborately in the Upanishads. The Vedantic method of spiritual growth means going through different stages of *sravana, manana* and *nididhyasana.*

Suppose one day you feel that in spite of all the material possessions you have in life, basically something is missing. The spiritual hunger of the soul comes to the front of your consciousness and you begin to feel a deep spiritual longing and passion for the absolute. What do you do? You want to follow the right path which will satisfy this yearning of the soul. You find a teacher, a spiritual preceptor or guide, who can tell you the right path to follow. The first stage is *sravana*—hearing, reading, being guided, exposing yourself to the word of truth. You listen to what your teacher has to say, and you read books of spiritual wisdom and inspiration. When you hear with a yearning soul, the right seed is planted in your fertile mind.

In *manana* you begin to think. As a result of hearing, your soul has been impregnated with the truth and you begin to think about its implications, its practical bearings, its significance. Questions and doubts arise in your mind. The teacher does not discourage this. A guru is not a dictator, just as God is not a dictator. God is a lover, a persuasive agency. A true teacher is also a persuasive agency and a not a coercive force. When you have doubts, questions, you need to tell your teacher without hiding or pretending anything. If you do not know, you do not know. The teacher understands this. This is the dialogue between the guru and the disciple. The teacher has all the patience of a parent in dealing with students.

After going through this *manana* stage of thinking, you become a philosopher in that you are organizing your ideas into a systematized world view. Yet even this is not enough. You may have become a philosopher, but you have not yet become a God-realized person. There is still a distance to go. In the next step of *nididhyasana* you have to meditate and go deeper into your being. You have to transform your intellectual understanding of the truth into a personal, direct, immediate, luminous apprehension of the truth or of God or of the absolute. Only meditation can do this.

Sravana can produce instant realization in some cases. Suppose an individual has already done a lot of thinking and reading. She has been striving for spiritual truth for a long time. She has been evolving, knowingly or unknowingly. She may have been practicing yoga without knowing it. She has come now to the right point. Her soul is ripe and she meets a teacher, as her inner being is ready for the truth. Just at the right moment, the teacher utters the word of truth to her. Just one simple statement, and immediately the student attains salvation or liberation.

Why does this happen? Plato's theory of reminiscence says that before the soul is born in this flesh, it has a glorious vision of truth. But when the soul is incarnated in the flesh, it forgets its previous experience. Eventually somebody tells him or her the truth, and immediately the person remembers. This is called the doctrine of reminiscence. As soon as a person remembers, he or she attains salvation.

However, mere experience is not enough for liberation. Experience must be evaluated properly; otherwise there is no salvation. You can go through some ecstatic, paranormal experiences, but if you do not understand them, there is no liberation. Over and over again a teacher says, 'Recognize this to be so and so.' In other words the instruction is to remember what the teacher has told you.

The whole expression, '*Bardo Thodol*,' therefore signifies

attaining liberation by hearing on the bardo or intermediate plane. The book discusses the important of higher, summit experience. But hearing is no less important. Hearing means proper recognition, interpretation, and evaluation of that experience on the basis of what you heard from the guru. In the absence of proper evaluation and recognition, the experience may not mean anything to you. You may come by some wonderful experience, miss its important significance, and therefore let it go.

This point has been developed highly in Kashmir Saivism in India. This is called the doctrine of recognition or *pratyavishna*. Let me give you an illustration. A child playing on a river bank suddenly finds a precious diamond and he is intrigued with it. He plays with the diamond, but after a while he gets tired and throws it into the river. What has happened? The child does not know its value.

By the grace of God you can have a diamond, some wonderful ecstatic experience of a lofty type, but you do not know what it is. You toy with this experience for a while and pass by without profiting or incorporating it into the texture of your psyche. Then the whole thing is lost.

Another child in the course of playing and wondering finds some colorful, fascinating pieces of glass. He is intrigued by them; he brings them home and treasures them. What is happening? He is fascinated by the colors and treasures them, but what he is treasuring is trash, nothing of much value.

This is relevant also to those who stumble into different experiences by taking drugs. If they are not fortunate or choose unfavorable circumstances, these experiences can be misleading and harmful. But if they are fortunate and use a drug under proper guidance, they may encounter some spiritual dimension. They will not benefit unless they recognize the experience for what it is and properly evaluate it, rejecting that which is irrelevant and assimilating what is relevant.

In the course of our search and exploration of the inner being, we may come across certain experiences which are fascinating and intriguing. They may not be the highest kind, but we may treasure them. We can recognize them properly if we remember what the teacher has instructed. We reach illumination on the basis of proper evaluation of different mystical experiences.

Thus we see the great importance of this doctrine of hearing. As we go through this or that experience we are asked to remember the characteristics of the diamond and the characteristics of a piece of colored glass. If we remember right, we will be able to recognize and evaluate. On the basis of such evaluation, we advance until we reach the highest goal of enlightenment.

Nirvana

Let us now consider the fundamental concepts which are at the foundation of the book. The ultimate goal of all spiritual effort — whether when we are living in this material world, or after death — is union with Being. We sprang into existence out of the bosom of the Supreme and our ultimate goal is to be reunited with the Supreme. That is the meaning of the word yoga — union. And this is the content of what Buddhism calls nirvana.

Let us look at the meaning of nirvana from different angles. As I said before, the literal meaning of nirvana is the 'blown out' condition or extinction. Many people think that this means evaporation into nothingness, and then they think, what sort of ideal is that? Then when we connect it to the Buddhist concept of *sunyata*, absolute void, it makes us doubly sure that nirvana is just nothingness. When we try to understand it through the analysis of verbal expression, we think that through meditation and spiritual unfoldment, eventually we are absorbed or annihilated in the absolute void. That creates a negative image in our mind. Some Western scholars have defined nirvana as the heaven of nothingness. The inevitable conclusion has been drawn that Buddhism is a form of nihilism, it teaches annihilation. We see how words can be tyrannical and misleading.

Let us try to find out the true meaning of nirvana and sunyata. 'Absolute void' means that ultimate reality is beyond all forms, images, and concepts of the human mind. When you reach that state of awareness all of your previous notions about God and soul are left far behind. Your previous conceptions are shattered. You discover a kind of reality which is unspeakable, which is incommunicable. From the standpoint of the little human mind, it is like an absolute void, the void of the sky, boundless blue, beyond all limited forms and images. When you reach nirvana, when you make an immediate experiential encounter with that immeasurable reality, you get annihilated, yes. Your little mind is transcended, and your egocentric existence is liquidated.

We can use an analogy of a wax man who wants to find out the essence of fire. He is fascinated by a big fire, so he goes close to it and pretty soon melts away. Who is going to find out what? Pushing the analogy a little further, out of the melting of the exterior wax emerges a man of gold, whom fire cannot burn.

This can give us a better picture of what happens. Through spiritual experience we enter into the cosmic flame of Being. Our egocentric existence, our ignorance and lack of knowledge of the truth, are melted away in contact with the fire of knowledge, the cosmic flame of truth. The wax of ignorance, the ego, melts away. Our wax body, the ignorant body, is annihilated. Yet out of the destruction of this ignorant body emerges the real self, the authentic spiritual being that we are, and which cannot be burned and destroyed.

There can be no true rebirth or liberation, without the liquidation of the ignorant, egocentric personality. This is the esoteric meaning also of the symbol of crucifixion and resurrection in Christian mysticism. Without crucifixion of the ignorant, particular being, there cannot be the resurrection of the eternal, universal being. The two go together. No resurrection without crucifixion. No liberation without liquidation of the ignorant self. This is the meaning of annihilation here.

Buddhist philosophy has made a good analysis of the nature of this ignorant self which is liquidated on reaching spiritual realization. According to Hindu-Buddhist philosophy, this ignorant, egocentric self is composed of four factors. Or, to put it another way, when nirvana is experienced, the four fires that cause suffering are extinguished so that peace is attained. Our little self is composed of these four fires.

These fires are the four constituent elements of our egocentric existence. The first is *avidya*, ignorance. Ignorance here means metaphysical ignorance — of the meaning of life. In living our lives in ignorance of the true meaning of existence, we grope in darkness and suffer. This is liquidated when we attain nirvana. We gain wisdom, an unclouded vision of the truth and of the meaning of existence.

The second fire is *asvida*, egotism, the small, selfish 'I.' Everyone says 'I am' — 'I am doing this, I am doing that, I am searching for happiness, I am striving for knowledge or power.' 'I am' is the common factor to all our speech. It is the centralizing principle of all our thoughts and activities. The little 'I' pins us down and lowers us in a small domain. When this gets dissolved in nirvana we have cosmic consciousness, an expanding consciousness. We pull down the barriers and experience a vast enlargement of our being.

Another element of our egocentric existence is *donda*, meaning conflict and duality. As psychotherapists tell us, most of our suffering is due to inner, unresolved conflicts of which we are often not fully aware. These conflicts cripple us and prevent a free flow of energy within us. When this fire gets dissolved, we experience the annihilation of all conflicts and the release of tremendous creative energy which lies dormant within us. When we rise above conflict, we experience a profound peace and serenity of mind.

The fourth fire is *dukkha*, meaning sorrow. *Dukkha* as sorrow is the pleasure-pain polarity, and from this wider standpoint, even our pleasures are sorrow. Buddha maintained that life is compounded with pains and pleasures, but both are evanescent. They do not last or endure. We go through the tears and laughter of our ordinary existence, but these fluctuate continually, leaving us in deeper sorrow. As the Upanishads say, only that bliss is real bliss which is eternal.

When we attain nirvana and these fluctuating pains and pleasures, tears and laughter are transcended, we experience what Buddhism calls *mahasukkha*, eternal and supreme joy. In Hindu philosophy it is called *ananda*, supreme bliss which is beyond the fluctuating polarity of pain and pleasure, joy and sorrow. How can it be eternal? Because, the great sages who have had this experience point out that this state is not dependent upon any external object.

Our ordinary pleasures of life are dependent upon external things. Let us say you crave a dish of ice cream. When you get it, you experience pleasure. But if somebody snatches it away from you, you feel pain. Here pain and pleasure depend upon an external thing. If you get something you want, you experience pleasure. If you are deprived of it, you experience pain. Whether painful or pleasurable, your experience is object-dependent.

Ananda is not object-centered. It is intrinsic to your very being. When you discover the inmost center of your own being, joy freely flows from the depths of your existence. Just by being what you are, you experience that joy. It is free and spontaneous and intrinsic to your whole being. Therefore, nobody can take it away from you. If anybody is to take it away from you, he or she has to destroy you.

Now we see the true meaning of extinction. Nirvana means the extinction of our egocentric existence which is composed of these four constituent elements. The transcendence or destruction of these four elements naturally gives rise to their spiritual counterparts. When *avidya* is destroyed, you experience wisdom. When *asvida* is destroyed, you experience a vast expansion of consciousness characterized by compassion and love. When *donda* is eliminated, you experience profound peace. When *dukkha* is destroyed, you experience supreme and eternal joy. That is the four-fold content of nirvana.

How is nirvana or mystic experience related to our sense of responsibility? In our social life, ethics demands that we have a strong sense of responsibility and duty. In discussions of the highest spiritual experience, it has been said that individuals go beyond all moral sense, beyond good and bad. Some people get the impression that since such individuals go beyond moral distinctions, then they have no responsibility anymore. Let us clarify this point.

There are three kinds of responsibility. One is socially conditioned responsibility. All of us are born in a particular social group or community. Every community has its own social-ethical mores and norms. This is right. This is wrong. This is good. This is bad. These ethical mores differ from community to community. Naturally we are conditioned by a particular society's existing ethical norms, and we have some ideas about right and wrong, good and bad. Based upon this socialized moral consciousness, we have a sense of responsibility. This is a conformist type of responsibility.

To give an example, let us say you obtain a new job in an office. Pretty soon you find the whole atmosphere of the office is uncongenial for you. You need the money, but you feel like a fish out of water. You do not like the boss and feel he is domineering. You do not seem to get along with the people. They have a completely different set of ideas from yours. They do not understand you, and you do not understand them. However, the office situation has its norms. You have a set of responsibilities to your boss and co-workers. This is conformist responsibility. If you want to keep your job, you must discharge your obligations there.

As long as you are there, you have to do justice to your sense of responsibility. Yet that responsibility has no absolute value. It has a relative value. If you choose to be in that job, you have to fulfill your responsibility. But you may decide that this is not the right job, place or atmosphere for you. You may try to get out of the whole place, the sooner, the better.

Then there is compulsive responsibility. Some people are always attempting to do something good. They are the busy do-gooders. They have a compulsion to fill up their minds with all kinds of responsibilities. This behavior may be an obsession, an inner compulsion, even though their behavior may look good. In their eagerness to do good, sometimes they are harming others. They spoil the game by being over-eager.

Psychologically, these people are running away from their own selves. They have not been able to come to terms with or face their inner being, so they run away by forgetting themselves in external activity. This is a neurotic kind of responsibility. True responsibility is not a compulsion. It will not be felt as a noose around your neck always dragging you on.

Then there is another kind of responsibility, which is free and spontaneous. This is when you no longer feel under a compulsion to do something, nor that your sense of duty or responsibilty is imposed by society. It is when you feel like doing something for your neighbor or friend just out of the fullness of love and joy in your heart — not that you have to do it, but you enjoy it. This is the responsibility of freedom, the responsibility of love, the responsibility of joy.

When you understand these different types of responsibility, you will understand how we transcend compulsive responsibility when we attain nirvana. We no longer have compulsion. Nor do we feel our duties are external or imposed upon us from the outside by some authority. When we attain nirvana, we experience the spirit of love and compassion. From the standpoint of Buddhist spirituality, this feeling of love and compassion is not just a sentiment or emotion; it is a function of liberation. You feel love because love is based upon your very being. You experience the indwelling presence of the One in all. You feel yourself in others and others in you. Love is the emotional tool of your ontological experience of the oneness of all existence. You feel like embracing the whole world. There is a profound responsibility in this experience. When you love your fellow beings, you want to do something for them, to share what you have with others.

Finally, there are three kinds of nirvana. In his book, *Peak Experience and Religion*, Abraham Maslow has distinguished low and high nirvana. I would like to add another. Nirvana, as I said, is experience of the oneness of existence, a realization that we all live and move and have our being in the medium of one cosmic reality. It is an experience of oneness.

There are different kinds of experiences of oneness. For example, at night when it is pitch dark, you do not distinguish one thing from another. Everything around you is enveloped in darkness. All differences are submerged in the darkness of night. You can have a feeling of oneness there. The German philosopher Hegel said that at night all cows are black. That is because blackness is all that you see.

In our psychic life, by some means or other, we may go back to what Freud called an oceanic feeling, a feeling of all being one submerged in the ocean. No differences exist there, or one is not able to distinguish one thing from another clearly. This is characteristic of the mind of the infant. It is a state of unspoiled innocence and has a joyful characteristic to it. But the trouble is that this is a primitive experience of oneness where intellectual distinctions have not yet emerged. Ethical distinctions do not exist properly. Let me call it the nirvana of night where distinctions are not distinctive, *per se*. It is a regression, a going backward.

Another kind of nirvana is the nirvana of the dazzling sun. The night goes and the sun appears. You stand in the open and the sun is up in the sky showing its brilliant light. You look at the sun with a sense of wonder. As you keep looking, your eyes are dazzled. You become so overwhelmed that you see only the sun and nothing else. Everything else disappears from your field of vision. When you attain this experience you feel Being alone is there and the whole world is unreal.

The highest kind of nirvana is mature nirvana. After you look at the sun for some time, your eyes outgrow the stunning and overwhelming effect. You look around and see things exactly as they are in the light of the sun. It is a normal, easy experience of things in all their diversity. You see things as they are in the light of truth. When the experience of the sun is assimilated into your being, you become spiritually mature and begin to understand things in their unique diversity in the master light.

This is what the Zen master meant when he said that first you see rivers and mountains. As you inwardly advance on the spiritual path, you may come to a point where you have a transcendental awareness, and for the time being, rivers and mountains disappear. The infinite diversities of the world vanish from your field of vision. You experience *sunyata* or nothingness. Once you have assimilated thoroughly the content of this transcendental consciousness, you become natural in your vision and integrated and mature in your understanding. You see rivers as rivers again, mountains as mountains again, everything just as it is in the light of the supreme truth that you have seen.

Nirvana, therefore, is not just a kind of subjective, delightful experience within you. Of course, it is full of joy, beauty and love, but there is much more to it. Nirvana also means ontological insight, understanding of the meaning of life and existence, understanding of the infinite diversities of this world.

Nirvana is incomplete without this insight. So it is subjective experience which is blissful plus philosophical, ontological understanding of the meaning of the whole world.

The Logic of Mysticism

Further understanding of the fundamental technique and logic of mysticism or the logic of the infinite can help us to unravel the mysteries within *The Tibetan Book of the Dead*. In the West, we are familiar with Aristotelian logic and understand things in terms of this. So often in reading Eastern mysticism we feel bewildered as it seems to be full of paradoxes. But if we have a key to its meaning, it begins to make sense again.

What is Aristotelian logic? It is the logic of either-or. We use it to make clear-cut distinctions and then consider which one is true. This is the intellectual approach. God is. God is not. These are opposite statements. People choose different camps, and a lot of heat is generated but often without any light.

When we read a book such as *The Tibetan Book of the Dead*, we find an avoidance of this kind of debate. Most of Western metaphysics and theology is based upon the application of this Aristotelian logic of either-or to the discussion of spiritual and philosophical problems. Either this is true or it is false. If somebody tells us that maybe both are true, we get puzzled. How can both be true?

There is a plane of consciousness in which both of these opposite statements may be true. We discover a wonderful viewpoint from which we can reconcile and harmonize apparently conflicting ideas. This spiritual standpoint gives us the key to the reconciliation of all opposites. We understand the significance of the great law of the unity of all opposites, which is God. In God, all opposites are harmonized. All discords and contradictions are reconciled in the nature of ultimate reality.

Does God exist? Does God not exist? God is. God is not. There is a polarization of human thought about this and the debate goes on. There can be no end to this debate if we cannot rise above this polarity and attain a higher plane of consciousness. From the spiritual standpoint, both of these opposites are true depending on what we mean. The main question is what do we understand by *God*? And what do we understand by *exist*? For example, by God some people mean a great grandfather type of magnified human form with a long, white beard and flowing garment dwelling somewhere up there in outer space, controlling the whole world from his golden throne with a golden rod in his hand. Those who accept our present-day scientific, philosophical and psychological knowledge would say that such a God does not exist. This is a concept of God in the image of humans. Instead of understanding God as the creator of humans, such people conceive of God as a creature of human imagination.

This is what Spinoza meant when he said that humans, being who they are, imagine God in their own image and think of God as a colossal human being endowed with excellent human qualities magnified to the nth degree. By the same token, if an elephant had imagination, it would conceive of God as the biggest elephant in the world. If a lion had imagination, it would conceive of God as the biggest and strongest lion in the world. So when we think of God as the biggest human in the world, in that sense, God does not exist.

The outcome of the debate also depends on what we mean by 'exist.' What do we mean when we say the table exists? We mean it occupies a definite position in the space-time continuum. It is out there in space, in time at such a distance from me or you. Occupying space-time is what we mean by existence. Just think about it. In this sense, certainly God does not exist. If there is any reality in God at all, God is not either in space or time. So from this standpoint, the idea that God exists is wrong.

However, if we go into the deeper realm of meaning, then certainly God exists. If, for example, by God we mean the unity of such higher values as truth, beauty, love, and peace, then God is the reality of all realities. We consider our own lives real in proportion to our approximation to such higher values. A great scientist may sacrifice his whole life in the pursuit of truth. A great artist may dedicate her whole life in pursuit of beauty. God is the value of all values, the unity of all these values, and in this sense the real of all that is real.

If we have the right understanding, God is real. If we do not have the right understanding, God is unreal. Our consciousness is the most important fact to consider here. The essence of mysticism lies in the inner growth of consciousness and a transformation of our whole outlook and perspective. So long as those are not there, it is all words and words and words, or in the language of Shakespeare, sound and fury signifying nothing.

What about a soul? Is there one or not? In the same way, it all depends on what we understand. This debate has been going on for centuries, and the only way to solve this problem is to rise up to a level of consciousness where both of these opposites can be reconciled. In a sense, every person has a soul, and in a sense, no soul.

In Buddhism, there is a theory called the doctrine of no soul or *anatta*. Let me briefly tell you what it means. One time Buddha gave this analogy. There was a man who was very excited and kept repeating loudly, 'I have fallen in love with the most beautiful woman in the land.' A passerby was impressed by the sight and inquired who the woman was. The man said, 'I don't know because I have not seen her.' But then he started exclaiming again, 'I have fallen in love with the most beautiful woman in the land!'

Buddha said this is the attitude of most people regarding the concept of their soul. They go into raptures over the immortality of the soul, but if you ask them what the soul is, they are dumbfounded. They do not know. Have you seen your soul? What is it? Can you describe it?

The man has fallen in love with the *idea* of the most beautiful woman. In the same way we fall in love with the idea of the immortal soul without seeing or knowing the soul. To fall in love with a mere idea, without grasping the reality behind it is a pathetic condition. The job of a spiritual teacher is to help turn the idea into reality.

Is there a soul or not? If we define the soul as an unknown spiritual substance within us, which is like a spiritual atom existing all by itself, then there is no such thing. In modern science the ancient concept of the atom as a self-existent entity has also been rejected. What is called atom is a whirlpool in a field of energy vibrations. There is no self-contained atom. In the same way, the ancient conception of the soul as a spiritual atom, contained within itself, sufficient onto itself, is wrong. Nothing can exist like that in this world. Everything is interconnected and interdependent. There is no self-contained entity. This idea of the soul has made some spiritual seekers selfish in their seeking, concerned only with their personal salvation.

But if by the soul we mean our sense of higher values or the spirit of love which is there in each of us, then there is a soul. Or if by the soul we mean our spiritual essence as an active center of the one Supreme Being, interconnected with all other spiritual centers, then there is a soul. The right understanding comes when we have this growth of consciousness which is the goal of true spiritual search and practice. We organize our life on the basis of love and selfless action, with that one end in view — a gradual evolution of our inner being, an unfolding of our outlook and a transforming of our perspective.

The Three Phases of Bardo

Let me briefly discuss the three phases of bardo experience, whether we understand it esoterically or exoterically. They are called *Chikhai bardo, Chonyid bardo* and *Sidpa bardo*. For the first four days the soul goes through the *Chikhai bardo*. Then from the fifth to fourteenth days it goes through the *Chonyid bardo*, and from the fifteenth day onward it goes through the *Sidpa bardo*.

First is the *Chikhai bardo*. As you step out of your physical consciousness, as a result of a pull of the higher consciousness upon you or through divine grace, you step into the *Chikhai bardo* and suddenly have the unclouded vision of the clear light of the infinite. This is the first experience. Before this we were in our physical consciousness and our outlook was limited. We were oppressed by so many things which are depressing in the world around us. Suddenly we step into a higher realm.

According to the book's theory, what happens to you as a result of this experience depends upon your karma. Many things can happen, and you can have different reactions to these experiences depending on your state of evolution, your readiness and your inner psychical preparation. Some catch a glimpse of this clear light, but do not think much of it; they bypass or ignore it. They experience a drowsy condition during these four days because they do not understand the significance of it. They see but still they do not see.

For example, it is like during the night as you are asleep and having a lot of dreams, some good ones and some bad ones. When the dawn comes, the sunlight enters your window and strikes you on your bed. As the sunlight strikes you, you wake up and catch a glimpse of it, but you are drowsy. The sun's light is uncomfortable to you. So you turn around and go to sleep again.

This is what happens. Some souls may catch a glimpse of the clear light of the infinite, but they are not ready for it; they cannot look at it. They feel uncomfortable so enter into a dreamy condition again. Others become dazzled and overpowered, blinded to such an extent that everything else disappears from their view.

Still others remember the instructions of the teacher. They see it and know this is their glimpse of the supreme truth, which is the ground of all existence. On the basis of this recognition, they begin to see the rest of the world with the help of the sunlight. This is a state of liberation. This is instant *satori*, which happens to those who are ready for it.

Plato in his *Republic* describes this same phenomenon in the simile of the cave. People dwelling in a vast, dark cave were chained hand and foot and with their faces turned to the wall, which was opposite to the mouth of the cave. By the opening of the cave was a highway with people going by. But the cave dwellers were living in darkness and did not know what was going on in the outer world. They thought the cave was the whole world, and they saw only the shadows of the people and animals on the walls. However, one day one of them was fortunate enough to break loose from the chains and saw the opening of the cave. As he came out, he discovered a whole new world of joy and beauty. This is the clear light. When we are ready, we discover a whole new world and become liberated.

A wonderful passage in the Upanishads says, 'This Atman, the truth, cannot be known by mere verbal discussions, nor can it be achieved by the weak mind.' In order to know the truth in its full glory, you have to strengthen and prepare yourself physically, mentally, and emotionally. 'Those who are not ready cannot bear the impact of that supreme light.'

Those who go through this period in a dreamy condition, feeling uncomfortable with the powerful light, enter into the next phase of the *Chonyid bardo*, the realm of hallucinations and dualities. This is the realm of heaven and hell, of opposites. For some time you may go through delightful experiences and see visions of peaceful deities, angels, gods, and goddesses. Suddenly it may all change and you may be exposed to wrathful deities and terrifying demons. You may go through a hellish experience. These are the polarities of experience of the *Chonyid bardo*.

According to *The Tibetan Book of the Dead*, even during this phase you can be liberated if you remember the instructions of your teacher. You understand that all these visions, whether gods or demons, actually are projections of the inner psyche. If you remember that these are not objective realities, you can maintain your inner peace and strength in the midst of all the changing experiences and become liberated. Otherwise your soul is oppressed by these experiences.

If you do not become liberated during this period, you enter *Sidpa bardo* from the fifteenth day onward. This is the realm of the Freudian unconscious. When you enter into *Sidpa bardo* you begin to have sexual images predominate the mind. Still if you correctly remember, even at this stage, the instruction of the teacher as to what is happening, you have a chance of liberation. But if you do not remember, you are reborn into the material plane again.

According to the exoteric meaning, the last vision in the *Sidpa bardo* is a man and woman in union. Then the soul enters the mother's womb and is reborn. From the esoteric standpoint, you have different types of sexual visions and images and come back again into physical consciousness and an ordinary life in which your actions and thoughts are largely determined by unconscious motivations such as the sex drive, the power drive and the ego drive.

Therefore, the next step from *Sidpa bardo* is to return to the routine life of samsara, or polarities. But even when one returns to the routine life, there is no need for despair. This is the great message of the masters. A central message of the book is to conquer the three 'd's' that torment us — namely death, duality, and despair. Although you may miss all chances of liberation and re-enter the routine life of ignorance, samsara is another opportunity for further development. You start life again, afresh, and begin to cultivate spiritual virtues. You try to reorganize your life toward the attainment of the ultimate goal, nirvana. Eastern mystics do not believe in the eternal damnation of any soul. All human beings are viewed as spiritual entities involved in a process of evolution. So, sooner or later, by going through different kinds of experiences, all human beings are destined to reach blissful union with the Supreme Being.

The Great Mantra

In order to appreciate fully the message of *The Tibetan Book of the Dead*, it is important to understand the spiritual significance of the great Tibetan mantra, 'Om mani padme hum.' In Tibetan Buddhism, this important mantra is the song of the Tibetan soul. Everywhere, throughout the length and breadth of the country, all those who are religious-minded continually repeat this mantra. The whole atmosphere reverberates with it.

A mantra can be important for meditation. It has been described as a golden thread or a golden rope upon which you can climb steadily to a higher level of consciousness. '*Man*' means to think. Man, the thinking being, perhaps has come from this. '*Tra*' is instrument. So '*mantra*' means the instrument of thinking. As the focal point of your meditation, a mantra can channel your psychic energy and elevate your consciousness. Through such intensification of your psychic energy, you achieve a spiritual breakthrough and soar beyond the utmost boundaries of the mind and intellect.

A great Tibetan yogi who had been practicing yoga for a long time had attained illumination and great yogic power. He tried his best to initiate his old mother into yoga, but she was busy in worldly affairs and had no interest in meditation or yoga. The only thing in which he succeeded was to get his mother to repeat the mantra, '*Om mani padme hum.*' Every day she used to repeat this mantra a little.

In due time, she passed away. Because her karma was not too good, she found herself in the abode of darkness and was miserable there, surrounded by malevolent, tormenting forces. With his yogic vision, her son could see the situation. Moved by compassion, he traveled to the nether world and was startled to see the condition of his mother. As soon as she saw her son coming to her, the mother remembered the mantra and started repeating it. According to this legend, immediately a column of light descended from above, and she was emancipated from hell.

This may sound strange and incredible. How can a mantra have such power? If we remember the psychological truth about heaven and hell, we can see this is possible. Heaven and hell are psychological experiences. Individuals are in hell when they forget the spiritual essence of their being. When they are estranged, they are in a realm of darkness; they suffer and are tormented. They are in despair. But as soon as they utter the mantra and remember the true essence of their being, the despair and suffering disappear.

It is like a child who experiences a nightmare and is groaning. The mother, upon hearing the groaning, comes and says, 'You are having a bad dream. Wake up! You are with me.' As this is heard, the child immediately wakes up from the bad dream and the hell disappears.

While living in the world, we go through heavenly conditions and hellish conditions. We go through emotional fluctuations. Sometimes, for example, we find ourselves on top of the world and full of self-confidence. When that mood passes, we may enter into the depths of depression. It may seem the whole world has lost its charm and the ground has been cut from under our feet. The point is that however low we are in our emotional condition, a mantra can give us a lift. If we remember and practice it, we allow the mantra to become a dynamic force in our consciousness. It can have a wonderful influence.

For example, sometimes people may feel life is meaningless. They may be so much in despair that they feel like committing suicide. A mantra can change that state of darkness. Also, in our life we often come up against undivine, hostile forces conspiring to destroy us. Life is a constant struggle against the forces of ignorance, death, and destruction. A mantra can give us divine armoring.

With the mantra, '*Om mani padme hum*,' Buddha reminded everybody that in essence we are *mani padma* — pure consciousness and pure love. Let me go into a detailed explanation of this mantra, because it is inherently important in this book and becomes especially efficacious when we utter it with attention to its meaning.

First is '*Om*' which is also sometimes written as '*Aum*.' According to the sages, this is the most sacred sound symbol of the supreme truth and covers the whole spectrum of sound variations. This is the original creative word which contains in seed form all potentialities of expression. As the creative word, it implies the Supreme Being.

The three letters stand for the fundamental Buddhist trinity. Philosophical importance is attached to the number three. In all religions in some form or other, three is expressive of the mystery of existence. In Christianity we have the trinity — God the father, God the son, and God the holy spirit. In Hinduism we have Brahma, Iswara, and Atma. In Buddhism the Buddha essence as ultimate reality has three forms of manifestation, namely, *Dharmakaya Buddha, Sambhogakaya Buddha* and *Nirmanakaya Buddha*. These three also relate to the three phases of experience of the soul.

Dharmakaya means reality as the eternal truth, as the transcendental silence, that which is inexhaustible and unfathomable, that which shines from everlasting to everlasting.

Sambhogakaya is the spirit of universal love, joy, and beauty, which are interrelated. These are the elements of supreme spiritual bliss. *Sambhoga* means spiritual enjoyment. It is interesting to note here that when you have a vision of the light and the truth, you feel within yourself love and compassion. Light and love go together.

Nirmana means constructed or constructed body. *Nirmanakaya* happens when you have a vision of the truth, the infinite light and the experience of love, joy, and beauty in your heart. You are reborn. You are no longer the same person as you were before. You cannot be. You are completely changed, with an entirely new personality. You have a new body which you receive from God.

The trinity here is truth, love and transformation. After the experience of truth and love, you go through a profound transformation of your entire being.

So you begin with 'Om' in the mantra. By uttering this, you reach out for union with ultimate reality. You express your deep spiritual aspiration for union with the divine. The most important characteristic of human nature is that we have a power to transcend ourselves. We have an urge within ourselves to reach out for something higher and greater and nobler than ourselves. The human being is a sythesis of the actual and the ideal, and we cannot be satisfied with our bare actuality. That is why John Stuart Mill said it is better to be a Socrates dissatisfied than a pig satisfied. Animals are satisfied with their condition. As humans, our life is glorious because we are not happy with our state of imperfection. Our glory lies in our divine discontent.

'*Mani*' literally means a jewel. In many contexts and especially in this mantra, '*mani*' also implies love and compassion. Love is visualized as a dynamic, creative element in us. When we experience love, we are not passive anymore. We want to serve those whom we love.

Love, as Buddha has explained, has four aspects. *Metta* means the spirit of universal brotherhood, friendship. *Mudita* means participation in the happiness and joy of others, which is not easy. Why is it not easy? Participation in the sorrow of others is easy compared to participation in their joys. When we see other people in distress, we have spontaneous empathy. But when somebody suddenly attains great glory, we often cannot wholeheartedly participate because of the great monster envy which dwells in the human heart. Until and unless we have the true spirit of love, it is difficult for us to participate in the joy and happiness of others.

Karuna is participation in the sorrow and suffering of others and trying to do something to relieve their distress.

Upekkha is indifference to the shortcomings of others. When we do not like people, we have a tendency to magnify their defects and shortcomings. When we love people, their defects do not matter that much. We ignore them, because who does not have shortcomings? True love alone can ignore the shortcomings of others. In the absence of true love, we do not see the good qualities; only the bad ones loom large in our mental vision.

Next is *'padme.' Padma* literally means lotus, which is the symbol of divine knowledge. So *'mani padme'* is the unity of love and wisdom, which is the essence of the spirit.

Padma also means the spiritual center in our own being. The heart center is called the heart lotus, the lotus in the heart. When this center in our psycho-physical system opens, we experience divine love and joy. That is why we say we realize God in our heart. Yogis tell us, 'Concentrate on your heart center.' Why? Because that is the center of love and devotion within us, symbolized by the lotus.

When our enlightened mind pierces the heart center and it opens, we become Buddha. Everyone has this potentiality. Buddhism tells us that Buddha dwells in the heart of each one of us. Buddha means the unity of wisdom and compassion. That is the substance of which our soul is made. When the heart center is opened, we become aware of the true spiritual essence of our being. We are enlightened and experience profound joy and beatitude. So that is one meaning of the mantra: 'May my heart center be opened by the power of consciousness so that I can attain enlightenment and experience beatitude.'

The meaning of '*Hum*' in this context is, 'May I be united with.' So another meaning of the mantra is, 'May I be united with the Supreme Being which is the unity of love and wisdom.' Another meaning is, 'May I express the glory of the infinite in my life and in human relations.' The spiritual ideal here has two sides. One is, 'May I be united with the Supreme.' Another is, 'May I manifest the glory of the Supreme in life.'

We have two movements of consciousness in our spiritual growth and unfoldment. As we practice meditation, we increasingly soar up to higher levels of consciousness. That is the ascending movement of our mind. Through spiritual practice we rise up to the highest level and catch a glimpse of Being. But ascent must be followed by descent. The balanced spiritual ideal demands that we come down, bringing with us something of the light, power and perfume of the infinite into our own finite existence, so we can transform our physical being into an image of the divine. We are images of the divine, so we must transform that potentiality into a living actuality. That is the ultimate goal of our spiritual effort.

This doctrine of mantra is connected philosophically with the doctrine of *Shabda Brahman*, which is found in Hindu and Buddhist philosophy and Christian mysticism. The theory of *Shabda Brahman* is expounded in the Upanishads around 1500 BC. It means Brahman, the Supreme Being, manifested as the creative word, as the cosmic sound vibration. That is the primordial manifestation of the Supreme. For example, we have in the Bible, 'And God said, "Let there be light." And there was light.' That is the creative word. It is creative because as soon as it is uttered, it is accomplished. There is no time gap here. Humans usually experience a time gap. We take a vow or make a resolve, and a lot of time may elapse before we accomplish it. But with the creative word, as soon as it is articulated it is self-accomplishing.

Later on in the West, this became known as the doctrine of Logos — the word which was at the beginning and which was with God and which was God.

From the doctrine of sound vibration, it follows that everything comes out of this cosmic vibration, and everything — whether it is a tree, an animal, a human being or an object — in essence is a configuration of vibrations of energy. This is not far from scientific theory. Science tells us that at the beginning was energy, a mass of vibrations. When these vibrations strike our mind, we experience them as sound. Since vibration is experienced as sound, everything has its sound. The essence of every human being has its own sound, too. If everything has its sound, then mantra becomes important. With the help of the right syllables and the right sounds, we can open the mystery of the universe.

You can see how the doctrine of mantra follows from the doctrine of *Shabda Brahman*. That is why in meditation it is good to have a mantra and to use it as the focal point of your concentration. Further, a mantra becomes especially powerful when it is given by a spiritual teacher. Why? Because when the word is suffused with the power of consciousness of a master, it becomes more efficacious.

One time the mother of a little boy had a problem. The boy ate so much candy every day that at dinner time he had no appetite. His mother could not control the situation and was greatly disturbed.

One day a great yogi came to their town. The mother took the boy to the yogi and told him the problem. The yogi said, 'Come to me one week from now. Then I shall advise you.' A week later the mother came again with the boy. The yogi took the boy aside, looked into his eyes and said, 'My dear boy, if you eat too much candy, it spoils your appetite and you don't have proper nourishment. You must control your appetite and lust for candy.' The way he said it and the circumstances in which he said it made a great impact upon the impressionable mind of the boy. The boy was then able to give up candy.

The mother began to think about it and went back to the yogi. She said, 'Why did you take one week? Why did you not give this advice right away?' The yogi said, 'When you first placed this problem before me, I knew it was not the time to give advice because I myself had a weakness for candy. So I took a week and eliminated from my system any lingering trace of desire for candy. At the week's end, I was master of myself in that respect, and I was in a position to tell him with authority that he must not eat so much candy.'

This is our common human experience. The same word may be spoken by different people. When it is uttered by one person, it makes no effect. But when it is uttered by some other person, it may have a great impact. What is the difference?

For example, many people talk about nonviolence, and often it makes no impression. But when Gandhi talked about truth and nonviolence, he galvanized a whole continent of 400 million people. What was the secret of his power? He spoke from the deep level of consciousness in which he lived. Consequently, his words of nonviolence became magical.

By this, you can see that a mantra is not just a series of words. The word must be suffused with the power of consciousness of the person who utters it. Then it becomes powerful. This is why a mantra given by a teacher is important. When we are hungry for the truth, a teacher can try to understand us and to feel the spiritual pulse of our being. A suitable mantra is selected which can become a magic word in our life and a power base of spiritual practice.

A spiritual teacher is sometimes called a doctor of the soul. How does he or she differ from an ordinary physician? Let me tell you a story. A well-known physician who was a skin specialist was making a lot of money. One day a friend wanted to know the secret of his success and why he decided to become a skin specialist instead of another type of doctor. The doctor said, 'There are three reasons why I decided this. First of all, in my profession I don't have to jump out of bed at midnight. Second, my patients never die from my treatment. And thirdly, my patients never get well.'

Doctors of the soul have a different orientation. Ordinary physicians may have a vested interest, so they have to have certain tricks which can keep them in business. But the most important criterion of illumined spiritual preceptors is that they must be free of all vested interests. They must be people of renunciation with no axe to grind. In being servants of God in a selfless sense of the word, their main concern is to help students stand on their own feet and discover their own ground of being. As soon as that job is finished, teachers are happy, even though they never see the student again. True spiritual teachers have great satisfaction when their students are entirely on their own and find their own truth of existence.

The Six Lokas

Earlier we discussed the great mantra, 'Om mani padme hum.' Now I want to discuss the concept of the six planes of existence or consciousness and call your attention to their correlation with the different syllables of the mantra.

The six lokas are the planes or levels of consciousness on which our mind can function. The ultimate goal of spiritual seeking is beyond these different levels of mental existence. The ultimate goal is integration with ultimate reality, with the purely spiritual dimension of existence, which is nirvana, the state of absolute enlightenment.

THE ESSENCE OF SPIRITUAL PHILOSOPHY

Let me tell you a story from Chinese folklore. An old man lived with his son in a beautiful house. Right in front of the house were two big mountains which cut off their view of the beautiful landscape beyond the mountains. The man felt bad about it and one day he made a resolve. He told his young son they must do something about it and uproot the two mountains. How to go about it? The old man suggested that they should start digging under the mountains. So the son agreed and they began to work every day from morning to dusk. Soon the man became known throughout the whole country as the grand old fool who was trying to sink mountains into the ground.

One day a wise old white man appeared on the scene. He saw these two persons at work and said, 'What are you doing here? Is it humanly possible to sink these two big mountains? Never! Give up this foolish project!' The grand old fool said, 'No, we shall not give up this project because we are superior to the mountains. Mountains, after all, are just so high. They will grow no farther. But we shall grow eternally. My son and I will dig all our lives. My son's children will dig all their lives. Their children will dig and then their grandchildren. This is our vow. We are eternal. We shall one day conquer these mountains, and they will sink.' When the grand fool said these words, some angels immediately appeared, took away the mountains and cleared the view. The grand old fool won the victory by virtue of sheer determination.

In our spiritual growth it is the same way. There are two big mountains which obstruct our vision of truth, *avidya* and *asvida*. *Avidya* is ignorance. *Asvida* is egoism. If we have strong determination, then by virtue of this, the spirit is bound to triumph over these two illusory mountains. Nirvana is seeing through these two mountains which obstruct our vision of the supreme truth. Nirvana is the ultimate goal, which is beyond all levels of mental existence.

In the mantra, '*Om mani padme hum*' there are six syllables corresponding to the different planes of existence. The first plane is called *sura-loka* or *deva-loka* corresponding to '*Om*,' the sphere of angels or gods and goddesses. Corresponding to '*ma*' is *asura-loka*, the realm of demons. Corresponding to '*ni*' is *naraloka*, the sphere of human beings. Corresponding to '*pad*' is *trisanloka*, the sphere of animal nature. Corresponding to '*me*' is *pretaloka*, the ghost land. And corresponding to '*hum*' there is *bikkhuloka*, the realm of utter darkness. I shall try to explain the subtle significance of each.

First of all, there is *deva-loka* or *sura-loka*, the realm of gods and goddesses. Its traditional meaning is supernatural kingdom. After death, those who have accumulated good karma go to *sura-loka*, which corresponds to the heavenly world of popular imagination.

The point to be noted here is that not even this is the ultimate goal. All of these lokas fall short of enlightenment or full liberation. There is an element of bondage and ignorance even in the realm of angels. With all their goodness, angels are not liberated because liberation is beyond good and evil. Angels are good, but they have not attained enlightenment by virtue of which they transcend the dualities of good and evil, right and wrong. They are good because they are conforming to some standard but they are bound in the meshes of samsara. As a result of this bondage, their existence on this plane is temporary. Enlightenment alone is permanent, and that is beyond good and evil, beyond right and wrong, beyond angels and demons.

What is the limitation of this level of consciousness? It is the fact that these souls are still in bondage and that this level is temporary. They have to come down from there as soon as they have used up their good karma. Everyone has a limited fund of good karma, just as our bank balance, however big, is still limited. According to this fund of good karma, we may be on this plane for a long or short time. Then we have to pass on.

Further, *The Tibetan Book of the Dead* claims that those who dwell on the *sura-loka* suffer from the illusion of permanence and perfection. In no temporal mode of existence or level of being can we have permanence. Permanence is beyond time. Permanence or eternity is not a category of time. It is an entirely different category of experience. It is a category beyond the limitations of time.

In one sense, this level denotes a supernatural level of existence which one can attain after death. However, in an esoteric sense it is a level of existence here and now while living in the body. All those who have attained some degree of illumination belong to this level. This refers to a particular segment of humanity, which cuts across all national and geographic boundaries. Every nation has some people who are more or less enlightened and who are the vanguard of civilization.

The next loka is *asura*. In the traditional sense *asura* is another supernatural level which is the plane of demons endowed with supernatural powers. But they do not use these powers for divine purposes. They are anti-divine powers. In mythological stories, we find these demons challenging the gods at every turn. They capture the kingdom of heaven and for some time they have a wonderful time banishing the gods from heaven. But again the wheel of fortune turns and they are vanquished. This is how it all goes on.

This has been called the realm of power and struggle. The psychological factor at the root of this is will to power, the power drive, the ego drive. Sometimes the demons are more powerful than gods, but their weakness lies in the fact that they are not pure. Power takes away from purity, and therefore, they are eventually defeated.

In the esoteric sense of *asura*, this is also a way to describe certain types of people who are full of a lust for power, who are ego maniacs or who have power mania. They operate in this world as despots, as dictators, as ruthless opportunists. As a result of this power drive, they acquire a lot of power, but they use it for their own self-aggrandizement at the sacrifice of human welfare and in utter disregard of the divine will.

Indian mythology says that even these demons are not lost souls. They are in a particular phase of their evolution. The most surprising thing is that sometimes these demons can realize God quickly. Once they fulfill certain conditions then they may rise to the pinnacle of power, success and glory. After all, energy is the basic thing. Demonism is just misplaced energy. It is energy gone in the wrong direction and applied in the wrong way. If we can somehow turn it around, it can be a tremendous richness for God. A virtue is positively placed energy, and a vice is negatively placed energy. If we can turn the energy of our vices around, the demonic in us becomes saintly. This is sometimes baffling to us.

For example, one powerful demon attained so much power through discipline and the practice of meditation that he challenged God. He began to live and act in an anti-God manner. However, certain things happened in his life so that his whole orientation was changed, and he became God-realized. There are several stories of this nature, just as in our history some of the greatest sinners have become saints. They suddenly experience a conversion of consciousness. It is all the play of energy.

The next level is *nara-loka*, the realm of normal human beings. It is called the realm of action. The psychological factor at the base of this loka is acquisitiveness and greed. In this connection let me tell you another story from the Upanishads. In ancient times a great teacher had a school in which children of humans, gods and demons studied together. During an examination the teacher called on one of the brightest students of the angelic kind. The teacher said, 'Do you understand the lesson?' The student nodded and said, 'You are saying to control myself.' He was right. As a result of his self-discipline and self-purification under the guidance of the great teacher, he had attained some insight into his own nature. Therefore, he said the guru had instructed him to control the supernatural, not to abuse it.

Then the teacher called on a student of the demonic type. The teacher again said, 'Do you understand the lesson?' The student said, 'You are telling me to have compassion.' The demonic student was going through a period of self-discipline and self-inquiry and he had realized that imbedded in his nature was a great obstacle, namely, his demonic cruelty. Cruelty is a powerful element in a demonic nature.

When the human pupil came, he understood the teacher to be saying, 'Give, share whatever you have with your fellow beings.' Why did he interpret it in that way? Because the human student, by virtue of his growing insight into his own nature, became aware that his chief weakness lay in greed. He wanted to possess, and therefore, he knew he must conquer this tendency. And the way to conquer it is to develop the spirit of sharing.

Then, the next level is *trisan-loka,* the realm of spiritual darkness, lethargy, and inertia. After death, by virtue of their own bad karma, some go into this realm where they sleep all the time. They do not feel like doing anything. They feel the heavy weight of their own inertia.

This category also applies to our human life. All of us at some time feel lethargic. This includes procrastination, laziness, always putting things off. This also applies to animalistic, primitive, crudely materialistic people who have no sense of higher values. All they understand is eating, being merry and making hay while the sun shines. That is all that matters to them.

The next level is *preta-loka*, the land of hungry ghosts and shadowy existence. Here again we can consider two meanings. One is that after death those who have strong, unsatisfied emotional attachments or vital attachments to material possessions hover around what they have left behind. Over and over again they look back and are not released from these bonds of attachment. Therefore, they are hungry ghosts or *pretas*. They are often depicted having huge bellies, but mouths and necks that are only the size of a pin-hole — they can never satisfy their huge appetites.

In many religions ceremonies are performed to release disembodied spirits from attachments and personal ties. It is believed that by the force of these prayers and ceremonies, the disembodied souls can be released from their bonds of attachment and pass on to higher planes on the road of evolution. Attachment holds down progress and growth. It is emotional fixation.

We also can see how this category applies to human beings living on earth. In *The Tibetan Book of the Dead*, this category essentially has been interpreted as neurotic. The most characteristic features of those who have strong neurotic tendencies are insatiable cravings and unfulfilled desires. Those who are emotionally fixated at some stage or other often cannot stand on their own feet or function independently. They cannot make their own decisions.

Finally, there is *bikkhu-loka*, the lowest region of darkness. One interpretation is the nether region, which is the realm of intense suffering and impenetrable darkness. The other meaning applies to human beings here and now, especially those who experience psychosis. This is a type of disturbance which goes beyond neurosis. It refers to those who suffer from spiritual darkness in such a way that they are cut off from a sense of reality and are alienated severely from the real world.

Remember that existence in any one of these lokas is temporary. For a time by virtue of their karma, people dwell here or there, but after the karma wears out, they move on. Even those who go to the lowest level should not lose heart.

The great message of hope is that all of these are passing planes of existence. As I remarked earlier, Buddhism and Hinduism do not believe in eternal heaven or eternal hell. Eternity is beyond heaven and hell. Immortality is beyond heaven and hell. It is a different category altogether, qualitatively different from the category of time and space. There is no such thing as eternal damnation because the spirit itself is essentially a spark of the divine. The very nature of the spirit is incompatible with eternal existence in any one of the lokas. It is all temporary suffering on account of bad karma. Here, therefore, the idea is that even the darkest clouds have a silver lining; even the darkest night is followed by dawn.

Finally by using this mantra, *Om mani padme hum*, we are relating to all these lokas; that is to say, we are sending out thoughts of compassion to them. We also are relating ourselves to the whole universe and sending love and good will. Further, while we send out thoughts of love to other fellow beings in the universe, we also are closing the gap of all these lokas for them. When we understand and place ourselves in rapport and communication with the different lokas, we conquer the dark forces by the power of love we send.

A byproduct of this is that the gates of these lokas also are closing for us. We are destroying the chances of rebirth in any one of them. We are following the path of self-transcendence toward the attainment of nirvana. As a result of this union with the spirit, we discover a new style and pattern of living, thinking and acting through the instrumentality of our own transformed body.

34

ASPIRATION AND DIVINE GRACE

Two things are essential for the realization of our spiritual effort. One is aspiration which is a push from below. Another is divine grace which is a pull from above. All great spiritual teachers are unanimous in their assertion that humans cannot attain liberation or enlightenment by their own unaided, individual effort. Something else in necessary. From the philosophical standpoint, divine grace or the pull from above is the impact of the pressure upon our minds of a higher plane of consciousness. The more you feel this pressure, the more you feel something wonderful is helping you. Without that you could not attain this lift in consciousness. When aspiration and divine grace combine, it is wonderful. When you have the right effort and when you receive the pull from above, this beautifully brings about the blossoming of your personality and the fulfillment of your spiritual potential.

Of further interest...

YOGA
The technology of ecstasy
GEORG FEUERSTEIN
Foreword by KEN WILBER

The impulse towards transcendence is intrinsic to human life. Nowhere has this drive found a more consistent and versatile expression than in India, whose civilization has spawned an overwhelming variety of spiritual beliefs, practices and approaches. The goal of Yoga, the most famous and globally widespread of India's spiritual traditions, is to take us beyond ourselves to the Absolute Reality, to the utterly blissful union of the individual self with the transcendental Divine.

In recent decades Yoga, once known only in the East, has spread across the world to become a household word. *Yoga: The Technology of Ecstasy* is a work of unparalleled scope that weaves the daunting complexity of five thousand years of Yoga into a single tapestry, outlining its relationship with other important Indian traditions and discussing the diverse forms it has taken in Hinduism, Buddhism and Jainism.

Speaking always to the contemporary reader, Georg Feuerstein offers a compelling and relevant articulation of Yoga's profound life-transforming value for modern men and women.

THE SEARCH FOR MEANING

The new spirit in science and philosophy

Edited by PAAVO PYLKKÄNEN
Foreword by MAURICE WILKINS

In an age when religion has lost much importance, where people are isolated, and where reality is largely shaped by mass media, many people feel that their life has little or no meaning. *The Search For Meaning* is a highly original and stimulating exploration in which people from various fields — biology, medicine, psychology and physics — come together to discuss concepts of meaning suitable for our own time.

This collection of essays, based around the work of theoretical physicist David Bohm, discusses the idea that meaning is not just a passive, ethereal quality, but that it actively determines what happens both in the mind and in nature. In order for humanity to survive, argue the contributors, radical change is vital and only a shift in what the world *means* to us will constitute a change in what the world *is*.

With contributions from academics around the world, this revolutionary book breaks much new ground in showing how a wider basis for human enquiry and creativity can be established in a true dialogue between the arts and science, philosophy and religion, in discovering the common role that meaning plays within them.